Urban and Regional Policy Analysis in Developing Countries

Edited by
LATA CHATTERJEE
Department of Geography,
Boston University,
Boston
and
PETER NIJKAMP
Department of Economics,
Free University,
Amsterdam

Gower

Published by
Gower Publishing Company Limited,
Gower House, Croft Road, Aldershot, Hants GU11 3HR,
England

British Library Cataloguing in Publication Data

Urban and regional policy analysis in developing
    countries.—(Issues in Southeast Asian security)
    1. Developing countries——Regional Planning
    I. Chatterjee, Lata   II. Nijkamp, Peter
    III. Series
    361.6'1'091724   HT391

    ISBN 0 566 00623 5

Printed and bound in Great Britain by
Biddles Ltd, Guildford and King's Lynn

Contents

Preface

This book is designed to demonstrate the potential of analytical methods and models for urban and regional policy analysis in developing countries. The first part of the book is devoted to a sample of policy issues which are of crucial importance in development planning. Then, in the next part, a set of modern tools (models, methods) is discussed in order to (1) critically judge the usefulness of conventional quantitative tools for policy analysis and to (2) pay attention to recently developed tools that are more appropriate for the specific problems of developing countries, especially those which have a poor data base.

Thus, this book brings together experts both in the field of practical development planning and of methods and models for policy analysis. It is hoped that this volume will serve as a breeding ground for new insights into, and new uses of suitable research methods in urban and regional policy analysis in developing countries.

It should be mentioned that this book is a follow-up to an earlier book in this area produced by the same editors (L. Chatterjee and P. Nijkamp, Urban Problems and Economic Development, Martinus Nijhoff, The Hague, 1981). But the present volume is much more policy oriented and aims at reaching also development planners who are practically involved. We hope that this book will be a useful vehicle for a better understanding and use of modern methods for policy analysis.

We would like to express our gratitude to all authors who have contributed to this book. Finally, our thanks go to Dianne Biederberg who carefully typed the manuscript.

Boston, USA   Lata Chatterjee
Amsterdam, The Netherlands   Peter Nijkamp
March 1983

PART A: INTRODUCTION

1 Urban and Regional Policy Design in Developing Countries

L. CHATTERJEE AND P. NIJKAMP

1. INTRODUCTION

Efficiency and effectiveness in urban and regional management are of
critical importance for rapid economic growth and equitable development
in the Third World. It is widely accepted by development analysts that
there exists a positive association between urbanisation and national or
regional economic growth. Nevertheless, recent history of unparallelled
urban expansion and of rural-urban discrepancies in developing countries
is the cause of the serious policy concern in the national and international community. The record shows that urban expansion has been accompanied by massive migration, open unemployment and underemployment, congestion in housing, education, transport and health facilities, and
overall deterioration of the urban environment. In addition, in many
cases, a dual development emerged leading to a decrease in the economic
potential of rural areas. While, to a large extent, these problems resulted from real resource shortages, both the urban and the rural situation is worse than the limited resources would warrant. This reflects
also the dismal record of urban management and decision making in major
urban and metropolitan areas of the developing world. In relatively few
exceptions where there has been a record of good policy design and management, it has been accompanied by rapid economic growth and better
distribution of real resources. In many countries, also the urban-rural
and urban-regional disparities tend to increase. There is, consequently,
a widespread agreement on the need for the improvement of urban policy
design and management in developing countries.
  Theoretically, efficiency can be improved through effective planning
and plan implementation. This has generated a considerable body of literature on urban and regional planning. While the benefits of planning
have been generally recognized, its practice leaves much to be desired.
Current urban and regional planning approaches emphasise goals and objectives and underemphasises the strategies required to achieve these
objectives. Attention to strategies and choice of instruments for trans-
lating objectives into reality are particularly crucial as there are
several formidable barriers to plan implementation. Serious social,
economic and political consequences are likely to follow unless urban
and regional development policy comes to terms with these barriers - such
as the chronic shortage of real and financial resources, the innapprop-
riate match between resources and goals, the inconsistency among various
goals, the paucity of control and enforcement mechanisms, inadequacy of
data and the like.
  In the light of the magnitude of the problem, currently there appears
to be the political will, at national and international levels, to make
the necessary changes. Not only are planning goals and objectives more

clearly stated, but also real resources are being channelled for the
improvement of urban and regional production and service delivery. It
is therefore crucial to discuss urban and regional policy design and
management alternatives at this juncture.

While several elements are involved in increasing the efficiency of
urban and regional policy design and management, this book singles out
two aspects: a) the lack of effective strategies for combatting the
problems, and b) the lack of adequate information that can permit accurate estimation of current and prediction of future conditions. Thus
this book addressed two crucial elements in urban policy design and
implementation - the selection of 'appropriate' or effective strategies
in industrial, migration, transportation and housing policy, and efficient information processing techniques.

The combination of these two elements hopefully provides a useful
addition to the literature, since literature on analytical techniques is
often divorced from the literature on policy design and program implementation. This has led to an unfortunate lack of dialogue between urban
policy analysts (usually academics) and decision makers (politicians and
public managers) in the developing countries. This can be contrasted
with the considerable dialogue found among the national planners and
economists. These two elements should thus be integrated if effective
urban strategies are to be designed.

Good management also requires efficient information processing as a
necessary prerequisite. Therefore, besides important policy issues such
as housing, transportation, migration and hierarchical planning, we discuss several analytical techniques that are appropriate for the type of
data more readily available to urban and regional decision makers in
developing countries. Much of the available data in developing countries
is: a) qualitative, that is, while precise numerical values cannot be
assigned to each variable, some of their attributes can be identified,
b) collected for some regular record keeping purpose. Those who have
worked in developing countries know that data is collected for a variety
of tasks on a regular basis. Such data sets for revenue collection,
marketing and sales information, licensing purposes, school and hospital
admissions, etc. are a valuable source of information that is usually
overlooked. This book attempts to increase the urban and regional
decision maker's ability to extract information from 'inadequate' data
sets. Some of these technques and policy areas in which they can be
applied, such as transportation, housing, industrial location, are discussed in this book.

This book is composed of two parts. Part A addresses various policy
issues, such as (multi)regional planning, housing, migration and transportation. Part B introduces a series of analytical tools that might be
used for operational policy analyses of urban and regional development
problems.

2. EXPERIENCE IN DEVELOPING COUNTRIES

The first part of the book will review existing experience, not as a
series of case studies or incidents, but as indicative of actions that
can be taken to attain desired objectives within the time, resources and
other constraints. Information will be provided on actual performance,
and policies will be assessed. The purpose will mainly be to analyse
the sets of actions or strategies involved in policy implementation.

A strategy can be defined as a set of actions that involve selection
of and sequencing of instruments used by an organisation to achieve its

desired ends. This implies choosing the right course (direction), ac-
complishing specific ends (effectiveness) and achieving them with minimum inputs of resources(efficiency). An effective strategy makes optimal use of the internal and external resouces it can muster to attain
its perdetermined objectives. It uses forces it can control (as instruments) to modify situational elements over which it has no control to
bring about the desired ends.

Strategies imply the use of appropriate instruments. The appropriateness of an instrument will vary and will be consistent with the available
resource of the institution - capital, labour, technology, etc. For
example in transportation policy, a pricing instrument, to be effective,
must be consistent with the enforcement capabilities of the organisation
and the consumption behaviour of households and firms.

Strategies to mobilise capital will vary with capabilities of finance
institutions, household savings behaviour and so on. In a like vein,
strategies for improving income distribution through better delivery of
basic needs will require a set of instruments that are consistent with
the sociopolitical and economic environment.

There is rarely a universal 'best alternative'. Effective strategies
will have some situationally specific elements, that need to be identified and assessed, and separated from the general characteristics, common
to any transportation, housing or health delivery system in developing
countries. The output from quantitative analysis should be useful in
providing informational inputs into the identification and measurement of
the various attributes of the specific situational elements that the
policy seeks to modify.

This book has selected several policy issues. It attempts to identify
factors, control mechanisms and impacts of policies with the objective
of interrelating analytical methods and quantitative techniques into the
discussion of policy design. The experience of several developing countries in a specific policy area - housing, infrastructure, urban development etc. - will be reviewed in the first part of the book.

3. NEW TECHNIQUES FOR URBAN AND REGIONAL POLICY ANALYSIS

The policy designer's ability to extract useful information from the
available data significantly influences the choice of instruments and
effectiveness of the policy. Particularly quantitative information permits parsimonious description of the current situation and selection of
reasonable, objective criteria for choosing among alternatives. This
recognition of the greater precision and efficiency of quantitative techniques for the practice of social and policy sciences has been reflected
in the impressive development of rigorous statistical and mathematical
models. While these models - explanatory or predictive - have been
fruitfully used to fit quantitative data to urban social, political, economic and geographic theory in the advanced economies, they have had much
lesser applicability in developing countries.

As indicated in greater detail in Part B of this book, models developed
in advanced economies are often unsuitable for developing countries for
a variety of reasons. First, mathematical and statistical models require
a large amount of information for their validation. Second, they impose
severe restrictions on the type and quality of data needed for successful results. Third, it is difficult to collect data for the express purpose of validating these models, since the costs of data collection are
prohibitive in developing countries. Thus, rarely are these urban and
regional models applied to developing countries, and where they have

been applied, the results have been mediocre.

On the one hand, this approach to quantitative analysis has led analysts to question the utility of conventional quantitative models. On
the other hand, it has resulted in the observation that developing countries have poor data bases. The resulting emphasis has been on qualita-
tively-oriented research. However, an alternative interpretation is
possible, viz. the observation that the current urban models are poorly
suited to the available data. The problem then is not the poverty of
the data per se, since data is often abundant, but the poverty and in-
appropriateness of the 'traditional' quantitative methods for analysing
the available data.

However, information considered 'qualitative' is increasingly becoming
'quantitative' as new mathematical and statistical tools are developed.
These newer quantitative methods are more appropriate for information
processing in developing countries. The chapters in Part B of this book
will discuss some of these newer and more 'non-traditional' quantitative
methods. In order to extract the several benefits that accrue from mathematical models it becomes necessary to shift these innovative techniques
adapted to 'data poor' conditions. Several of these models can use
'soft' imprecise data and there is increasing interest in the exploration of these models for policy design.

A synthesising chapter on rationalising regional and urban policies
from the viewpoint of such new analytical techniques will conclude this
book. Altogether this volume aims at providing an operational framework
for strategic and effective urban and regional policy analysis in developing countries.

PART B: POLICY ISSUES

2 Urban and Regional Policy Issues in Developing Countries: An Introduction

L. CHATTERJEE

Urban areas are rapidly expanding in most developing countries. As
urban growth reflects the spatial consequences of economic and structural transformations occurring in developing countries, the pace of urban
growth is likely to continue in the near and intermediate future. The
impact of this growth on urban employment, housing, transportation,
health and energy needs have been documented in several books (Chatterjee and Nijkamp 1982, Linn 1982, Safa 1982). In addition to the current
problems this growth is causing for urban management and service delivery, the urban growth is raising critical issues about the design of
urban development policy and the determination of national/regional
spatial strategies, as governments attempt to minimise these costs of
development.

Urban and regional policy analysis, addressed to the management of
these development impacts, has two components – the scientific and the
political. Unfortunately, the area of intersection between these two
components is still rather small. At the scientific level, policy analysis has increasingly become rigorous. In the last two decades, it has
developed an impressive array of analytical and quantitiative techniques
that can address complex decision environments. These policy analytic
methods are primarily used for decision making in the private sector and
for business management (where goals, objectives and the decision environment is relatively more simple than in the public sector). Policy
analytic studies, using quantitative techniques, are not widely used for
policy making in the public sector. Rather, actual policies result from
negotiation, bargaining and compromises at a political level. Policies
result from these processes between impacted interest groups, and conflict management methods are more influential than studies of economic
efficiency or effectiveness or the use of optimality criteria.

The practical consequences of this lack of interaction between the
scientific and the political elements has been particularly severe in
developing countries that possess limited resources for policy analysis
but burgeoning claims on them. The ability of the public sector to use
its resources efficiently and to improve employment, housing, transportation, i.e. the quality of the urban environment (broadly defined), is
increasingly falling short of requirements. Further, there has not been
much convergence between the analytic and the practical elements of
policy making even though C.P. Snow alerted the intellectual community
more than two decades ago to the dangers inherent in the polarisation
of the branches of knowledge (Snow 1959). Since then, analysts have
stressed the need for dialogue and interdependency between the scientific community and policy makers; yet the complex dialectic between the
two groups has not permitted this dialogue, at substantive levels, in
urban and regional policy in developing countries. The quantitative

tradition is often viewed by policy decision makers as being overly
simplistic, lacking comprehension about the complexities of the decision
processes in pluralistic worlds. It has also been difficult for the
decision makers to comprehend the analytics and the practical importance
of what the scientific community has been saying. The gap between the
two groups has increased, rather than decreased, over the years.

This volume accepts the logic of the utility of increased dialogue
between the two 'cultures' and discusses the policy practice issues in
the first section. Given the massive task of mobilising societal resources for promoting sustained development, few governments have devoted the attention necessary for devising systematic strategies for
addressing urban and regional problems. Institutions concerned with
municipal or regional administration are inundated with daily crises and
their capacity to anticipate and plan for the future is limited. Unless
these new sprawling urban populations are appropriately integrated into
the national and regional economy, and their needs met, it is likely
that economic progress will be slowed and blocked. Moreover, urban
areas often account for half the national product; hence inattention to
these problems will have adverse effects on labour productivity and economic growth, causing reduced urban efficiency.

As a consequence, a large analytical literature has developed in the
last two decades, to devise broad strategies that combine desired social
objectives (pertaining to equitable growth), with the imperatives of
limited resources. Policy prescriptions have dealt with the choice
among alternative instruments that might be used to achieve equitable
growth at low levels of income. Of the several areas of policy intervention that have received attention in the urban and regional policy
literature, the following four strategic perspectives have been pursued
here:
a) the development of mechanisms and management structures to facili-
    tate interregional development at various levels of planning;
b) the discussion of rational rural urban migration policy, since in-
    come growth in the urban area, in the long run, is dependent on com-
    plementary economic growth in rural areas;
c) mechanisms for the provision of affordable housing, with appropriate
    sanitary and related public services;
d) the interdependence between public investments for physical and
    social infrastructure and private sector production decisions, in
    order to promote rapid economic development.
In these areas of urban and regional policy, as in other aspects, the
policy analyst has been interested in the systematic exploration of the
attributes and impacts of policy interventions. Traditionally, the
policy analyst has been interested in either the ex ante choice of a
course of action (analysis for policy), or the assessment of a course of
action that has been undertaken (analysis of policy). This dual emphasis on ex ante and ex post analysis of policies has encouraged the development of analytic techniques, using a variety of socio-economic
variables, to aid the selection and the evaluation of alternative policies and instruments. At the same time, this focus on policy selection
and evaluation (often connected through feedback loops and resource
flows as in systems models), has resulted in a lack of methodological
attention to the variables influencing the process of implementation,
particularly the variables describing the political, institutional and
organisational contexts in which these policy instruments have to be
operationalised. Complex processes which affect outcomes are ignored as
in deterministic models, or in stochastic models probabilities based on
prior experience have to be assigned by the decision maker. In reality,

however, there are several decision makers, and the probabilities will depend on particularistic events, i.e., they have to be determined sequentially and incrementally.

While the quantitative analytic tradition had ignored the context and process of decision making, the political science and public administration disciplines have paid considerable attention to these elements. Their focus has, however, been on the descriptions of organisations, classification of organisation behaviours under varying political environments, conflict resolution and decision processes under uncertainty conditions. Less attention has been paid to the connection between these elements and policy design, policy content and ex post evaluation of policy implementations (that can provide guidelines for more efficient resource use). Rather, they have focussed on explanation and description of decision processes and have paid inadequate attention to policy prescriptions under conditions of resource scarcity and high levels of uncertainty characterising decision making in mixed economies.

The quantitative analytic tradition in urban and regional policy analysis, if it is to be of greater use to its clients, i.e., urban and regional decision makers at various levels of the decision chain, has to combine both these traditions. Since the poor adoption of recommendations of policy analytic studies in developing countries (i.e., the weak link between policy analysis and policy making) results from this neglect of aspects of critical importance to the administrator and the manager, greater attention must be focussed on these elements describing the intermediate stages between ex ante and ex post assessments. A partial cause of the lack of attention to implementation issues devolves from the shortcomings and restrictive assumptions of traditional techniques. However, analytic techniques developed recently have greater ability to incorporate variables that describe the complex decision environments and thus narrow the gap between theory and practice.

The papers prepared for this section provide a wealth of information about policy practice and a set of common messages. First, they emphasise the messiness of the decision environments and the ambiguity of the results. Second, they imply that interactions between analysts and policy makers, on a continuing basis, is essential if policy analysis is to be used by policy makers (as the parameters describing the decision system continuously change and adapt to pressures in mixed economic systems). Third, while expert help in policy selection is important, the analysts can play a useful role in helping the policies to be implemented. This will require a continuing process of monitoring, adding and eliminating elements, not all of it requiring quantitative assessments. In mixed economies with a combination of precise (e.g. technological) and imprecise (e.g. political) information, analysts will have to combine qualitative and quantitative information for policy purposes.

The first paper in this section, by Misra and Prantilla, describes the supranational and national regional planning efforts in South East Asia, from an institutional perspective. In critically examining the elements of regional cooperation, they highlight the nature of political realities that confound policy implementation. In spite of clear definitions of goals and objectives, the selection and design of a number of policy instruments, the creation of a multination organisation - the Association of South East Asian Nations (ASEAN) - to implement these instruments for regional growth and equity, they note that the results have not been as desired. They conclude that though the four ASEAN countries have ex ante or ex post analysis of their regional plans these studies are limited in their capacity to improve the planning and implementation of regional development strategies.

They adopt an evolutionary approach, and trace the changing definition of regional planning in this global region. Regional planning went through three clearly identifiable phases of role definition, following trends of regional planning in advanced economies. In the first place, there was an emphasis on balanced national development, through the efficient use of local resource endowments, and river basin management was its primary instrument. In the second phase, this was replaced by an advocacy of increased efficiency through promoting unbalanced or uneven spatial development, with growth centres as the primary instruments. The current emphasis has the dual objectives of increased productivity (efficient growth) and equitable distribution (for meeting basic needs); multilevel spatial planning for interregional integration is its primary instrument. They point out that the combination of efficiency and equity objectives have been defined at supranational (equitable and efficient development of member nations) and at national (integration and development of provinces) spatial levels.

The ASEAN was established to strengthen the bonds of regional solidarity and encourage regional economic cooperation so as to accelerate industrial growth and eliminate problems of 'poverty, hunger, disease and illiteracy'. Trade instruments, particularly preferential tariff arrangements, were designed to promote industrial development. Their sectoral approach to regional cooperation is evident from the organisational structure of the ASEAN. The ASEAN countries have also adopted subnational planning goals, although each country has defined the approach to spatial planning differently, as befits their differences in political systems and urban and regional geography.

The primary relevance of this paper to this volume it is delineation of the problems of regional cooperation that derive from their plan formation and operationalising systems. The authors note that the regional development plans of the four ASEAN countries follow the economic model of setting objectives, and use a top down implementation approach, with usual sectoral biases. They question whether the complementary and synergetic aspects of regional development activities are captured by this approach. The main focus of the criticism has been on issues of operationalisation, the limited ability to identify programmes and projects and lack of mechanisms for integrating the regional development plans into the budgetting process.

What are the methodological implications of this paper? Only a few are highlighted here. First, traditional analytics stress coordination and integration based on knowledge of complementarities, tradeoffs and current resource distribution. The establishment of ASEAN reflected this approach, and it was established to provide a central coordinating institution. However, Misra and Prantilla show that the policies and results were based on conflict resolution. For example, they note, "intersectoral conflicts in the formulation of regional development policies and strategies ... occur during the process of policy and strategy formulation. Regional conflicts are ironed out during meetings and workshops help for that purpose".

In such a context, the notion of a single decision maker, known tradeoffs and the like, will not be very useful. The actual decision process required incremental decisions, with interaction among several decision makers and where tradeoffs emerged during a process of negotiation. The spatial planning decision environment, at the supranational and national levels was ill-defined, filled with ambiguities, and mixed with some elements of precision (i.e., resource distributions), and others of imprecision (attitudes of other decision makers). In such situations, the newer analytic methods using qualitative and quantitative data or fuzzy sets are mote appropriate.

Project identification posed problems. For example they state, '...
regional development plans include projects identified by local government units as well as those identified by individual agencies operating
at both local and regional levels', in which, 'the identification of
programs and projects can only be inferred' from the end results. Such
an approach to project identification is not only wasteful, but it leads
to a proliferation of plans without any formal criteria for prioritisa-
tion. Since cost benefit or effectiveness criteria were not particularly useful, and project selection resulted from an interactive process,
man machine gaming simulations can be particularly useful in such decision environments. The analyst can provide the decision maker with
information on the costs of accepting particular strategies. Thus
interactive methods which allow swift outputs (for example as is possible using microcomputers and simple models), will allow a practical combination of concepts of economic efficiency and political feasibility.
There is need to focus on analytic methods that will permit analysts to
provide inputs in a decision context where decisions depend on interactive processes.

Sundaram discusses the arguments for multilevel planning in India and
its implementation experience in four States - Gujarat, Maharastra,
Karnataka and Uttar Pradesh. Multilevel planning recognises the efficacy of differentiating planning activities according to the appropriate
spatial level of impact. It is in partial response to the recognition
of the gap between plan formulation and realisation in developing countries, and thus it addresses some of the issues raised in the Misra-
Prantilla paper (even though described in a different context). The
multilevel planning approach has been adopted in India also in the interests of decentralised decision making, since at a theoretical level
at least, more responsive plans can be made. Multilevel planning can
be more cost effective, as costs of information should be reduced, and
responses to interventions can be monitored more easily. It could increase distributional benefits through a better delivery of services.

Sundaram describes, very briefly, the planning process in India as a
two way linkage between the Centre and the State, in which State plans
are finalised through an iterative mechanism. The States have built up
their own planning machinery in order to negotiate with the Centre and
thus the first state in decentralisation is fairly well established.
It is at the third level - district level - that planning is not well
established, and the experimentation in the four States is of particular
value. The procedures vary between the States and reflect the degree of
autonomy granted to the lower levels. These procedures are described in
detail in this paper.

The politics of multilevel planning become evident as the mechanisms
for district planning are discussed. While the logic of decentralised
planning cannot be faulted, the actual implementation 'bristles with a
number of problems, bottlenecks and constraints'. In common with Misra
and Prantilla, Sundaram points out that it is the operational aspects of
decentralisation, including both financial and administrative decentralisation, that is a key to success. Since these aspects require innovation and changing of old procedures, technical expertise can be of
considerable help.

Sundaram emphasises the need for technical help for the effective
operationalisation of multilevel spatial planning. The type of technical expertise that will be appropriate can be inferred from Sundaram's
comments. 'Decentralised planning is not a one time planning operation.
It is a relay and re-relay process in which the micro units, through a

13

repetitive process of change seek continuous convergence to the dynamic path of stable equilibrium ...' Thus programming using multicriteria and multilevel formulations, combining interactive and iterative adjustment mechanisms, can be particularly helpful. Or the last stage in the process is the integration of the plans of the several spatial levels. This requires nesting procedures. 'It would require the establishment of organisational and communication links among the different hierarchic levels so as to facilitate reciprocal interaction, exchange, cooperation and resolution of conflicts,' and 'the problem of consistency is essentially solved by consciously seeking to develop and build plans at each spatial level within the framework of the plans of higher level.' Thus the application of nested hierarchic models will allow interlinkages and harmonisation of plans.

However, Sundaram emphasises that for democratic countries, such as India, technical help is not the only requirement, and that mechanisms should embrace also social and political elements, for a technically sound plan without political support is not likely to be implemented. Since political support implies interaction with decision makers who are not very technically qualified (at least at lower levels), it is important that the techniques mix formal and informal devices, qualitative and quantitative information, i.e. have to be formulated under conditions of data and other uncertainties.

Sundaram's documentation of the complexities of hierarchic integration between and within implementing institutions in mixed economies, and the existence of several semi-autonomous agencies for plan implementation in the various sectors has also another message for the choice of appropriate methodology. Such decision frameworks imply that there is likely to be considerable variation in behavioural compliance among implementing officials, i.e., the system is only loosely integrated. In such contexts not only is it important to emphasise interactive and iterative solutions, but also the iterative systems must be non-deterministic, since a current state is likely to give rise to a set of possible next states, rather than to a unique next state.

The three following papers address policy issues in specific sectors – agriculture and migration, housing delivery for low income groups, and public expenditures and their impact on regional production enterprises. They each address some aspects of the transformation processes occurring in developing countries. A major change in developing countries is occurring in the farming sector, where adoption of productivity enhancing innovations has caused labour to be released from agriculture. Due to a lack of local employment opportunities in rural areas, large scale migrations to urban areas is common in most developing countries. The migration issue is thus important on a regional planner's agenda. One consequence of this migration is the lack of adequate housing opportunities in urban areas, and a serious planning problem centres around the delivery of low cost housing. A major impact of inadequate housing and related physical and social infrastructure, i.e., transportation, power, health and educational facilities, has been on labour productivity. So there is a clear interdependence between public expenditures and regional economic growth. The final paper in this section provides a framework for analysing these interdependencies.

Chaudhury's paper deals with the interface between rural and urban areas, as it describes the characteristics of rural-urban migration in Bangladesh, particularly the effects of migration on the income and assets of migrants in the urban and their rural settings. In spite of several studies on migrant characteristics, and the theoretical statements on the effect of income on migration flows, there is little empirical documentation of the actual benefits received by the migrants and their impact on the society they leave. It is generally assumed that it is the perception of economic benefits in the short and long run (through intergenerational transfers) that motiviates migration. Yet there is little measurement of the actual income gains received by the migrant and the migrant's kin in the rural area. Chaudhury's paper is particularly useful as it measures these gains both in monetary and human capital terms.

In common with other studies of migrant characteristics, he shows that out-migration is a selective process, and the two groups with the highest rates of migration are the poorest and the wealthiest in the rural areas. A similar dual pattern can be found with reference to the educational levels. Migrants are drawn from illiterate groups and those with higher levels of education. He discusses the special problems that derive from this selective migration, particularly the drawing off of the younger and more able members of the rural community, for the age bias tends to reinforce the skill bias in migration.

His special contribution relates to the estimation of the monetary effects of migration. He shows that the process tends to increase disequilibrium, as the major beneficiaries of migration are the upper income groups. The nature and consequences of this is traced for rural areas, where increasing concentration of land holdings os partially financed by the remittances of the migrants. Since the benefits from migration is positively associated with income, migration increases income disparities. Since the costs of migration are negatively associated with income, the weaker members of society bear the costs inordinately. Chadhaury shows, whichever indicator one chooses to measure the impact of migration on the migrant, that migration tends to worsen the income distribution (through the incidence of the differential costs and benefits borne by the different income groups). Thus migration tends to intensify poverty through land concentration in the rural areas, rather than reduce poverty through a labour adjustment process. While all the migrants benefitted in monetary terms, the true impacts on their real income could not be estimated.

National and regional economic development and manpower policies have seldom been connected in policy. While this paper does not evaluate any specific policy, it has some policy implications. A clear implication is the need to improve the current limited employment opportunity in rural areas. Programs to help the small farmer are necessary, and these programs should include acquisition of non farm skills and increased opportunity for off farm earnings in rural areas (so as to augment farm incomes and thereby reduce the pressures for migration). There are also implications for employment creation for the out-migrants in urban areas, for migration will continue due to the structural transformations occurring in developing countries. A greater access to opportunity has to be encouraged for the migrant as the system tends to reward the higher skilled and upper income migrants, originating from the upper income farm households.

The importance of focussing directly on the lower income groups, instead of waiting for trickle down processes, has been clearly established in the development literature. It is in the interests of those living in relative poverty as also in the interests of those in the receiving regions. Increasing congestion, environmental deterioration and other health and productivity related problems deriving from congestion have been well documented in the urban environmental literature. A powerful case can be made for designing policies specifically for the poor.

15

Chatterjee focusses on a specific policy developed for the poor and analyses its record, particularly the constraints that inhibited the development of effective strategies for increasing housing investment and improving the housing conditions of currently deprived households. In this paper she uses a systems framework to analyse the housing delivery system, to identify its structural components and to highlight the contradictions that must be addressed so that housing strategies for poverty alleviation can be meaningfully implemented. She applies this framework to the design of a low income housing finance system that is more likely to reach the target groups.

In common with Misra-Prantilla and Sundaram she notes that development strategies (in this case as applied to housing) will be effective only if their design and implementation are consistent with the overall organisational, institutional and fiscal framework of individual regions. Several attempts to decrease housing poverty through the adoption of equity oriented instruments such as sites and services, provision of public housing or low income finance systems have not been as effective because of the inconsistencies between the attributes of the instruments and the organisational, institutional and asset distribution system in which they were implemented. She uses the Brazilian experience in the implementation of a low income housing finance policy to illustrate these points.

Housing finance in its conventional form benefits only a few because of the long term, large debt ratio, and risk associated with the character of housing investment. Mortgage instruments designed in the context of these attributes are not suitable for the poor because of the mismatch between their earning patterns, level of education, savings behaviour and these conventional instruments. While the Brazilian program design showed the desire for aiding the poor, an analysis of the allocation of funds revealed the difficulty of meeting this objective. The data shows that the share of the lower income groups have consistently declined since the sixties. The Brazilian Housing Bank's emphasis on creating specialised programmes for low income groups and the adoption of concessionary interest rates did not permit effectiveness in meeting the objectives.

Chatterjee claims that the conventional instruments fail because they ignore existing asset distribution, savings incentives and institutional mechanisms of the poor. She advocates the design of instruments should be based on mechanisms that exist among these groups and provides an illustration from studies conducted in a variety of countries. However, for the success of these institutions it is necessary to integrate them hierarchically with the formal system, otherwise the existing dual system will be perpetuated in the capital market. Thus vertical integration and a multilevel approach to housing finance is required.

Planning in developing countries has undergone an immense range of experimentation. Both Sundaram and Chatterjee advocate a decentralised approach to planning delivery, if lower income groups are to benefit. Increased localism and grass roots participation will be practical if appropriate institutions are developed, and they are situated within the overall systemic context. While experts can provide input and technical assistance, ultimately it is the people directly involved who will have to make the decisions. Thus here too an interactive approach is called for, with analysts presenting options within the interests and cultural attributes of these groups.

In hierarchic systems, implementation - i.e. translation from knowledge to practice, from designing of strategies to incorporation into an ongoing organisational system is always difficult, incremental and time consuming. An orderly linear process is not likely to occur. In common with the Chaudhury paper, the notion of undesired change and discontinuities are important.

Lakshmanan and Elhance focus on the crucial role played by public investments, in physical and social infrastructure, in improving welfare of individuals and the productivity of both producer and consumer capital. They note the two kinds of effects - the amenity demand effect and the amenity supply effect, and suggest that the latter which derives from the attractiveness of the region for industries outside the region are particularly important for regional economic growth. In developing countries where public investments are below threshold levels, productivity is below the potential level given existing stocks of capital, due to its effects on labour.

Consequently, a major thrust of development policy in developing countries has been to increase public expenditures for infrastructure development in order to increase the productive potential and the income of these regions. After reviewing the literature on the interdependence between public expenditures and the growth of productive enterprises, they present a model that is capable of assessing the contributions that public investments of various types make to the productivity of enterprises in a region. Since they suggest that some types of public investments may play a greater role in output determination in the earlier stages of regional growth while others may be more important at a later stage, it is important to be able to assess ex ante the contribution of different regional public investments so as to optimally deploy scarce resources. The model they provide is capable of doing this assessment.

Their model explicitly incorporates social overhead capital into regional production behaviour without imposing a priori restrictions on substitution possibilities or model parameters. Their article forms a bridge between the first part of the book, dealing with policy practice and the second part that deals with policy analytics.

REFERENCES

Chatterjee, L.R. and Nijkamp P. (eds), Urban Problems and Economic Devel-
   opment, Sijthoff and Noordhoff, Alphen a/d Rijn, 1982.
Linn, J.F., Cities in the Developing World: Policy for Equitable and
   Efficient Growth, Oxford University Press, New York, 1982.
Safa, H. (ed), Toward a Political Economy of Urbanization in Third World
   Countries, Oxford University Press, New York, 1982.
Snow, C.P., The Two Cultures and the Scientific Revolution, Cambridge
   University Press, New York, 1959.

3 Emerging Trends in Regional Development Planning: The Southeast Asian Experiences

R. P. MISRA AND ED. B. PRANTILLA

1. AN OVERVIEW

Until the 1960s regional development planning had two purposes. First, it aimed at better utilization and management of natural resources of a country. The spate of river valley projects promoted in the fifties in the LDCs and in the thirties in the USA meant, in essence, the actualization of the concept of regional planning for resource development. Second, it was a reaction against the neglect by the national governments of regional and local interests on the one hand and natural and social identities on the other. As such it was a subnational process designed to evolve spatially balanced national development. The balance was guided by considerations of regional cultural affinities and the peculiarities of natural endowments. It however, cut across national boundaries when commonality of interests and interdependences were caused by natural forces. The case of Mekong River valley project could be cited as an example.

The 1960s saw a marked shift in regional planning theory and practice. Natural resources and culture were no longer the bases for regionalization nor the central concern of regional development planning. It emerged perhaps from the realization that except in very early stages, natural resources and cultural traits alone did not determine the pattern and structure of development. The flow of goods and services and the spatial location and structure of their production and consumption are equally or more powerful than natural or cultural forces in determining the quantity and quality of economic development. The empirical evidences of lumpiness of human activities especially the manufacturing ones, and circular tendencies for the growing areas to grow further and poor areas to get poorer, also strengthened the moves to take regional planning outside the exclusive province of physical planning.

All this ultimately gave rise to Regional Science as an analytical discipline cutting across conventional disciplinary boundaries. Armed with the language of mathematics and charged with a missionary zeal, Regional Science made unprecedented inroads in economics and geography. Its influence on other disciplines was not inconsiderable. But the very strength of Regional Science ultimately proved to be its weakness. Its preoccupation with quantitative analysis led to overgeneralization, and acceptance of overly restrictive assumptions to facilitate mathematical modelling. Its emphasis on efficiency led to a neglect of equity issues.

In the early 1970s, regional development planning was neither a physical planning discipline, nor was it coterminous with Regional Science. It recognized that national or regional economic growth, even if feasible, did not necessarily ensure better distribution of fruits of development among individuals and groups of people. Spatial policies and strategies could be the means and not ends of a more egalitarian development process. The 1970s was also the period during which the newly independent countries realized the importance of cooperation among themselves regionally, as well as globally, to overcome the hurdles they might face in the future. Some of these countries tried to form regional groupings for defense and/or economic cooperation while at the same time formulated national regional development strategies to minimize internal regional disparities.

By the 1980s, regional development planning, at least in Asia, emerged as a multilevel planning and development discipline. It became a tool to integrate socio-economic space. Thus it encompassed regional entities constituted by a number of national states on the one hand, and subnational units constituted by a few small communities on the other. Consequently, regional development planning is being adopted as one of the main instruments in Southeast Asian countries to mobilize the resources of the country to the optimum capacity and to ensure a minimum level of equity in socio-economic development. This paper reviews the approaches and methods of planning these countries are using collectively and individually to restructure their economies. Only four ASEAN countries - the Philippines, Indonesia, Malaysia and Thailand - have been selected for case study, as dependable data on other countries are not readily available (figure 1). Currently all ASEAN countries, (except Singapore which is an island state), have evolved a well conceived governmental organization to prepare and execute regional development plans. Each country is divided into regions and subregions for multilevel regional planning. The success of ASEAN as a regional grouping of five Southeast Asian nations has made these countries a good laboratory for analyzing the theory and practice of regional development.

Regional planning per se is not new to Southeast Asia. It was introduced in some of these countries in the form of river basin planning in the 1950s and 1960s [1]. The Mekong River valley project is still on the agenda of the ESCAP. It was also adopted as a means to chart the development of major metropolitan regions like Manila, Bangkok, and Jakarta. They were, however, isolated cases designed to better utilize the natural resources of the country or to control the expansion of large urban centres [2]. Some attempts at population redistribution were also made in the colonial period [3], but none of these could be considered as elements of a systemic planning and development process aimed at rearticulating the spatial economies of these countries.

What is presented below is a review of the approaches and methods of regional development planning in these countries identifying the gaps which must be filled in order that regional planning serves the purpose it is meant to serve i.e. (1) to increase productivity, and (2) distribute the fruits of economic development equitably so that mass poverty is eradicated and resources of the country are optimally utilized.

2. SUPRANATIONAL REGIONAL COOPERATION

Five island and peninsular countries of Southeast Asia established the Association of Southeast Asian Nations (ASEAN) in 1967 for strengthening the 'existing bonds of regional solidarity and cooperation'. The countries signing the Bangkok declaration were the Philippines, Indonesia, Malaysia, Thailand and Singapore. The association was formed to ensure 'stability and security from external interference'. To realize this objective, the signatories decided to 'accelerate the economic growth, social progress and cultural development' and to settle any disputes

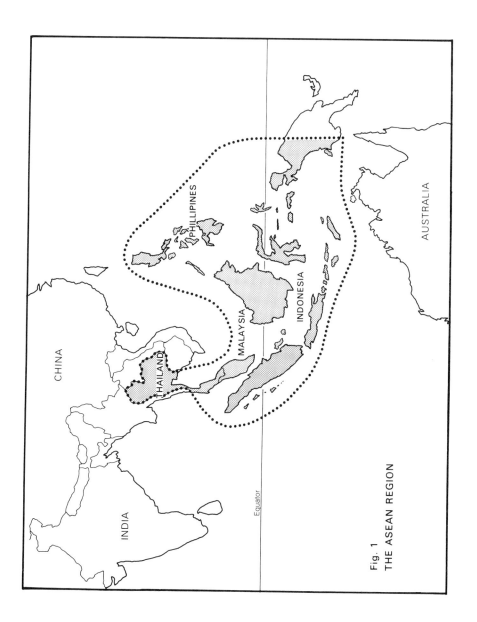

Fig. 1
THE ASEAN REGION

arising among them through peaceful means [4]. It sought economic cooperation to eliminate 'poverty, hunger, disease and illiteracy' in the
member countries.

The Bangkok declaration represented the growing desire on the part of
developing countries to disassociate themselves from the hegemonistic
ambits of the two superpowers and to seek cooperation among themselves
to generate a self-reliant development process. It is pertinent to note
that almost all the governments which originally opted for membership
were anti-communist and highly authoritarian. The ASEAN, although
launched in 1967 reached maturity only after the declaration of ASEAN
Concord and Treaty of Amity and Cooperation in Southeast Asia in 1975 [5].
Even though the original purpose behind the formation of ASEAN was political, since 1977 economic cooperation overshadows other roles. The
Preferential Trading Agreement (PTA) signed in 1977 was designed to promote trade among the member countries [7]. The commodities included in
the preferential list are primary as well as industrial. By mid 1981
as many as 6,581 items were exchanged carrying none or nominal tariff.

Another area of economic cooperation is the ASEAN Industrial Project
(AIP) which launches projects for meeting the shortage of essential
commodities. Projects based on regional raw materials are given preference as they save foreign exchange and create employment, e.g. urea,
superphosphates, potash, petro-chemicals, steel, soda ash, new print and
rubber products [8]. AIP projects are joint ventures of ASEAN members;
the host country meets two-thirds of the cost and the remainder is met
primarily by the other four countries (with Singapore's share being
nominal).

Yet another instrument of economic cooperation is the ASEAN Industrial
Complementation (AIC). Under this arrangement certain products of an
industry are allocated to participating countries and receive tariff
preferences. Other participating members cannot set up new production
facilities or expand existing ones for a period of two to four years
(depending on whether the product is old or new).

The other areas of cooperation are energy, food, banking, transport
and communications, science and technology, environment and social development. For each of these, there is a committee either under the
aegis of the ASEAN Foreign Ministers or the ASEAN Economic Ministers.
In all, there are nine such committees. Figure 2 gives the organizational structure of the ASEAN in 1981.

3. PROBLEMS AND PROSPECTS OF ASEAN REGIONAL COOPERATION

The ASEAN has made efforts in the direction of economic and political
cooperation. This section examines the sources of its strengths and
weaknesses and identifies problems which may create internal convulsions
in the future. Economic cooperation among the ASEAN countries is building up at a slow speed. For example, there is no spectacular change in
trade flows among the ASEAN countries although one does notice slight
shifts since 1976 (table 1). There is no major shift in the rate of
intra-ASEAN trade to the total foreign trade of these countries. In
1970 the ratio of intra-ASEAN to Total Foreign Trade was 17.0. In 1978,
it declined to 13.5 and rose again to 18.6 in 1980. This is largely
because the ASEAN countries (except Singapore) are exporters of primary
goods and there are little complementarities. Thus they compete among
themselves for the export market. For example 70% of Indonesian export
consists of crude oil and another 28% of timber, rubber, palm oil, tin
and petroleum. The Philippines export sugar, coconut oil, copper,

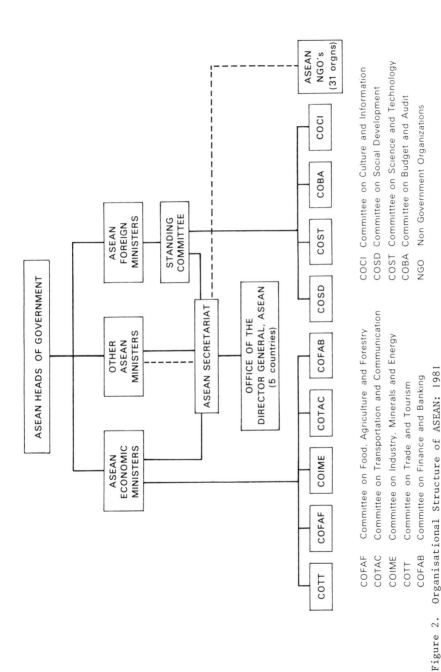

COFAF Committee on Food, Agriculture and Forestry   COCI Committee on Culture and Information
COTAC Committee on Transportation and Communication   COSD Committee on Social Development
COIME Committee on Industry, Minerals and Energy   COST Committtee on Science and Technology
COTT   Committee on Trade and Tourism   COBA Committee on Budget and Audit
COFAB Committee on Finance and Banking   NGO   Non Government Organizations

Figure 2. Organisational Structure of ASEAN: 1981

23

Table 1

Trade Relations Among ASEAN Countries and between ASEAN and the rest of the world

	Total	To DC	To LDC	To ASEAN
Indonesia				
1975	925	900	720	1,171
1980	2,935	2,645	3,930	4,905
Malaysia				
1975	320	280	350	360
1980	1,085	940	1,230	1,125
Philippines				
1975	270	255	450	450
1980	675	550	1,956	2,930
Singapore				
1975	485	2,215	2,185	–
1980	1,755	6,725	8,935	–
Thailand				
1975	310	400	140	265
1980	925	1,200	665	890
ASEAN				
1975	450	525	535	615
1980	1,455	1,525	2,245	2,305

DC   – Development Countries
LDC   – Less Developed Countries
ASEAN Countries: Increase in exports with 1966 as base = 100

Source :   United Nations, Yearbook of International Trade Statistics
           and ESCAP, Foreign Trade Statistics of Asia and the Pacific
           1975-78.

timber and copra, and Thailand exports rubber, rice, sugar, maize and tin.

Cooperation and integration are possible only if the cooperating entities are at the same level of achievement, are themselves integrated internally and have complementary economic structures. Some of the ASEAN countries do not have any of these. The Philippines is pursuing an export oriented industrialization policy, while Indonesia and Malaysia are set on import substitution policy.

There are also problems in the area of political cooperation. For example, there are differences between Thailand and Malaysia over the communist and Islamic insurgencies on the border and between Singapore on the one hand and Malaysia and Indonesian on the other over the issue of free navigation through the Malaccas.

In matters of external dangers, the perceptions of ASEAN countries are not the same. Philipines and Indonesia are concerned about the threat from China and of recent Japanese defense build-up. Thailand however,

considers Vietnam to be the main source of trouble. All this has led
to a situation where despite heroic efforts, there exist simmering problems with the potential of blowing up to great proportions once the
unifying forces, especially the external threats, are eased even slightly. It is difficult to predict at this stage the chances of success for
the ASEAN. Whatever the end result, the ASEAN is an interesting experiment in supranational regional planning and is likely to prompt other
countries to join regional economic groupings for national defense as
well as economic development.

4. SUBNATIONAL REGIONAL DEVELOPMENT PLANNING

The ASEAN countries countries have adopted subnational planning goals.
Since the organic link which must exist between national-planning and
local planning, (both of which have received prior government attention), is not well developed, regional planning has been viewed as an
important link in spatial economic development at the subnational level.

Delineation of regions. Regional delineation in the four ASEAN countries was done arbitrarily. The precise set of criteria upon which
the regions were delineated is not available, and has to be inferred
from the development plans of these four countries. Table 2 provides
a profile of the average population and size of regions in the four
ASEAN countries. There is no consistent size or pattern between
regions within each country. However, there is one similarity.
   In each of the four countries there is a primate city. This is particularly marked in Thailand, Indonesia, and the Philippines, and to a
lesser degree Malaysia. Thus, the Central Region of Thailand, which includes Bangkok, accounted for approximately 60 percent of the country's
gross national product (GNP). The Central Region also has the highest
GDP growth rate relative to the other regions and the highest per capita
income in the whole kingdom.
   In the Philippines, Southern Tagalog Region which included Metro
Manila (before the latter was separated to form the National Capital
Region), leads the rest of the country in almost all the economic indicators. It is the most industrialised region, has the highest per
capita income, and has the best social service facilities. Hence in
1974, Southern Tagalog accounted for 18 percent of the agriculture gross
domestic product (GDP) of the country, 63 percent of manufacturing, 30
percent of construction, 75 percent of transportation, communication,
storage and utilities, 64 percent of commerce, and 54 percent of services.
   The presence of a large primate city also characterises Indonesia.
While primacy is not critical in Malaysia, the Central Region which
includes Kuala Lumpur) also mirrors the significant effect of the largest city in that country.
   In terms of administrative set up, the Philippines and Indonesia have
a multilevel planning framework. Thus in the Philippines, there are
municipal development bodies, city planning and development boards, provincial development councils, regional development councils, and finally
there is a central planning and policy making body known as the National
Economic and Development Authority (NEDA) headed by the President of the
Republic. The central planning body of Indonesia, known as the National
Development Planning Board (BAPPENAS) has a similar structure, with
planning bodies (BAPPEDA) at the provincial level and planning units at
the regional or kabupaten and the municipal or katamadya levels of the

government in various parts of the country. The main development region (MDR) of Indonesia, at present, seems not to have yet acquired a distinctive development planning body of its own separate from the BAPPENAS.

Thailand and Malaysia, however, seem to present a different approach. Relative to the Philippines and Indonesia, Thailand and Malaysia have highly centralised planning bodies. Thus, the National Economic and Development Board (NESDB) of Thailand and the Economic Planning Unit (EPU) of the Prime Minister's Office in Malaysia have divisions which take care of regional development planning. The regions of Thailand and Malaysia do not have a singular body unique to the region which will do the planning, coordination, project implementation, monitoring and evaluation of the progress of development in the region. Subregional development bodies however, exist in both countries, i.e., the state and the subregional development authorities in Malaysia and the changwats and the amphoes in Thailand. Tables 3 to 6 present the regional delineation of the four ASEAN countries. A region is defined as a relatively contiguous land mass which is in approximately uniform stages of development,

Table 2

Profile of Existing Average Administrative Units, ASEAN countries, 1979

Item	Indonesia	Malaysia	Thailand	Philippines
National				
Population	142,900,000	13,100,000	45,400,000	46,700,000
Area (km^2)	1,919,000	330,000	514,000	300,000
Region				
Population	36,000,000	2,183,000	11,375,000	3,890,000
Area (km^2)	480,000	55,000	128,000	25,000
Number	4	6	4	12
Province		(state)		
Population	5,500,000	936,000	641,000	354,000
Area (km^2)	74,000	24,000	7,000	2,300
Number	26	14	71	132
Municipality	(Kabupaten/ Katamadya)	(district)	(district)	
Population	565,000	18,200	71,000	32,000
Area (km^2)	7,600	4,600	800	210
Number	253	72	642	1,445

has similar resources and economic activities, and is dominated by a single metropolitan area. In practice a region consists of one large state or a group of small states.

In the Philippines, the regions are delineated for 'administrative, planning and management purposes with special attention paid to the problems of regional equity and existing administrative, political and ethnic boundaries'. Originally, the number of regions was eleven. In 1975 however, the clamour for a separate Muslim Region gave rise to Central Mindanao Region (Region XII) which was carved out of the Northern and Southern Mindanao Regions.

The regional delineation of Indonesia is geared towards a growth centre strategy. As a result, the country is divided into four main develop-

26

ment regions (MDR) supposedly to 'ensure the efficient achievement of
regional development in harmony as well as in balance, among the sectors within each development region and among development regions'.
The criteria used in delineating an MDR focus on the interrelationships
between trade, production, finance, services and other economic activities. Provinces are units of MDR. Administrative boundaries and organisations of provinces are unaffected by the regional grouping.

Table 3
Regional Delineation in Malaysia

Region	States	Regional Area km^2	Population 1980
Northern		32,180	4,453
	Kedah Perak Perlin Pulau Pinang		
Central		16,350	3,449
	Federal Territory Melaka Nederi Sembilan Selangor		
Eastern		63,910	2,190
	Kelantan Pahang Trangganu		
Southern		19,000	1,730
	Johor		
Sabah		71,860	876
	Sabah		
Sarawak		124,490	1,278
	Sarawak		
Total		327,790	13,976

Source: Government of Malaysia, Fourth Malaysia Plan 1981-1985,
         (Kuala Lumpur: 1981), p. 99; and Government of Malaysia,
         Third Malaysian Plan 1976-1980, (Kuala Lumpur, 1976), pp.
         144 and 208.

Table 5 reveals that an MDR in Indonesia can be as large or larger
than the whole of the Philippines or Malaysia. The four MDR's, however, are further subdivided into ten development regions. The MDR of
Indonesia does not have a development planning body of its own, nor a
plan. Instead annual regional consultations are held in each of the
four main development regions for all member BAPPEDA and representatives of the Regional Development Division of BAPPENAS and central government department to mark the initiation of the annual budget cycles.
The BAPPEDA then return to their respective provinces and work with

Table 4
Regional Delineation in the Philippines

Regions	Provinces	Regional Capital	Region Area km²	Population 1977 (million)
National Capital Region		Metro Manila	2,806	4.970
Ilocos	Abra, Benguet Ilocos, Norte, Ilocos Sur, La Union Mt. Province	San Fernando	21,568	3.281
Cagayan Valley	Batanes, Cagayan Ifugao, Isabela Kalinga-Apayas, Rueva Vizcaya, Quirino	Tuguegarao	36,403	1.934
Central Luzon	Bataan, Bulacan Nueva Ecija, Pampanga Tarlac, Zambales	San Fernando	18,278	4,210
Southern Tagalog	Batangas, Cavite, Laguna Marindugue, Occidental Mindoro, Oriental Mindoro, Palawan, Quezon Rizal Ramblon	Metro Manila	44,707	5,214
Bicol	Albay, Camarines Norte Camarines Sur, Catanduanes, Masbate Sorsozon	Lagaspi	17,632	3.195
Western Visayas	Aklan, Antigue Capiz, Iloilo Negros Occidental	Iloilo City	20,223	4.146
Central Visayas	Bohol, Cebu Negros Oriental Siguijor	Cebu City	14,951	3,387

Table 4

Regional Delineation in the Philippines (continued)

Regions	Provinces	Regional Capital	Region Area km^2	Population 1975 (million)
Eastern Visayas	Leyte, Southern Leyte Eastern Samar, Northern Samar, Western Samar	Tackloban City	21,432	2.599
Western Mindanao	Zamboanga del Sur, Zamboanga del Norte, Basilan, Sulu, Tawi-Tawi	Zamboanga City	18,685	2.047
Northern Mindanao	Agasun del Norte, Agasun del Sur, Bukidnon, Camiguin, Misamis Occidental, Misamis Oriental Surigao del Norte	Cagayan de Oro City	28,559	2.313
Southern Mindanao	South Cotabato, Davao del Norte, Davao del Sur, Davao Oriental Surigao del Sur	Davao City	31,580	2.714
Central Mindanao	Lanao del Norte Lavao del Sur, North Cotabato, Maguindanao Sultan Kudarat	Cotabato City	23,024	2.071
Total			299,847	42.071

Table 5
Regional Delineation in Indonesia

Region	Provinces	Regional Capital	Region Area km²	Population 1975 (million)
MDR*A	D.I. Aceh, North Sumatera West Sumatera, Riau	Medan	320,782	14.834
MDR*B	D.K.I.Jakarta, West Java Central Java, D.I.Jogjakarta, East Java, Benkulu, Lampung South Sumatera, West Kelimantan, Jambo	Jakarta	464,885	67.652
MDR*C	East Kalimantan, Central Kalimantan, South Kalimantan, Bali, West Nusa Tenggara	Surabaya	446,711	33.451
MDR*D	Northern Sulawesi, Central Sulawesi, Southeast Sulawasi, South Sulawesi, Maluku, East Nusa Tenggara, West Irian	Ujungpadang	794,676	16.649
Total			2,027,054	132,586

*Main Development Region

Table 6
Regional Delineation in Thailand

Region	Number of Provinces	Area km²	Population 1979 (million)
Northern	17	170,031	9.493
Central (including Bangkok)	9	21,074	8.138
Eastern	7	36,391	3,337
Western	8	46,106	3.576
Northeast	16	170,237	15.792
Southern	14	70,212	5.715
Total		514,051	46.051

Source of Population Data: Phisit Pakkasem, 'Role of Urban System in National Development in Thailand', in National Paper presented at a Seminar on Urbanisation and National Development, UNCRD, Nagoya, Japan, 20-28 October, 1980.

local agencies in preparing preliminary project proposals for the
national consultations involving all development regions during the last
quarter of the calendar year. Development budget allocations from the
central government are apparently channelled directly to the provinces
which have a certain extent of autonomy and responsibility in planning
and managing their development projects. The MDR at present may be
serving only as a framework within which the central government as well
as the provinces can coordinate and integrate development policies and
programmes in the area.

Regional delineation in Thailand has recently changed. Whereas in the
Fourth Five Year Plan of 1977-81 there were four regions in the country,
currently there are six. The question of homogeneity, culture and sociopolitical factors were considered in the delineation of the regions besides purely economic and planning factors.

Regions in Thailand function the same manner as in Indonesia. Since
government agencies do not operate according to regional divisions, the
changwat or the province is more operational than the region in terms
of planning and implementation of the programmes and projects. The
regions, nevertheless, are used as the basic framework for formulating
regional development policy, such as the closure of regional income gaps
and allocation of government expenditure.

The Philippines also adopted the growth centre approach as a strategy
for regional development. The regional capital of each of the twelve
regions was also designated as the growth centre. The designation of a
growth centre for each region corresponds to a higher hierarchy referred
to as the Tripolar Urban Strategy. The basic argument behind this
strategy is the simultaneous development of two urban areas to act as
counter-magnets to Metro Manila. The counterpoles in this strategy are
Metropolitan Cebu in Central Visayas and Metropolitan Davao in Southern
Mindanao. Thus, 'three hierarchies of urban settlements will be developed; the first around the Manila area, the second around CEBU City area,
and the third around the Davao City area'. Regional growth centres are
expected to develop in relation to the three metropolitan areas.

The formal designation of a growth centre for each region in the
Philippines contrasts with that of Malaysia. Regions in Malaysia identified in the Fourth Malaysia Plan do not mention their regional capi-
tals. Instead, growth centres seem to be more identified with the state,
and a state may have more than one growth centre. Studies regarding
growth centres in Malaysia, therefore, were conducted state-wide, as
exemplified by their master plan studies. Nevertheless, the objectives
of the two countries is to spread urban development and reduce the concentration of population in already congested areas. In addition, dis-
persing economic growth to a national urban network, underlined their
regionalisation strategy.

While regions were delineated in the four ASEAN countries using different criteria all have given prominence to regional development and
planning during the past years. Moreover, what is unique in ASEAN
countries is the use of regionalisation and regional development planning as a means for integrating the country.

5. THE REGIONAL DEVELOPMENT PLANNING PROCESS

The four ASEAN countries do not follow similar approaches in formulating
their regional development plans. In the Philippines, a regionally
based institution is mandated and responsible for formulating regional
development plans. Indonesia, Thailand and Malaysia formulate their

regional development plans either through their central planning offices or use the services of foreign consultants. Planning studies done by consultants, although invariably of high quality, may not actually be strictly categorised as plans. They provide the government with an excellent analysis of the development potentials of the region, alternative development strategies and even a listing of projects which a government may further investigate as to their feasibility. A number of these studies are available, for example, the South Thailand Regional Planning Study by Hunting Technical Services Ltd., the East Indonesia Regonal Development Study by the Government of Alberta, Canada, the Kedah-Perlis Development Study by Economic Consultants Ltd., in Malaysia, and the Western Region Planning Study by the Halcrow-ULC Ltd. in Thailand. While most studies use the conventional approach, the Institute for Planning and Development of Israel, faced with a scarcity of data in Northern Thailand, developed the Concepts-Strategy-Projects (CSP) approach (also known as the Themes-Strategy-Projects approach), which focussed on key issues and projects. It was observed, however, that the CSP does not produce a comprehensive plan in the strict sense of the word.

These planning studies rarely give the time frame within which recommendations should be implemented. It could be presumed however, that these are long term 'plans' because they analysed the development potentials and alternatives of the region. This approach contrasts with countries that produce five, ten and twenty-five years development plans, wherein the five year plan contains specific projects by sector, along with the budgetary requirements for the plan period.

A systematic approach to analysing the process of regional development planning in the four ASEAN countries, would require the planning process to be divided into four parts: (1) diagnosis; (2) policies and strategies; (3) programmes and projects; and (4) coordination and integration systems.

Diagnosis. This part of the regional plan generally focusses on analyses of existing conditions in the planning area, particularly on identifying problems, regional needs, resources and potentials. The depth of an analysis is directly proportional to the data available. Judging from the reports categorised as di gnostic, all four ASEAN countries seem to be spending their time and money on this aspect of the regional plan.

The diagnostic phase of regional development planning in the four ASEAN countries makes use of simple statistical methods, e.g., central tendencies and dispersion methods, simple regression and correlation, location quotient, shift share analysis, and an extensive use of tabular and graphic analyses. Population data are handled via ratio methods, and specific age projection is done by standard interpolation techniques such as Karup-King or Sprague Fifth Difference Formula. Deficiency in food and social services are usually identified through the use of norms, e.g. comparing the daily requirement of calories or food with actual consumption, standard pupil-teacher ratio in elementary grades to actual pupil-teacher ratio, standard population-doctor ratio versus actual population-doctor ratio, etc. Projections of population requirements in food and social services are standard estimation procedures, e.g. elasticity of demand coefficients were used in the Nusa Tenggara Timur Development Plan of Indonesia.

Regional development objectives and targets can be expected to be influenced by the diagnostic phase. There is an ongoing debate however, on the structuring of plan objectives. There are two schools of thought: the standard economic planning approach, and the corporate planning approach. The regional development plans of the four ASEAN countries are following the economic planning model of setting objectives, e.g. 'to increase income, to achieve equitable distribution of income, to increase employment, and preservation of environment'. Criticisms of this type of objective setting are: (1) the lack of specificity, i.e. the same set of objectives could be used by any regions of any country in the world; (2) validation of this type of objective is difficult, i.e., it is hard to measure whether it has already been attained, and (3) its usefulness to policy and strategy formulation and identification of programmes and projects are limited. Thus, the main focus of the attack is on operationalisation issues. Indeed, an objective such as, 'to have an equitable income distribution' may contain the egalitarian philosophy of the country and its concern for its citizenry, but does not offer any idea on how to achieve that objective.

Policies and strategies. The existence of a strong central government set up and the establishment of government ministries along functional lines have more or less dictated a generally top-down policy formulation with the expected sectoral bias for the regions in the four ASEAN countries. This is especially true in the case of Thailand and Malaysia, and to some degree in the Philippines and Indonesia. In the case of the Philippines, a feedback mechanism is provided and the local government units can reach the policy makers via the local and regional planning agencies. In addition, the twelve regional development plans contain policy recommendations and strategies for consideration by the central planning body.

Regional development plans of the four ASEAN countries use their national development plan policies and strategies as parameters. At the regional level, however, there is no clear indication whether the region's own policies and strategies take into consideration the policies and strategies of other regions. Indeed questions may be raised on whether the complementarity and synergetic aspects of regional development activities are completely taken care of by the present generation of regional plans.

For countries with operational regional development bodies, policy and strategy formulation may be done in consultation with other government agencies and local executives. The final adoption of regional development policies and strategies at the regional level is usually done with the regional development body in session. For example, in the Philippines, the Regional Development Council of the region has to pass a resolution approving the plan. The resolution automatically becomes an integral component of the document.

Intersectoral conflicts in the formulation of regional development policies and strategies are expected to occur during the process of policy and strategy formulation. Regional conflicts are generally ironed out during meetings and workshops held for this purpose. The vertical reconciliation of policies and strategies, on the other hand, is solved via the sectoral hierarchy or by the central coordinating body of the government. As a rule, however, the solution of regional-national policy conflict is largely biased towards the latter.

Programs and projects. The four ASEAN countries exhibited various approaches and a different understanding of the programs and projects phase of regional development planning. Thus, the Five Year Regional Development Plans of the Philippines contain specific projects by sector, including project description, priority among projects, schedule of implementation, and estimated budgetary requirements. On the other hand, the regional development planning studies have minimal project content and only specify alternative development strategies for the region.

Programs and project, when identified, are usually confined to government financed activities. The twelve regional development plans of the Philippines, for example, have a limited number of projects under the private sector, although lately the translation of these twelve regional development plans into their equivalent regional development investment programs have forced regional development planners in the Philippines to search for a mechanism that will affect the so-called public-private sector interface. The issue, however, is far from being settled. The same observation is also evident in the regional plans or studies of Indonesia, Malaysia and Thailand.

Coverage of programs and projects content of the regional development plans in the four ASEAN countries also varies. Some plans, like the planning studies in Malaysia, present only a few major projects. On the other hand, the regional development plans of the Philippines give an exhaustive listing of every government agency program and project proposed for the region in question.

Identification of programs and projects can only be inferred from the development plans of Indonesia, Malaysia, and Thailand. In the Philippines, project identification seems to permeate at all levels of the regions's government machinery. Thus, the regional development plan includes projects identified by local government units as well as those identified by individual government agencies operating at both the local and regional levels. To direct this complex activity, the Regional Development Council issues the policies, strategies and priorities of the region to government agencies and local government units to guide them in identifying programs and projects. The identified programs and projects later undergo the region's selection and evaluation process before they are included in the plan.

Those who are seriously watching the efficacy of regional development planning will be looking for results and not the number of plans issued. Thus, as planners become aware of the implementation issues expected, attention to project development as a vital component of regional planning will be intensified.

Integration and coordination. There are three major goals: (1) description of how the regional planning body interacts with various government agencies at the regional and national levels during the process of plan formulation; (2) the process by which the regional development body integrates the local government's and agency's plan with the regional development plan; and (3) a monitoring system to keep track of the progress of plan implementation.

Although it may only take account of public investments, regional development planning necessarily implies integration and coordination of development activities of government entities both at the regional and national levels. A description of how this will be done is usually ignored in the regional development plans of the four ASEAN countries. There were initial attempts in the Philippines, e.g., the twelve regional plans for 1978-82 and 1982-87. Attention was devoted to development administration in the plan formulation process, including a suggested scheme for interagency and hierarchical interactions. Nevertheless, integration and coordination in a particular country is seldom articulated in the plan but may be ingrained in the bureaucratic set up and formalized in a system of degrees and circulars that the executive of the country issues from time to time. Lack of attention to integration and coordination mechanisms in the regional development plans of the four ASEAN countries, therefore, does not necessarily mean the non-existence of such mechanisms in the country.

6. REGIONAL BUDGETTING

Budgeting is traditionally excluded from the model, however, as regional development planning in the four ASEAN countries focusses on public investments it is important to consider budgeting as an activity in which planners have to take active part. Development plans cannot be implemented unless they are translated into their budgetary equivalent and are approved for execution by the government. The government budget in addition to financing the maintenance and operation of the government system, mobilises the resources of the public sector to implement the programs and projects scheduled for development in a given year. For any government financed project or activity, to be implemented it must be included in the approved government budget.

It is difficult to assess the extent of regional budgeting practised in Thailand, Malaysia and Indonesia. Malaysia, which established regional development authorities that formulated regional plans, seems to provide a centrally generated budget consisting of grants and loans for each authority. Development projects implemented by other government departments in the same region are independent of the regional development authority. Indonesia appeared to be operating also in a similar framework, with grants and other subsidies given to provinces and regions.

Regional budgets in Thailand appear to be solely determined at the national level, and to some extent the same may be said of Indonesia. The amount of public funds going to the regions in this sense may hinge, by and large, on the political strength of the region's representative in the national body.

Budgeting at the regional level has become necessary following the Philippine's acceptance of regional development planning. Thus, all ministries and agency heads were instructed to have their regional offices formulate their respective budgets in conformity with the priorities established by the Regional Development Councils. The Regional Development Councils in turn are directed to recommend to the National Economic and Development Authority and to the Ministry of the Budget a system of priorities for the allocation of budgetary resources for programs and projects of national government offices in the region in accordance with the regional development plan.

Giving the responsibility to the regional level for determining the inclusion of programs and projects in the national budget places stress on the coordinative and integrative powers of the regional development bodies. But it also provides a framework for plan evaluation. To achieve this, the Regional Development Councils of the Philippines conduct sectoral workshops with representatives from different ministries and local government units and discuss priority programs and projects for all provinces, cities and municipalities of the region in accordance with national and regional objectives and policies. The outcome of the workshops is presented later to the Regional Development Council in session for deliberation and approval. Finally, the Ministry of the Budget conducts a regional budget hearing where the Regional Development Council presents a summary of the region's strategy and priorities, followed by a presentation and discussion of each ministry's or agency's regional budget. The Ministry of the Budget then integrates the regional budgets with the national budget and presents it to the Parliament for deliberation and approval. The revised regional budget is generally sent back to the Regional Development Councils for reprogramming and reprioritisation before final approval by the President.

It is evident that the four ASEAN countries do not underestimate the role of the budget in development. On the other hand, a number of important issues do not seem to receive the kind of attention needed for policy and decision makers to exploit fully the powers of the regional budget. At the top of the list is the apparent neglect of a workable planning and budgeting interface. It is, for example, considered a matter of procedure to assume that the plan is the basis of the budget. However, to what degree a budget attains the prescription in the plan is, by and large, a matter of conjecture.

This brings us to another important issue, i.e., budget evaluation relative to the objectives of the plan. To a large extent, budget evaluation at present, excluding the usual political acceptability criterion, generally focusses on affordability and efficiency, i.e., whether the cost of an activity is acceptable and within the budget ceiling, and whether its per unit output cost is within the standard set by the government. Although, to some extent, the zero base budgeting (ZBB), performance budgeting, and planning-programming-budgeting system (PPBS) may have evaluative content vis à vis the plan, these are generally localised project by project in orientation. Thus, a regional development plan may have a targeted agricultural output growth of 10 percent per annum, but there is no way of knowing whether the budget for the agricultural sector can achieve such target. The problem of course, could be made easier if the target growth rate of, say, the agricultural sector output can be reduced to: (a) the area to be irrigated; (b) the number of extention workers necessary; (d) the amount of seeds and fertiliser needed; and (d) the overhead costs, etc., which are easily translated into their budgetary equivalents. So far however, the present planning-budgeting relationship has not taken this direction.

The lack of adequate evaluation of the correspondence between the plan and the budget to a large extent may have been compounded by the seemingly scarce technical papers or studies of budget evaluation regarding development. Generally, papers written on this subject limit themselves to the role of the budget in planning and on the budgeting process.

Finally, there is a tendency among planners not to translate their proposed development strategy into cost terms. This is completely at variance with those in the government budget office where all activities must be translated into their corresponding cost terms and specific budgetary object expenditures classified. Doubts could even be raised, in fact, on whether regional development planners fully understand their respective country's budgeting process, or whether they can translate their regional development plans into their equivalent budgetary language.

Implementation

Planning becomes a meaningful activity only if it leads to implementation. Otherwise, a plan becomes an end in itself instead of an instrument for achieving the development objectives.

The process that starts with planning and ends with implementation is undeniably long and complex. Indeed, where planning explores the various alternatives open to the regional economy, implementation

requires the setting up of political and administrative measures to
mobilise manpower and financial resources and entails the involvement
of various government agencies, local government units, and the people
to prepare and execute programs and projects. In particular, effective
and efficient implementation of programs and project entails the stream-
lining of institutional and interagency linkages to effect coordination
and integration of development activities. Similarly, a system for promoting popular participation has to be set up and made operational to
achieve linkage with prospective clienteles of development programs and
projects.

Except in Malaysia, where authority type regional development bodies
plan and implement projects, planning agencies in Indonesia, Thailand
and the Philippines do not perform the role of implementing programs and
projects. Separation of planning and implementation bodies may be considered debatable, but most policy makers and students of development
see this as necessary in order to prevent undue concentration of power
in one group, particularly in the planning ministry of the government's
bureaucratic machinery. This condition requires planners to argue their
case with other ministries and the Parliament, and to guarantee a 'give
and take' situation between planners and implementers.

In addition, coordination and integration functions without implementing powers will ensure that regional planners request and listen to the
opinions of implementing agencies on alternative strategies for the
region. Accordingly, to gain support for the plan, planners have to
discuss the plan with local government leaders and private sector representatives, a process which may not be necessary if planners have
implementation powers. This, however, does not mean that planners have
a lesser role during the implementation phase. By anticipating problems and providing corrective measures on the implementation of programs and projects, planners can become invaluable to line agencies of
the government. A number of failures in program/project implementation
for example, can be traced to poor or inadequate planning.

In the Philippines, the regional development bodies participate in
implementation from the budgeting process to process monitoring. The
Regional Development Councils are furnished with copies of quarterly
releases by the Ministry of the Budget on funds to major implementing
agencies in the region and, therefore, have more or less an exact knowledge of the flow of public expenditures in the region. Information
contained in the quarterly releases from the Ministry of the Budget also
indicates to what province the money is going, hence, cause for delays
on any provincial project can be immediately traced. Regional Development Councils also keep track of the progress of each major project and
its own monitoring system, but do not interfere with implementation
activities. Indeed, the interest of the Philippines' Regional Development Councils in monitoring essentially revolves around the activita-
tion of the regional machinery, in case an implementing agency encoun-
ters problems that need assistance.

At present, however, one of the most interesting as well as challeng-
ing aspects in implementation is how to obtain popular participation.
Basically, not all types of development projects warrant active participation on the part of the population. Popular participation, however,
becomes an extremely important dimension when proposed programs and
projects are directed towards solving the problems of a particular community. In this instance, it becomes necessary to have the community
leaders, or even the community itself participate in project planning.
Popular participation is easily achieved when people identify themselves with the program or project. It is observed in Southern Mindan-

ao, Philippines, for example, that community leaders will do their utmost to ensure the success of the project once they consider it as the 'village's own' activity.

A number of projects illustrate popular participation efforts. In the Philippines, the Masagana 99 would have had limited success without the active participation of the rice farmers; or the Barangay Road Program that gives the village leader the primary role in farm-to-market road construction. Popular participation is also the essence of gotong royong in Indonesia, and in the development schemes of Malaysia and Thailand. The four ASEAN countries, however, have yet to match the outstanding performance of the Republic of Korea with its Saemaul Undong.

Planners and policy makers unfortunately have not been able to fully harness and exploit the strategic importance of popular participation in planning and implementing development projects in the ASEAN countries.

Evaluation of Regional Development Plans

Theoretically, regional development plans could be subjected to two kinds of evaluation: (1) ex ante evaluation, or before the plan is submitted for government approval, usually the Parliament; and (2) ex post evaluation, or after the plan or portions of the plan have been implemented. Ex ante evaluation looks at the internal consistency of the plan and ideally should determine (a) whether the programs and projects can achieve the plan targets, and (b) whether the plan will produce the most desirable resource allocation pattern during the plan period. Ex post evaluation, on the other hand, determines whether: (1) the variables behave as expected in the plan, i.e., the objectives of targets are achieved; and (2) the actual impact of the plan is favourable to the population. Ex post evaluation serves as an important input in the next planning cycle.

Currently, ex ante evaluation of regional development plans as practised in the four ASEAN countries is essentially limited to assuring that regional development plans reflect the objectives, policies and strategies of the national development plan. Since regional development plans are generally formulated according to the guidelines issued by the national government, only minor changes are usually needed to make regional development plans consistent with the national plan. As such evaluation is embedded in the policy process and is seldom a source of a problem in actual practice. However, the absence of an overall programs and projects evaluation relative to the objectives or targets of the regional development plan does not ensure that the listed programs and projects in the plan will attain the objectives or targets.

All four ASEAN countries conduct periodic evaluation on the state of their regional and national economies. Although these can be considered as ex post evaluations of the plans in these countries, the absence of a set of validation criteria, i.e., standards from which the evaluation may be made, casts doubts on such evaluations of the operation of the plans. Existing ex post evaluation criteria employed by Indonesia, Malaysia, Thailand and the Philippines are generally biased towards aggregate economic variables at the regional and national levels. This conforms with the ex post evaluation practice of regional development plans in other countries. Reports on the lengths of roads constructed, number of hospitals built, and school houses erected are available. While these reports provide evidence about activities there is less indication of their impact, i.e., whether the road served its purpose, or the hospital improved the health of the people, or the school improved the community's level of education.

Ambiguities regarding the impact of regional development planning is less true of Malaysia whose efforts to alleviate the condition of depressed regions are shown to produce significant results. Malaysia coefficients of regional inequality for the years 1971, 1980 and 1985 showed a sustained decline on both the weighted and unweighted indices (Table 7) a strong indication that regional incomes are moving towards convergence. This movement towards convergence of regional incomes accompanies the impressive performance of Malaysia in its poverty reduction efforts. Indeed, the incidence of poverty in the country has declined progressively from 49.3 percent in 1970, to 43.9 percent in 1975, to 37.7 percent in 1976, and to 29.2 percent in 1980.

Table 7
Coefficients of Ineqiality, Malaysia, 1971, 1980, 1985

	1971	1980	1985*
Malaysia			
V_u	0.4026	0.3873	0.2752
V_{uw}	0.3515	0.3304	0.2410
Peninsula Malaysia			
V_u	0.3962	0.3800	0.2640
V_{uw}	0.3771	0.3530	0.2517

* Based on forecasted income from the Fourth Malaysia Plan

Source: William James, 'By-passed Areas, Regional Inequalities and Development Policies in Selected Southeast Asian Countries', Asian Development Bank Economic Staff Paper No. 4, Manila, 1981, p. 30.

$$V_w = \frac{\sqrt{\Sigma(y_i - \bar{y})^2 \, f_i/n}}{\bar{y}}$$

$$V_{uw} = \frac{\sqrt{\Sigma(y_i - \bar{y})^2 / N}}{\bar{y}}$$

where : y_i = average household income in region i
$\bar{y}$ = national average households income
f_i = population of the ith region
n = total population
N = number of regions

The Philippings provides a contrasting picture. In spite of Government poverty alleviation policies, no significant change is observed. Data for 1971 and 1975 revealed that the incidence of poverty may have worsened not only in the rural areas but also in Metro Manila. Thus, the percentage of families below the poverty line for all regions increased from 38.7 percent in 1971 to 45.3 percent in 1975. Of all regions, a dramatic change perhaps is seen in Metro Manila, where the incidence of poverty increased from 9.1 percent in 1971 to 30.9 percent in 1975. The increasing incidence of poverty is partly due to the increase in skewness of intraregional income distribution. This is evident from the alarming jump in the ratio of average family incomes in

Manila between 1975 and 1978 relative to the rest of the country. Accordingly, the increasing per capita income in each region, coupled with increasing or constant poverty incidence implies a worsening of intra-regional income distribution structure.

In spite of the descriptive evidence cited, a precise verdict cannot be made on the performance of regional development planning in the four ASEAN countries. For that, improved models or techniques to evaluate the impact of regional development planning have to be developed.

7. SUMMARY AND CONCLUSIONS

This paper discussed regional development planning in Indonesia, Malaysia, Philippines and Thailand. The development problem faced by Thailand, the Philippines, Indonesia and Malaysia are similar to some degree. And this similarity is clearly reflected in their attempts to form a regional group - the ASEAN. The progress of ASEAN as a regional cooperation venture at supranational level, was reviewed. The review traced the history of the ASEAN and identified its strengths and weaknesses. The ASEAN was primarily formed for defense but gradually its orientation shifted to economic cooperation. Cooperation in various fields has increased even though several problems have yet to be resolved. Unless the economic cooperation among the countries overrides these problems, the ASEAN will have a bleak future.

All four countries exhibited concentrations of economic activities in one or two urban centres. Thus, aggregate economic indicators hid regional income gaps. The incidence of poverty in two of the four ASEAN countries is high, and some of their regions are considered depressed. The governments of the four ASEAN countries were aware of these problems and had by and large employed a similar strategy in searching for answers to their socioeconomic problems. Accordingly, the four countries have adopted regional development planning, in addition to national planning, in recent years, to address the problems of income disparity. Consequently, the machinery for regional development planning has been laid down. Operationally, the system has yet to be tested.

The adoption of regional development planning also caused the four ASEAN governments to divide their countries into regions as units of regional development planning. Except in the Philippines where a development body at the regional level formulates and coordinates the planning and implementation of a regional development plan, the other three ASEAN countries use their regions only as frameworks for regional policy formulation and implementation. For example, Indonesia's Main Development Regions (MDR) which undeniably had the potential for development, seem to be currently limited to serve as fora for provincial coordination of programs and projects.

Due to their recent appearance regional development plans produced by the four ASEAN countries are essentially of the first generation type. These regional development plans range from a master plan/planning study type (Malaysia, Thailand and Indonesia) to a comprehensive type (the Philippines). The master plan/planning study type essentially focus on alternative development strategies for a region and a set of projects for development. The comprehensive type as seen in the Philippines is essentially a mini-national plan with intensive project listing. Currently, with the exception of Malaysia, wherein the spatial and physical components are coordinated, regional development plans in the four ASEAN countries have limited spatial content, and interregional relations in the plans are either weak or absent. The plans also focussed largely on public investment, although the role of the private sector in development

40

is recognised.

The four ASIAN countries do not clearly exhibit the mechanism by which regional development plans are integrated into the budget process. The Philippines addresses this issue and conducts an annual regional budget hearing at which the budget proposal of each government agency in the region is evaluated relative to the regional development plan. Indonesia also conducts consultative meetings where the proposed budgets of provinces in a region are discussed. Nevertheless, the interfacing of regional development plans with the budget process has still to be developed.

Evaluation of regional development plans in the four ASEAN countries, where on an ex ante or ex post basis, is in its initial stages. Studies are limited, however, on how this evaluation may be done to improve the planning and implementation of regional development plans.

NOTES

[1] These were prototypes of Tennessee Valley Authority in the USA.
[2] The concept of urban regional planning was derived from urbanised societies of Europe especially the United Kingdom.
[3] This refers to the transmigration process in Indonesia and the expansion of plantation agriculture in Malaysia.
[4] State secretariat of the Republic of Indonesia, ASEAN Summit Meeting, Bali, 23-25 February 1976, pp. 39-50.
[5] Ibid.
[6] The Treaty of Amity and Cooperation in Southeast Asia, Chapter 1, Article 2, ASEAN Summit Meeting, Bali, 23-25 February 1976, p. 46.
[7] ASEAN National Secretariat (Indonesia), ASEAN Document s.l.n.d., pp. 4-5.
[8] Declaration of ASEAN concord: B.2; Joint Press Communique of the Heads of Government, Bali, 23-25 February 1976.

4 Multilevel Planning: The Indian Experience

K. V. SUNDARAM

I.   INTRODUCTION

The limits to central direction of development efforts, and the desirability of encouraging planning and development management at sub-national
levels through decentralisation, have been increasingly recognised among
many developing countries today. A number of these countries now seem
to feel that the gap between plan formulation and its realisation in
their sub-national areas could be filled by a decentralised process of
decision making and popular participation. Consequently, planning
strategy is being reoriented towards sub-national and local level planning [1,2]. In countries like India, the search for an appropriate
methodology to enmesh planning from the top and planning from below
through a two-way linkage in the planning process is going on. New
policies and institutional changes necessary for developing efficiency in
a two-way planning process are also being devised. In short, the issue
of decentralisation in the form of multilevel planning seems to be at
the heart of the development strategies for the 80s. This better appreciation of the relevance of multilevel planning notwithstanding, the
methodology for such planning through a two-way linkage in the planning
process is still in a formative stage [3]. This paper proposes to discuss some of the crucial aspects of this methodology and the constraints
faced in its implementation. The Indian experience in operationalising
the multilevel planning process has many important lessons to offer in
this context.

2.   MULTILEVEL THEORY

The greatest merit of multilevel planning lies in its ability to tackle
the problems of the areas at sub-national levels with greater understanding and perception. At the national level, these problems are seen
as through ground glass, in a hazy and in a highly aggregated manner
through broad indicators of development. With multilevel planning, however, a sharpened focus is possible and the understanding of problems
gains in clarity and content. Consequently, the solutions devised also
become more meaningful and specific from the viewpoint of the area and
the community. The proximity to an area, which sub-national level planning makes possible, also means greater access to information. In an
optimal system decisions are taken at a spatial level, where information
could be obtained with relative ease, speed and authenticity at a lesser
cost and where responses to interventions could also be spontaneous and
effective. Thus multilevel planning understood in a system-theoretic
sense is a cost effective approach.

The efficiency of a multilevel planning approach also derives from the fact that it rests on the principle of 'function sharing', as it tends to differentiate activities according to the territorial levels where they could most effectively be performed. This 'territory function' nexus attains its acme of performance efficiency in a multilevel set up, as function sharing logically contributes to functional efficiency. In fact, one of the important steps in the multilevel planning process is the identification and demarcation of activities which could most effectively be performed at different levels.

Multilevel planning rests on the principle of 'area development'. This would imply greater efficiency of resource use, and better use of regional and local skills and manpower resources. The area development approach would ensure that those goods and services would be produced in areas which have a comparative advantage. This would encourage specialised production. Such specialisation would lead to an inter-area flow of goods and services, leading to a migration of the various factors of production, so that the cost efficiency criterion is satisfied. When regional and local resources are activitated, due to decentralised plan formulation and implementation, national resources are augmented in terms of better supply and quality. This aspect of better supply, i.e. delivery, needs to be emphasised because the distributional gains could be maximised through multilevel planning. In the context of the current orientations of development planning, with its emphasis on growth with distributive justice, especially to the rural poor, the role of multi-level planning is particularly significant. Thus the decentralised plan formulation and implementation not merely helps to increase the economic product but also to achieve distributional equity in the provision of basic minimum needs and services to the disadvantaged sections of the community and thus better the conditions of the rural poor.

Multilevel planning also increases the 'linkage effects' of development, primarily because of its reliance on the area approach to development. Thus from the technological point of view, the linkages between small and large enterprises are intensified and the diffusion of technology from the central level to the sub-national levels takes place in a systematic manner, ultimately leading to the optimal utilisation of resources. A concomitant effect of such development is increased local employment generation. Enhanced local employment opportunities will tend to reduce city-ward migration and will contain the population in the rural areas. This will not only regulate the accelerated rate of urbanisation but will also change the whole pattern of urbanisation in the country by developing the entire rural urban continuum at each point. In inducing all these changes, it may be seen that multilevel planning performs a trigger function and therefore must be seen as providing an essential input to development.

Perhaps the greatest disadvantage of multilevel planning lies in its ability to reach the people and draw their effective participation in development. Since multilevel planning is intended to bring about an enlarged redistribution of opportunities, it would imply more effective popular participation providing considerable opportunities for the people to take part in societal decision making in contributing to development and in benefitting from the fruits of development. By the term 'popular participation', it is not merely the association of elected representatives of the people which is intended, but more especially (in the context of the present day objectives of multilevel planning), the association of the majority of the population characterised by low incomes, low educational levels and restricted or non-existent opportunities. A decentralised territorial framework facilitates the access of the rural

masses to the decision making bodies. This however has to be deliber-
ately brought about by effecting appropriate changes in our institutional framework. This is because the representative bodies of elected
people in most developing countries today are dominated by the elites in
society.

3. LIMITATIONS OF MULTILEVEL PLANNING

The numerous advantages cited above like the better perception of developmental problems, greater access to information, function-sharing and
greater efficiency of resource use, skills and manpower and greater
degree of public participation, etc., no doubt emphasise forcefully the
logic for decentralised planning. While one may eulogise these virtues
of decentralisation, it is necessary to know that such decentralisation
also bristles with a number of problems, bottlenecks and constraints in
its implementation. These problems, bottlenecks and constraints come
to the surface only when we seek to experiment with decentralised planning in an area. Such experimentation has been tried in India. In the
present context, our analysis of the Indian experience will be limited
to four states, vis. Maharashtra, Gujarat, Karnataka, and Uttar Pradesh,
where inspired political leadership as well as a highly motivated bureaucracy have been instrumental in taking some concrete steps towards
decentralised planning. At this state, it should be emphasised that
this 'twin alliance' is an important prerequisite if multilevel planning
is to be translated into action in a realistic manner in any part of the
world. We cannot help observing that 'multilevel planning is a pawn in
the power game'. There is much truth in this observation and it at once
serves to explain why multilevel planning has not caught up with the
same degree of enthusiasm in all states in India.
    Apart from the above mentioned political and bureaucratic commitment
to decentralisation, which is a necessary condition, there are certain
other prerequisites or desiderata for multilevel planning. It is perhaps necessary to take note of all these before we examine the Indian
experience in some depth.
    As mentioned earlier, one of the first steps in the multilevel plan-
ning process is to define with precision, the functions among the various area levels. Developmental functions have differing geographic
scope. While developmental activity can be performed in perfect isola-
tion, it is possible to identify activities that can be best performed
at particular area levels and also to take note of their linkages with
the activities at the other area levels. In this way, an interlinked
and interdependent planning process can be established. This is the
basic idea in a multilevel planning set up. The identification of the
exclusive functions at the different area levels constitutes therefore
the first step of 'Functional Decentralisation'.
    The mere task of demarcating or assigning appropriate functions to
various levels would amount only to an exercise in 'breaking the bulk'
i.e. deconcentration. If this is is to have any meaning, it should be
accompanied by the assigning of adequate powers and responsibilities to
the different area levels to enable them to perform the designated
functions with ease and efficiency. This takes us to some other operational aspects of decentralisation, which include financial decentrali-
zation and administrative decentralisation. Financial decentralisation
includes an exercise in disaggregation of financial resources from the
central level to the other area levels. This, in turn, calls for certain rules and criteria, as interregional allocation of resources have

45

to be necessarily based on a proper understanding the relative levels
of development among areas and must give due weightage to this and various other factors.

Financial decentralisation to an area level also requires for its
efficient administration, the establishment of suitable budgetting and
reappropriation procedures. For many countries with a centralised planning system, 'area budgetting' in itself is a major innovation. It involves a movement away from the traditional procedure of channelling
funds through sectoral departments and agencies which is a vertical procedure, to channelling funds directly to the horizontal area levels in
the country. This calls for changing old procedures by removing some
powers of control from established centres and creating new centres of
power. Such changes are not easy and call for considerable administrative reforms in any country.

Decentralised planning is not a one-time planning operation. It is a
relay and re-relay process in which the micro-units, through a repetitive proces of change, seek continuous convergence to the dynamic path
of stable equilibrium for the entire macro system. What is therefore
required is an iterative adjustment mechanism which can constantly align
the plans at the sub-national levels to the national plan at each round
of implementation. This iterative process is very important because the
goals and objectives in a decentralised planning structure may tend to
conflict between different area levels and the resolution of these goal
conflicts is necessary for ensuring harmonised planning for development.
This adjustment mechanism would consist of an appropriate planning machinery at each one of the sub-national levels where planning functions
are sought to be decentralised. While considering a multilevel planning
framework for a democratic country like India, further complications are
introduced. For a more technical machinery alone is not sufficient, although this is important. The adjustment mechanism at the territorial
level should also include a public participation forum as well as a plan
approving body, in accordance with all norms of democracy. One of the
lacunae noticed in many developing countries is the absence of such a
mechanism embracing technical, social and political requirements. Sometimes the people's consultative council alone may be there without a
technical planning machinery, or only a technical machinery without the
support of the people's organisation. While in one case, this leads to
the formulation of a loose need-based plan without proper technical
analysis and determination of priorities, in the other, it results in a
technically sound plan in the nature of a bureaucratic exercise which is
not informed by and responsive to public opinion. Both are not adequate.
In a multilevel planning framework, therefore, one has to lay great emphasis on the development of a proper institutional mechanism for planning, that can meet the technical, social and political requirements of
a country, as appropriate. Only when such a mechanism is available, it
will be possible to organise effectively the iterative process of consultation among the hierarchic levels of planning and relay and re-relay
of various planning parameters (e.g. output targets, materials quotas,
manpower requirements, financial allocation, preferred priorities, etc.),
and ensure a smooth multilevel planning process.

The last stage in a multilevel planning process is what is called the
'nesting operation'. This implies integrating the plans of different
spatial levels into a unified frame, so that these plans are harmonised.
The iterative process mentioned above brings this harmonisation; but in
order to move in this direction, an effective dialogue between the lower
levels and successive higher levels will have to be established in well
defined terms. All these requirements again underline the need for

appropriate institutional arrangements. Thus it may be seen that multi-level planning is quite a demanding operation and its effective operationalisation will depend on a number of parameters.

With the above theoretical background, we may now examine the Indian experience.

4. THE INDIAN EXPERIENCE

It is necessary to preface our discussion about the Indian experience with a brief account of the important features of Indian planning. The Indian planning process operates within the framework of a federal, democratic structure. Under the Constitution of the country, certain legislative and fiscal jurisdictions of the Central and State Governments have been defined. Economic and social planning has been termed a 'Concurrent Subject', in which both the Centre and well as the States are the active partners. This situation thus warrants planning at least at two levels; this, however, is not enough, as the States are too large physical entities for effective planning and implementation. Below the State, the Districts (numbering 413) and the Blocks (numbering 5004) have emerged as distinct levels of administration. They are also considered suitable spatial levels for delegating the planning functions. They are, however, yet to realise this role effectively. Between the top two layers of administration, i.e. the Central and the States, certain decentralised practices of planning have already crystallised over the years. These consist of a mixture of formal and informal devices of an interactive nature.

The two-way process of planning between the Centre and the States is worked out in three stages. First, a perspective plan is prepared at the Central level for a period covering 10 to 15 years. The long term perspectives of growth and consistency in the economy are indicated in this plan. At the second stage, the five year plan is worked out with specific details of various activities and projects to be carried out over a period of five years. The third stage consists of the annual plan which lists out details of all the activities to be carried out in the next one year, the corresponding budgetary provisions being indicated under the annual budgets. It is through the annual budgets that the plan is made operational and seeks the approval of the legislature both at the Central and at the State levels.

At the State level, the preparation of perspective plans has not been systematically resorted to, although some States have done this exercise. The Five Year and the Annual Plans, however, are prepared by all the States. For these exercises, the States take their broad direction from the Central perspective plan and the national five year plan. These plans are finalised after an intense interactive process between the Planning Commission and the States. In this process, the Planning Commission provides broad guidelines and also indicates the financial parameters within which the Plans have to be formulated. The States prepare their plans on this basis and then a dialogue ensues at two levels (a) the official level through Working Groups etc. and (b) the political level with the Chief Ministers of States. Thus after an iterative process of discussions and negotiations, the plans of the States are finalised. This two-way planning process is now institutionalised and has become a permanent feature. In order to prepare themselves for the dialogue with the Planning Commission and also to augment their negotiable strength, the State Governments have built up their own State machinery for planning which makes the necessary analyses and puts together

the various departmental programs of the State. One may say that this
first stage of decentralisation of the planning process between the
Centre and the State is now fairly well established, although there
could be scope for further refinements and improvements.

The planning process below the State level, however, is less established. For many states in India, it is at present a mere disaggregation of
the State level budget, programs and physical targets to lower order administrative units wherever possible. However, a few States in the country e.g. Maharashtra, Gujarat, Karnataka and Uttar Pradesh have made
remarkable strides in decentralising the planning function to the district level. The experience gained in this context is discussed here.

Functional decentralisation

All the aforementioned four States have viewed district planning as a
two-way approach and evolved procedures to operationalise this approach.
The first and foremost step in this approach concerns the State which
has to provide certain important guidelines in which the scope and functions of the district plan are to be clearly specified. For this purpose, the states that have attempted multilevel planning have divided
developmental schemes in their state into State sector schemes and the
District sector schemes. The District sector schemes are really those
in the residuary sphere in the sense that whatever is not specifically
included in the State sector belongs to the District sector. By and
large, the criteria for determining whether a scheme belonged to the
State sector or the District sector are (a) the location of the program;
and (b) the areas which are to benefit from the program. Generally the
State sector schemes are intended to promote the general socioeconomic
interests of the people of the whole state, while the District sector
schemes would benefit mainly the people of the particular District. In
actual practice, the application of such criteria may not be very clear
cut, and may pose some problems as there may be schemes whose benefits
may cut across several district boundaries. In such cases, the proportion of the benefit to the district in relation to the state as a whole
is taken into account for deciding its classification. Illustratively,
the following list provides an idea of the demarcation between the District sector schemes and the State sector schemes:

District sector schemes	State sector schemes
Agricultural production	Generation and distribution of power
Soil conservation	Major and medium irrigation projects
Forests	Major and medium industries; in-
Fisheries	vestment in corporate bodies
Animal husbandry	University education
Marketing	Professional and technical educa-
Minor irrigation	tion
Small scale and rural industries	State and national highways
Ayacut development under minor	Ayacut development under major and
irrigation projects	medium projects
Primary and secondary education	Ports and inland waterways

Financial decentralisation

While organising the multilevel planning process, a crucial information
that the State level should provide to the district level relates to
the ceiling of resources within which the districts have to plan. In
the absence of a clear cut indication of the outlays available for dis-

trict planning, the latter tends to become a mere catalogue of district needs. In the procedures that have been evolved in Maharashtra, Gujarat, Karnataka and Utter Pradesh, there are subtle differences which reflect the degree of autonomy granted to the local level. Broadly the concept of financial decentralisation consists of dividing the total plan out-lay of the state into two categories; via: (a) an indivisible pool, which indicates the resources available for state sector schemes and (b) the divisible pool which indicates the resources available for district sector scheme. Detailed exercises done in the four States shows that broadly 30% to 40% of the Plan outlays constitute the divisible outlay apportionable between districts. For further distributing this divis-ible outlay among various districts in the State, each State has adopted certain objective criteria giving weightage to different factors.

In Maharashtra, for instance, the criteria and the scale of weightage adopted for interdistrict allocation of plan outlay are as follows:

Item	Percentage allocation
1. Total population	60
2. Urban population	5
3. Population of scheduled castes and scheduled tribes, etc.	5
4. Backwardness in :	
a) agriculture	5
b) irrigation	4
c) communications	5
d) industries	5
5. Special problems of	
a) drought prone areas	3
b) coastal districts	1.5
c) forest areas	1.5
6. Unallocated amount for meeting special problems	5
	100.00

An important component in the above allocation is a 5% unallocated sum which is retained at the State level of meeting special problems. In Karnataka, this is as much as 25%. Recent trends in Maharashtra indi-cate increasing erosion by the State into the 'Divisible pool of plan outlay'. This is reflected in the gradual shrinking of the proportion of this outlay from the original 40% (when the scheme of decentralisation was introduced) to 26% in 1982-82. A notable development in this con-text is the emergence of another component of the 'divisible pool' for accommodating what may be called the 'State level district sector schemes'. This illustrates sharply the sort of contrary pulls which affect the proces of decentralisation. While the justification for such erosion may be a genuine need to provide some correctives from the state level, to ensure certain overall priorities, one may also see this de-velopment as a reaction to the procedures that have tended to circum-scribe the manipulative power of the vested interests at the State level.

The earmarking of district allocations on this matter, leading to a decentralistion budget system, has no doubt ensured the availability of plan funds of a certain order on the basis of some rational criteria. Nevertheless it does not follow from this that it has conferred the necessary degree of autonomy regarding the utilisation of plan funds at the district level. This is because most of the allocations indicated to the districts are already pre-empted for various departmental schemes and are provided in the budgets of the sectoral departments. The actual decision making in regard to these departmental schemes rests with the departmental heads at the state level. This makes a mockery of district planning because the districts do not have any free allocation or 'untied funds' available with them, which they can operate on their own for implementing schemes that are felt as necessary and important at the district level. The case of Maharashtra illustrates this point. The following extract from a case study of district planning in Maharashtra is significant.

> Here (i.e., Maharashtra) what is actually being done is only allotted to the district (i.e., 'district budgeting') within the ceiling of resources. The set of schemes which constitute the district plan are those which are not determined by objective analysis and study, but have been arrived at by consensus in the meetings of the District Planning and Development Council and, therefore, subjective in nature. They are not organised around an inner logic of their own. They mainly rely on an aggregational exercise based upon the proposals of the Department agencies. The district plans, therefore, may not answer the rigorous tests of internal consistency, intersectoral complementarity, or criteria of efficiency. The district planning staff do not conduct any studies on their own or project alternative plans or do any impact analysis or evaluation of on-going programs. Thus, there is very little analytically informed decision making in regard to selection of projects in the district plan.

> There is also very little scope or manoeuvrability that is left to the district planning bodies for the planning of new schemes. The district plans carry with them the burden of the past - of on-going schemes and committed expenditures - and do not permit any drastic alteration of priorities and schemes. Some chopping off of redundant or irrelevant schemes and pruning of expenditure may be possible in any situation. But to identify those weak spots and to give effect to any changes in the face of departmental pulls and pressures, requires technical competence of an order, which is not available today at the district level.'

This constraint in decentralised planning has been sought to be tackled in the Gujarat scheme of decentralisation by planning a certain quantum of funds at the disposal of the District Planning Boards. In this context, the divisible outlay available for district level schemes is further divided into three categories:
i)   80% of the provision is retained for normal schemes to be proposed by the sectoral departments;
ii) 15% of the outlay is provided for schemes suggested by the district planning boards to respond to local needs and exploit local potential; and
iii) the remaining 5% is earmarked as provision towards an incentive to raise additional financial resources at district level.

The above method adopted in Gujarat may be seen as a halfway response to the pulls and pressures operating in the context of decentralised planning. The allocational formula seeks to compromise the interests of both the Departmental bureaucracies and the local planning authorities. It also serves to underline the residual character of district planning and the little manoeuvrability available to the district planner to plan for the local needs. Ideally, if local level planning is to have any

meaning, all funds flowing into the local area must be pooled together
and placed at the discretion of the local level authority. This does
not happen because the departments are not prepared to give up their
hold on financial resources, which give them much power and prestige.
An excuse that is normally given is that the districts do not have adequate planning capacilities in the sense that at the district level today there is no sound technical planning machinery capable of formulating the district plan on systematic lines. This situation is now being
sought to be corrected through a 'capacitation approach'. The Planning
Commission has recently (from January 1983) launched a scheme for
strengthening of planning machinery at the district level which is intended to assist the districts to augment their planning capabilities.
It will, of course, take some time for the districts to induct adequate
technical talents into their planning machinery and to bring about a
reversal of the planning process, conforming to the needs of a multilevel planning system. The essential point to be noted is that some
efforts have been initiated by the Centre in this direction.

5. THE MECHANISM FOR DISTRICT PLANNING

It is when we come to the question of the mechanism for district planning that the politics of multilevel planning comes glaringly to the
surface. Power equations at the political level and the apprehension
of the bureaucracy of losing their importance seem to be the major in-
hibiting factors for decentralisation. The experience in setting up
suitable mechanisms for district planning amply demonstrates this point.
In Karnataka and Uktar Pradesh, the District Planning Committees are
headed by the bureaucracy (usually the District Magistrate) and their
composition indicates that these are mostly official-level committees
with little or no representation of the public. More interesting, however, are the changes that have been brought about in Maharashtra and
Gujarat [4]. These States were the forerummers in introducing democratic decentralisation by setting up a Panchayati Raj (i.e. local self-
government) system including the Zilla Parishad (i.e. District Council)
at the district level. Despite the existence of these institutions, the
planning function has now been entrusted to other newly created bodies.
    In Maharashtra, this is a body called the 'District Planning and De-
velopment Council (DPDC)' with a Minister in the State Government as its
Chairman, the Divisional Commissioner as its Vice-Chairman, and the District Collector as its Member Secretary. The President of the Zilla
Parishad is only an ordinary member in this body.
    In the case of Gujarat, a 'District Planning Board (DPB)' has been
constituted with a Minister of the State Government as its Chairman and
the District Collector as its Vice-Chairman. In this set up also, the
District Panchayat President is only an ordinary member. This new set
up has come into existence since 1981. Prior to that, the District
Planning Body had the District Collector as its Chairman and the President of the District Panchayat as its Co-Chairman.
    The frequent shifts in the position assigned to the local level poli-
tician in the District Planning set up bring out clearly the power
struggle inherent in the multilevel planning process. In the present
political climate, it is significant that both in Gujarat and Maharashtra,
the State level politician has been preferred to head the local level
planning body. According to Dantwala this is a 'retrogression in the
much publicised drive towards decentralisation in planning'. For such
retrogression, he offers the following explanations:

1) The State leadership, whatever may be its rhetoric, is averse to the idea of decentralisation mainly out of political consideration of preventing the emergence of rival political force at the district level, belonging to the same political party of a party in opposi- tion.
2) The line bureaucracy at the state headquarters is not reconciled to the idea of dilution of its departmental authority implied in the establishment of a horizontal decision making body entitled to alter or amend departmental plans in the name of integration.
3) In the very nature of things, there are genuine limitations to de-centralisated planning and people's participation.' [5]

6. THE MECHANISM OF THE COORDINATION OF PLANS

In this section of our study, we may consider the problems in the integration of plans at different territorial levels. Earlier we referred to this step in the multilevel planning process as the 'nesting procedures'. These are very important because multilevel planning for any territorial level is not to be regarded as an isolated exercise, but as an interlinked activity. It would require the establishment of organisational and communication linkages among different hierarchic levels so as to facilitate reciprocal interaction, exchange, cooperation and resolution of conflicts. It is only through such interaction that it would be possible to ensure consistency and coordination between planning activities at various levels. The problem of consistency is essentially solved by consciously seeking to develop and build the plans at each spatial level within the framework of the plans of the higher level. The efficacy of multilevel planning would ultimately depend upon how effectively the iterative procedure involving downward and upward steps is organised.

The experience of implementing the two-way planning process in the State of Karnataka has served to highlight some deficiencies which tend to impede the harmonisation of plans. This experience revealed that the schemes works recommended by the District Development Council underwent thorough modifications at the State level while finalising them. This was due to the following reasons:
i) The sectoral priorities determined by the districts did not coincide with the sectoral priorities decided at the State and National levels.
ii) Even within a particular sector, varying priorities were given for different programs. This did not tally with the budgetted outlays. Hence, these proposals had to be modified to bring them to the budgetted outlays.
iii) The locations proposed in the District plans could not be adhered to at the Government level, since the latter had taken locational decisions without reference to District Plans.

All the above inconsistencies may be attributed to the lack of intense consultations and feedback between the District bodies and the State level. In this context, the importance of the iterative process involving the relay and re-relay of information between the local level and the State level cannot be overemphasised. The Karnataka experience clearly showed that when this iterative mechanism is weak, the Plans of the lower level units do not realistically mesh into the plans at the higher levels and therefore tend to become a wasted effort.

7. CONCLUSION

The Indian experience in multilevel planning, as it has evolved during
the last two decades clearly points to the fact that there are certain
limits to decentralisation. These limits are of three types: political,
administrative and technological. According to Dantwala 'one can assume
that the political and administrative obstacles can be removed through
better understanding and open debate. That the obstacles are removable
is not questioned, thought it would need much more than good sense to
remove them'.[5] This observation summarises in a nutshell the magnitude of the problems that confront us while seeking to operationalise
a multilevel planning system.

NOTES

[1] Local level planning is increasingly becoming an important issue in
    South and Southeast Asian countries. See 'The Practice of Local
    Level Planning: Case studies in selected rural areas in India, Nepal
    and Malaysia' (ESCAP, Bangkok, 1980).
[2] United Nations Asian and Pacific Development Institute - Local Level
    Planning and Rural Development - Alternative Strategies (Concept
    Publishing Company, New Delhi, 1980).
[3] Misra R.P. and Sundaram, K.V., Multi-level Planning and Integrated
    Rural Development in India, Heritage Publishers, New Delhi, 1980.
[4] Sundaram, R.V., District Planning - The Cast of Maharashtra', in
    Misra, R.P. and Sundaram, K.R., Multi-level Planning and Integrated
    Rural Development in India, Heritage Publishers, New Delhi, 1980.
[5] Dantwala, M.L., Two-way Planning: Logic and Limitations - A Crici-
    cal Review of Indian Experience, Paper prepared for FAO Regional
    Office for Asia and the Pacific, Bangkok, 1983.

5 Migration, Mobility and Income Distribution: Some Evidence from Bangladesh

L. H. CHAUDHURY

1. INTRODUCTION

Migration has been viewed in classical/neo-classical analysis as an equilibrium mechanism. An important implication is the reduction in the economic gap between the rich and poor that would be achieved through the
removal of surplus labour from rural areas. The lower income households
would benefit through a filter mechanism. However, in this study we offer
an alternative hypothesis which posits that intrarural inequality is the
main cause, and a serious consequence of rural out-migration [1]. Increased intravillage inequality produces a dualistic pattern of migration.
Deficit farmers and landless labourers who find it extremely difficult to
be absorbed in the local economy, tend to be pushed out, and wander in
search of wages. They are likely to end up in low paid, insecure marginal urban employment, given their low education, resources, fewer contacts. But the children of prosperous farmers (pull migrants) are
attracted to urban areas for capital and skill acquisitions, and to further their economic position. This dualistic pattern of migration will
foster further inequality within rural areas and between the 'push' and
'pull' migrants.

2. FURTHER ELABORATION OF THE HYPOTHESIS

Rapid population increase in villages of many developing countries, particularly in Asia, have adversely affected the land/man ratio. This
pressure on land, coupled with deteriorating purchasing power due to high
inflation rates and declining real income (Alamgir 1974) and lack of non-
agricultural opportunities in rural areas has resulted in increased
landlessness and concentration of land-holdings in fewer hands in rural
areas. In Bangladesh during 1961-74, the percentage of landless agric-
tural labourers increased from 18.9 percent to 24.9 percent and the percentage of owner cultivators declined from 34.7 percent to 31.1 percent
(Bangladesh Bureau of Statistics 1977). According to the 1977 Land Occupancy Survey of Rural Bangladesh, 11 percent of the households in
Bangladesh are totally landless and 48 percent of the households own at
most 0.99 acres of cultivable land (Tomasson 1977). Decline in the proportion of own cultivators and increase in landless agricultural labourers indicates the continuous alienation of land from the poor peasants
during the last decade. The net losers in these land transactions are
particularly the marginal and small peasants, because they are likely to
be the worst victims of the prevailing galloping rate of inflation (Bose
1973) and heavy indebtedness (IRDP 1977). Consequent land concentration
in fewer hands results in the top 5 percent of the households owning 20-
30 percent of the cultivable land holdings in rural areas (IRDP 1977).

Increased intra village inequality produces a dualistic pattern of migration. Deficit farmers and landless labourers who find it extremely
difficult to be absorbed in the local economy, tend to be pushed out,
and migrate in search of work mostly in other rural areas. But the children of prosperous farmers (who could be absorbed locally) are attracted
to urban areas for capital and skill acquisition, and to further their
economic position. Their surplus income due to intrarural inequality
helps them finance the costs associated with this pull migration. Thus
both 'push' and 'pull' migration are the twin children of intrarural inequality.

This dualistic (push and pull) pattern of migration is likely to further increase inequality in rural society in view of the differential
nature of the migration streams. The 'push' migrants are likely to
travel a short distance as they are poor and cannot afford to meet the
initial cost of long distance moves and search for work in urban areas.
'Push migrants' who manage to reach urban areas are also likely to end up
in low-paid, insecure marginal urban employment, given their low education, resources and fewer contacts. Therefore, the push migrants are unlikely to acquire extra incomes and/or skills to improve their living
conditions or that of their families. 'Push migration' can at best save
a poor-deficit migrant from destitution and deeper poverty. In contrast,
the better off 'pull migrants' can afford to move long distances in
order to acquire either higher education (as a step to secure better
urban jobs), or to seize the best earning opportunities to which their
earlier education and/or contact have given them access. The pull migrants will, therefore, tend to acquire skills, extra income and send
larger remittances.

Migration, as long as it follows the above pattern, may foster further
inequality within rural areas and between the 'push' and 'pull' migrants.
The greatest benefits from migration will be reaped by pull migrants and
their rich families, while for the poor migrants, migration may be merely a mechanism for bare survival.

Drawing from the above discussions, the following hypotheses are advanced and tested in this study:

1. The propensity to out-migrate from rural areas will be higher among
   those households who are poor and also among those who are rich.
2. The benefits of higher education, occupation, and economic mobility
   will accrue more to the 'pull' than to 'push' migrants in view of
   higher education, resources and other endowments of the former than
   the latter.
3. Income of the 'pull' migrants is likely to be higher than the 'push'
   migrants. Human capital factors, particularly education, skill levels
   and contact are likely to be the major determinants of urban income.
4. The higher the income, the greater the remittance. Therefore, the
   'pull' migrants are expected to remit more money (at least in absolute
   terms) to their rural kin than the 'push' migrants.
5. Higher remittances received by the families of 'pull' migrants will
   increase intrarural inequalities through higher propensity on their
   part to acquire more land and other assets in rural and urban areas.
   The higher the acquisition of assets by 'pull' migrants, the higher
   the changes of widening economic disparities between the 'pull' and
   'push' migrants.

The above hypotheses are tested in this study by employing data at
household and individual level from 68 villages in MymenSingh, two
villages in Faridpur, and the Dacca metropolitan area. The procedures
for data collection are described in Appendix A.

3. THE DUAL MIGRATION STREAMS

The characteristics of the individual migrants from MymenSingh Survey are discussed first. There were 245 out-migrants who constituted 22.7 percent of the total population of the study villages. The out-migration rate was similar to that obtained in other village studies in Bangladesh (Chaudhury 1983, and Chaudhury and Curlin 1975). Of the total out-migrants, 67 percent were females. The female migrants, with two exceptions, moved to other rural areas due to marriage and were excluded from the present analysis due to their involuntary and socially determined migration. This left 81 adult male out-migrants for the analysis. Table 1 compares the socioeconomic characteristics of the migrant and migrant families with those of the study population.

The following conclusions emerge from the findings in Table 1. Demographically, the migrants are primarily concentrated in young adult ages (29-39 years), a finding corroborated in other studies. With respect to education, two broad conclusions emerge. First, the overall education level of the migrants (64 percent) and the migrants families (41 percent) is higher than that of the non-migrant study population (27 percent). There are fewer illiterates among the migrants in comparison to non-migrant families; and the percentage of the migrants with secondary and high secondary education far exceeds the corresponding figure for the non-migrant study population. Second, amongst the migrants, the distribution between various education categories form a U-shaped pattern: with higher propensity to migrate among the illiterates and those with high levels of education.

With respect to landholding a bi-modal pattern of migration emerges with a higher proportion of out-migrants among the landless and higher landholding groups. Although the migrant families account for 4 percent of the total households, for the lowest and highest landholding groups, the corresponding figures are 5 percent and 9 percent respectively.

Economically, the migrants are better off than the non-migrant study population. The median yearly income of migrant and non-migrant households from all sources is found to be Taka 3264 and Taka 2354 respectively; the difference may be attributed to the effect of remittance as will be discussed later. Amongst the migrant families, the distribution between income categories once again assumes a U-shaped pattern and the proportion of migrants originating from the lowest and highest income categories is higher than those originating from the middle income categories. Even when we look at the migration rates among the income/asset groups, the following pattern emerges: while the migrant families constitute 4 percent of the total households, for the lowest and highest income migrant families the corresponding figures are 28 percent and 10 percent respectively.

So both in number of migrants and as a share of the households, the lowest and highest income/landholding categories contribute most to the migration stream. These findings show that the migrants primarily originate from two distinct economic classes - the economically poor and economically rich families of the rural community. This conclusion is further reinforced by data from Faridpur (Chaudhury, forthcoming).

The economic consequences of these divergent patterns of migration within different social classes is examined in the following section.

4. ECONOMIC CONSEQUENCES OF MIGRATION: MOBILITY

Mobility in this study is measured in terms of changes in the levels of

Table 1
Some Socio-economic Characteristics of the Migrants/Migrant Families and
Study Population at Source
(Mymensingh Study)

Variables	Migrants n	%	Migrant Families n	%	Study n	Population %
Age						
10-19	18	22.22			1022	34.46
20-39	47	58.02			1157	36.75
40+	16	19.75			969	30.78
Total	81	100.00			3148	100.00
Average Family Size				5.67		4.84
Education[1]						
Illiterate	29	35.80	226	58.88	2865	72.07
Primary	10	12.34	77	19.94	645	16.45
Middle	19	23.45	48	12.43	403	10.13
Secondary &						
higher secondary	23	28.39	35	9.06	53	1.33
Total literate	52	64.19	160	41.45	1110	27.92
Total	81	100.00	386*	100.00	3975*	100.00
Land-holding status						
(acre)						
Landless			30	37.03	575	32.91
.01-1.0			16	19.75	554	31.71
1.01-2.50			10	12.34	352	20.14
2.51+			25	30.86	266	15.22
Total			81**	100.00	1747**	100.00
Occupation (Head of						
the Household)						
Farming			26	32.01	966	55.30
Agricultural labour			34	41.97	466	26.68
Non-agriculture			21	25.92	315	18.01
Total			81	100.00	1747**	100.00
Yearly Income from all						
Sources (Taka)						
1800			20	25.64	71	4.04
1800-2999			15	19.23	1019	58.31
3000-4199			14	17.94	379	21.71
4200+			29	37.14	278	15.91
Total			78***	100.00	1747**	100.00
Medium annual income			3264		2354	

[1]   Population 5 years and above
*   Total Population
**   Total number of households
*** There are three non-respondents.

58

education, income and occupation from pre to post migration period.
(These were determined by asking the migrants their levels of education
and income and types of occupation in rural areas prior to migration to
town and their current position on these measures in urban areas.)
Given the differential background of the migrants, it may be hypothesised
that upward mobility will be largely achieved by the 'pull migrants', i.e.
those who originate from higher socioeconomic classes, for reasons advanced earlier such as higher education levels, and longer waiting periods
for acceptable employment and better connections [2]. Economic necessity
on the other hand will force the 'push migrants' to accept low income employment, as the scope for upper mobility on their part is very limited.
This is supported by data obtained from Dacca and Faridpur studies.

Education mobility

There has been considerable improvement in the level of education of the
migrants from the time when they left their places of origin to their
present situation in urban areas. This educational advancement is observed among the migrants from both Faridpur and Dacca Studies (see Table
2). For example, among the migrants from Faridpur, the level of illiteracy declined from 31 percent to 29 percent and the proportion attaining
education 10th grade and above increased from 16 to 27 percent. In Dacca,
the level of illiteracy declined from 35 percent to 33 percent and those
who have received education 10th grade and above invreased from 21 to 24
percent from pre to post migration period. It would be interesting to
know who they are. According to the hypothesis, we would expect educational advancements to be highest among the 'pull migrants' or those originating from higher socioeconomic classes. This is supported from data
of both study areas. For example, in the Faridpur study 80-94 percent of
migrants, with less than primary education prior to migration, were unable to increase their education after migration, whereas 36 percent of
those who had a 6-9 grade education prior to migration were able to get
at least 10th grade education (see Table 3). This is also corroborated
from the Dacca study, where 22 percent and 27 percent of the migrants
with 10th and 12th grade education prior to migration were able to increase their education levels, contrasted to only 5-7 percent among those
with 0-5 grade education (see Table 4). These statistics suggest that
educational benefits are likely to be reaped by those with some prior
education [3]. The data on land holding status of migrant families shows
a positive relationship between education level of the migrants and the
size of holdings of their families (Table 5). Therefore, one can infer
that it is probable that educational benefits accrue to the 'pull
migrants', i.e., the children of the richer farmers who are able to acquire some education prior to their migration.

Occupational mobility

There has been considerable shift in the occupation structure of the
migrants from pre to post migration period. For example, among the migrants from Faridpur, we find that farming was the most important source
of employment prior to moving to urban areas (see Table 6). This was
followed by agricultural labour and small business or shop keeping.
Nearly 8 percent of them were unemployed and 41 percent were students.
But in urban areas only 2 percent of the migrants remain unemployed
after moving to town, the majority of them were absorbed in the tertiary
or informal sector (i.e., as non-agricultural labour, rickshaw/cart
puller, domestic servant, hotel boy, etc.), and government services,

Table 2

Percentage distribution of level of education of the migrants in rural area before migration and in urban area after migration.

Level of education	Faridpur Study		Dacca Study	
	Before Migration	After Migration	Before Migration	After Migration
Illiterate	31.3	29.4	34.5	32.9
Below 5 grade	19.6	15.7		
5 grade	11.1	9.8		
1-5 grade			27.9	26.6
6-9 grade	21.6	17.6	16.6	16.3
10 grade +	15.7	27.4	20.9	24.1
Total %	100.0	100.0	100.0	100.0
N	51	51	661*	661*

* 25 cases who have had non-institution/religious education were excluded from this table.

Table 3

Percentage distribution of the current level of education of the migrants in town by their previous education level (i.e., when they first moved from rural to urban areas)

Faridpur Study

N = 51*

Level of** education (Before migration)	Level of education (after migration, i.e., current level in town)					
	Illiterate	Below Primary	Primary	6-9 grade	10 grade & above	Total
Illiterate	94.0 (15)		6.0 (1)			100.0 (16)
Below primary		80.0 (8)	10.0 (1)	10.0 (1)		100.0 (10)
Primary			50.0 (3)	17.0 (1)	33.0 (2)	100.0 (6)
6-9 grade				64.0 (7)	36.0 (4)	100.0 (11)
10 grade & above					100.0 (8)	100.0 (8)
Total	15	8	5	9	14	51

* The table is based on data obtained from the respondents i.e., the migrants: out of 112 migrants from Faridpur only 51 male migrants could be contacted in Dacca City.

** The determining questions of past and present level of education were
   (i) what was the highest grade of education that you had completed prior to moving out to urban areas?
   and
   (ii) what is your current level of education (i.e., highest grade completed) in urban areas?

Note: The figures in parentheses refer to number of cases.

Table 4
Percentage distribution of the current level of education of the migrants
in town by their previous education

Dacca Study

Level of education (before) migration	Level of education (after migration)						
	Illiterate	1-5 grade	6-9 grade	10 grade	11-12 grade	B.A.College Degree	Total
Illiterate	95.61 (218)	1.75 (4)	1.32 (3)	0.44 (1)	0.88 (2)		100.0 (288)
1-5 grade		92.97 (172)	3.24 (6)	1.62 (3)	1.62 (3)	0.54 (1)	100.0 (185)
6-9 grade			90.00 (99)	6.36 (7)	1.81 (2)	1.81 (2)	100.0 (110)
10 grade				77.77 (63)	8.64 (7)	13.58 (11)	100.0 (81)
12 grade					73.33 (22)	26.66 (8)	100.0 (30)
College						100.0 (27)	100.0 (27)
Total	218	176	108	74	36	49	661*

Note: The figures in parentheses refer to number of cases.

* The table excludes 25 cases who have had non-institutional/religious education.

Table 5
Mean land holding of head of households of migrants by level of education
of the migrants.

Faridpur Study

Level of education of the migrants (before migration)	Mean land holding (in acre) of head of the migrants' households
Illiterate	0.70
Below primary	0.31
Primary	2.11
6-9 grade	5.75
10 grade & above	9.64

followed by business and manufacturing industry.

An almost similar pattern of structural changes in occupation is
noticed among migrants in Dacca metropolitan area. Among the Dacca migrants, the major sources of rural employment were farming, followed by
agricultural and small business. Forty-seven percent of them were unemployed and eleven percent were students and/or dependents. (This high
rate of pre-migration unemployment may be overstated and difficult to in-
terpret given the conceptual problems associated with measuring unemployment.) However, after migration 41 percent and 27 percent were in manufacturing and government services and less than 2 percent remained unemployed among the Dacca migrants. While employment increased for both
types of migrants, the Faridpur study shows that of those who had moved
from rural areas as students, a majority of them were absorbed in civil
and administrative services and businesses in urban areas. In contrast

Table 6
Percentage distribution of occupation of the migrants before migration in rural areas and after migration in urban areas.

Faridpur and Dacca

Occupation	Faridpur		Dacca	
	Occupation before migration %	Occupation after migration %	Occupation before migration %	Occupation after migration %
Farming	23.53 (12)	–	26.38 (181)	–
Agricultural labour	9.80 (5)	–	6.27 (43)	–
Non-agricultural labour	7.84 (4)	25.49 (13)	4.95 (34)	16.61 (114)
Business	9.80 (5)	15.68 (8)	3.93 (27)	11.22 (77)
Student/dependent	41.17 (21)	7.84 (4)	11.07 (76)	1.02 (7)
Mill workers, i.e. manufacturing, industry	–	17.64 (9)	–	41.98 (288)
Government/Commercial Farms	–	25.49 (13)	–	27.26 (187)
Retired	–	5.88 (3)	–	1.17 (8)
Unemployed	7.83 (4)	1.96 (1)	47.37 (325)	0.43 (3)
Beggars	–	–	–	0.29 (2)
Total %	100	100	100	100
N	51	51	686	686

to this situation, a majority of those who were small scale farmers and day labourers in rural areas found themselves as cart/rickshaw pullers, day labourers or at best mill workers in urban areas. The student migrants originated from families having on an average 12 acres of land, in contrast to less than three acres of land owned by households of the latter two groups. Moreover, 70 percent of the students had 6-9 grade education and above prior to moving our to urban areas. Whereas, the absolute majority of the farmers and day labourers had less than primary education (Chaudhury, forthcoming).

Income mobility

Respondents were asked about their monthly income from all sources before and after migration. The determining questions were (1) what was your

monthly income from all sources prior to migration from rural to urban
areas? (2) what is your current monthly income from all sources in urban
areas? Weekly and daily workers were asked the average number of days
employed in a week and the average number of hours worked in a day respectively; and to state their cash and/or in kind income. The cash and
in kind payments were converted to a monthly equivalent based on actual
work history. Information was also sought on income from other sources,
e.g. income from investment, bank deposits, gift and remittances. These
annual incomes were also converted into monthly equivalents and added to
work income.

The total monthly income of migrants shows increase from the pre to
post migration period. Average monthly income of migrants from the Dacca
survey increased by 1089 percent from Taka 70 to Taka 832 [4]. This can
be expected in view of the increase in employment opportunities, age,
education, experience and contacts and also a majority of those who were
formerly students and/or unemployed now joined the labour force.

According to the hypothesis, one would expect the 'pull migrants' to
enhance their income more than 'push migrants' due to their higher educational background. This was substantiated by the Dacca data. Data on
monthly income, from all cources, in the pre and post migration period
and by education level is present in Table 7.

It shows a strong positive relationship between education and income of
the migrants. As expected, income increases with the level of education
and the a erage income of a high school graduate is approximately 200
percent higher than of an illiterate migrant. It is interesting to note
that whereas the average income among migrants did not vary significantly
by education level prior to migration [5], after migration the difference
in incomes among education categories varies significantly (at .0001
level). While the average incomes of less educated migrants increased by
700 percent (65 percent in real terms), for the high school graduates and
above (12th grade and above) this was at least 2592 percent or 406 percent
in real terms. While incomes have increased for all migrants, the greatest rewards of migration accrued to the higher educational/occupational
categories. Similar trends can be observed with respect to the relationship between occupation and income. The average income of a higher level
professional/executive is 279 percent more than a day-labourer. Differences in mean incomes among occupation groups were found to be statistically significant as determined by one-way analysis of variance [6].

Table 7
Average monthly income of migrants before and after migration by current
level of education

Dacca Survey

Level of Education (current)	n	Income* before (Taka)	Income** after (Taka)	% change (absolute)	% change+ (real)	Index illiterate = 100 (after migration)
Illiterate	218	74	648	775.67	64.86	1.00
1-5 grade	176	82	695	748.0	58.53	1.07
6-9 grade	108	55	790	1336.0	169.09	1.22
10 grade	74	73	1124	1439.7	189.04	1.74
12 & above	85	70	1400	2592.3	405.76	2.16
Total (ave.)	661	70	832	1088.57	122.85	

* F value = 1.016 not significant. ** F value = 12.190 significant at
.0001 level as determined by one-way analysis of variance.
+ Note: Current income was adjusted for average inflation during 1968-80.
        (See footnote 4).

Determinants of urban income

Monthly income of a migrant in an urban area is likely to be determined
by his/her education, occupation, age, contact, family size, duration of
stay and number of working adults in the household.

The net effect of each of the above independent variables on monthly
income was estimated through a dummy variable regression. Here, each
dummy variable represented a single subclass of a factor and an individual
was assigned a value of unity if he belonged to the subclass. Each subclass of the variable was considered as a separate regressor (Feldstein
1966).

The use of the dummy variable regression does not involve making any
assumptions about the linearity of the effect (Suits 1957). The relationship between the dependent (e.g., logarithm of monthly earnings) and the
independent variables (education, age, etc.) is analysed by ordinary
least squares. The general model used is one of the following form:

$$Ln_{ij} = A_0 + \Sigma_i b_i E_{ij} + \Sigma_i c_i O_{ij} + \Sigma_i d_i A_{ij} + \Sigma_i e_i M_{ij} + \Sigma_i f_i F_{ij} +$$
$$+ \Sigma_i g_i W_{ij} + \Sigma_i h_i D_{ij} + \Sigma_i k_i C_{ij} + \Sigma_i l_i R_{ij}$$

where:
Ln_{ij} = log monthly income i of migrant j
E_{ij} = education level i of migrant j
O_{ij} = occupation category i of migrant j
A_{ij} = age group i of migrant j
M_{ij} = marital status i of migrant j
F_{ij} = family size i of migrant j
W_{ij} = number of workers i of migrant j
D_{ij} = duration of stay i of migrant j
C_{ij} = city i of migrant j
R_{ij} = relation i of migrant j

ANOVA was used to examine the interaction effect between the explanatory variables, but no significant interaction was noted. The net effect
of each of the independent variables on log of monthly income is shown in
Table 8.

The explanatory variables accounted for 47 percent of the variance.
The effect of the variables for each category is shown in Table 8. Education (human capital enhancement) emerged as the most important factor for
explaining the monthly income of a male migrant [7]. Since 'illiterate'
was selected as the reference category, consistent higher returns to education investment is indicated by the increasing value of the coefficients. The second most important variable for explaining monthly income
was occupation status. The omitted category here was the highest occupation category and it shows the decline in income associated with lower
occupations. Migrants in the informal sector had lower incomes than
those in the formal sector (both manual and clerical). The other variables - marital status, duration of stay, family size, and contact in
town - were also significant in explaining monthly incomes of male migrants.
This analysis clearly suggests that migrants with higher education are
likely to be the most economically successful in urban areas [8].

Table 8
Adjusted effect of education, occupation, age marital status, family
size, duration of stay, number of adult workers in the family, contact
& migration stream on income of a migrant (Dacca Survey)

Independent Variables	Regression Coefficient	S.E.	F-ratio
EDUCATION			
Illiterate	-	-	-
1-5	.022	.020	1.18 n.s.
6-9	.061	.024	6.22 *
Secondary	.135	.031	19.06 **
Higher Secondary & Above	.195	.033	33.22 ***
OCCUPATION[1]			
Higher level Professionals/ Executives	-	-	-
Business	-.127	.042	46.36 ***
Junior level Professionals/ Executives	-.168	.040	17.36 **
Mill/Skilled Workers	-.217	.039	30.85 ***
Informal/Tertiary	-.286	.040	9.74 **
Sales & Clerical	-.299	.043	48.16 ***
Retired	-.301	.094	10.29 **
MARITAL STATUS			
Single	-	-	-
Married	.122	.028	19.15 **
Widowed/Separated	.034	.091	0.13 n.s.
AGE			
Less or equal 20	-	-	-
20-29	.228	.071	10.19 **
30-39	.243	.073	10.86 **
40-49	.231	.075	9.37 **
50 & above	.290	.077	14.21 **
FAMILY SIZE			
0-1	-	-	-
2-3	.025	.038	0.44 n.s.
4-5	.083	.026	9.64 **
6-7	.085	.027	9.98 **
8-9	.163	.040	16.00 **
10-16	.129	.055	5.37 *
DURATION OF STAY			
20-34 years	-	-	-
9-19 years	-.037	.023	13.71 **
1-9 years	-.088	.021	3.05 *
RELATIVES IN URBAN AREA			
No	-	-	-
Yes	.048	.051	9.42 **

R^2 46.66   14.47

+   Adjusted for the effect of all the variables in the table and also
    for five other additional variables - (1) number of days worked,
    (2) number of female workers, (3) migration stream (4) number of
    male workers, (5) residential status. Coefficients of these addi-
    tional variables are not presented in view of their insignificant
    contribution for explaining income.
*   significant at .05 level
**   significant at .01 level
***   significant at .001 level
n.s. not significant

NOTE: Illustration of occupation categories.
1. Higher level professionals and executives: (a) medical doctor; (b)
   lawyer; (c) senior officers in government; (d) senior executives in
   industries and commercial firms.
2. Junior level professionals and executives: (a) teacher; (b) priest;
   (c) land surveyor; (d) personnel in armed and police services; (e)
   land revenue collector; (f) accountant; (g) cartographer; (h) super-
   visor in a mill/factory; (i) compounder; (j) librarian.
3. Sales and clerical: clerks in government and commercial offices, mail-
   men, salesmen in shops, store keeper.
4. Mill or skilled workers: Labourers in mills/factories, carpenter,
   mason, tailor, driver, machine operator, book-binder, goldsmith,
5. Service/informal/tertiary sector: boatman, fisherman, day-labourer,
   rickshaw-puller, cart-puller, domestic servant, hotel boy, guard,
   gate-keeper, porter, sweeper, errand boy.
7. Business: vegetable and fish business; owner of pharmaceutical shops,
   tea stalls, rickshaws and taxis, contractor.

Remittance

Remittance, or the transfer of cash and other resources, is a major consequence of migration. Remittances from the migrant to the rural household are important for they may (1) constitute an important source of
income for the consumption fund, (2) help production by permitting the
reclamation of prior leased out land, debt repayment, increased land
holdings and payment for other capital inputs. These remittances are
likely to increase the standard of living of the rural household and
affect its attitude toward migration.

It appears from Table 9 that a sizeable majority (60%) of the migrants
remit money to their kin [9]. The proportion of remitters at first increases and then declines with the increase in income [10].

Table 9
Pattern of Remittances: Dacca Survey

Monthly Income	N	Migrant Remitters (%)	Average Monthly Remittance
< 400	99	59.59	128
401-600	252	70.12	147
601-800	146	68.49	191
801-100	72	50.00	314
1001-1500	63	39.68	276
1500	48	31.25	361
Average		60.00	187

For Volume of Remittances F Ratio = 3.34 and is significant at .02
level.

While the average remittance is Taka 198 per month, migrants in the two

66

lowest income categories send less than the average. In contrast, migrants in the upper income categories remit approximately twice the average. The difference in volume of remittances is statistically significant.

Impact of remittance on income of migrant families

It would be interesting to examine the impact of this differential remittance on the rural economy by 'push' and 'pull' migrants. Unfortunately, this impact cannot be assessed for the migrants of the Dacca survey since no information on their families in rural areas was collected. However, data from one of our surveys may shed some light on this subject. The Mymensingh survey collected data on the volume of remittance received in a year by migrant families. The data are presented in Table 10.

The median remittance received by a migrant household is found to be Tk. 565. However, there is a wide variation among households in terms of receiving remittance. Thus 21 percent of the households received Taka 1900-2299 as remittance in a year as against 10 percent and 16 percent of the households receiving less than Tk. 300 and Taka 300-699 respectively as remittance in a year.

Table 10

Percentage Distribution of the Yearly Remittance Received by the Migrant Households (Mymensingh Survey)

Remittance Received (in Taka)	n	%
00	22	29.73
299 or less	7	9.46
300 - 699	12	16.21
700 - 1099	7	9.46
1100 - 1499	4	5.40
1500 - 1849	6	8.11
1900 - 2299	16	21.62
Total Median = 565	74*	100.00

* There were 7 non-respondents.

A large quantum of remittance is sent by the 'pull migrants' to their families. The migrants in the formal occupation category (pull migrants) and 'day labourers' (push migrants) were found to remit on an average Taka 1850 and Taka 600 per annum respectively to their families. This variation in money remittances by the above two categories of migrants may be explained in terms of differences in place of work, educational achievement, and income which are interrelated variables. Amongst the 'pull migrants' those who belong to the 'formal' occupation category [11] 89 percent had education beyond middle level (6 grade and above), 72 percent worked in urban areas and had median annual incomes of Taka 3804. The corresponding figures for the 'push migrants', i.e., those who are reported as 'day labourers', are 30 percent, 10 percent and Taka 1374 respectively. From the above findings it appears that those migrants who have higher education, work in urban areas and also have higher incomes, remit more money to their rural families than those migrants who have low education, work in rural areas and earn less.

Impact of remittance

Remittance accounts for 16 percent of the total annual income from all

sources for the migrant families. It is an important source of income
for some families and it may increase income inequalities and social
differentiation in the village (if the beneficiaries of higher remittance are those families who are already the prosperous members of the
community). We shall test the above hypothesis by examining the socio-
economic background of the migrant families, employing data from the
Mymensingh Survey.

It may be noted that the families sending the pull migrants are also
the richest in the village in terms of land ownership, income and consumption levels. Those of the families sending out push migrants (those
who are in the occupation category 'day-labourer') are relatively poor.
The percentage of landless households among the rich and poor migrant
families are found to be 15 percent and 68 percent respectively. The
corresponding proportion for the entire sample is 33 percent. Conversely, 52 percent of the rich migrant families have more than 2.50 acres of
cultivable land but none of the poor migrant families own as much as
2.50 acres. Housholds owning more than 2.50 acres of cultivable landholding were found to be 15 percent in the entire sample. Median total
annual income if found to be Tk. 4800 and Tk. 2400 for the rich and poor
migrant families respectively. The corresponding figure for the entire
sample is found to be Tk. 2354. We have earlier noted that the rich
migrants (those in the formal occupation category) remit at least three
times as much money as the poor migrants to their rural families. Moreover, remittance constitutes 23 percent and 12 percent of the total
annual income of the rich and poor migrant families. From the point of
view of remittance, the above findings imply that the households in
receipt of high remittance are also those who are relatively prosperous
compared with their neighbours. One of the consequences of the higher
levels of remittances received by the prosperous families could be further accentuation of the unequal distribution of incomes within the
village community. Indirect evidence to this effect is found in land
transactions by the rich and poor migrant families. During 1970-1975
33 percent of the rich migrant families bought new land as opposed to 7
percent of the poor migrant families. The net sum of transactions of
land during the aforesaid period was found to be 9.20 and 1.75 acres for
the rich and poor migrant families respectively. The inflow of cash remittances may have directly helped the more prosperous migrant families
to purchase new land and lead to further income inequality in the rural
community.

Remittances also play a positive role in raising the income levels of
the migrant families and particularly helping the poor migrants from
slipping further into poverty. The median yearly income of the migrant
families excluding remittances were only 10 percent higher than the
median income for the whole sample, but the difference in median income
increases to 28 percent when remittances are included in the annual income of the migrant families [12]. The major share of this increase
accrued to the rich migrant families [13]; nevertheless some of the
benefits also trickled down to the poor migrant families. The median
yearly income of poor migrant families is found to be Tk. 2400 which is
very close to the median annual income of the sample. However, the
income level of the poor migrants would have been only Tk 1884 per annum
if remittances were not added to their income. Remittances raise the
poor migrant families above the level of the poorest.

Impact of urban income on asset acquisition

Migrants' remittances can be used for consumption or to help in the

further enhancement of the asset position of the migrant family. Since
the higher income urban migrants originate from the higher income rural
households, these larger remittances are likely to be used for asset
acquisition. Increased assets, particularly land, will widen the gap
between the 'push' and 'pull' migrants and through the process of cumulative causation increase income inequality.

The Dacca Survey provides an estimate of the property acquired by
migrants in urban and rural areas (Table 11). As land is the most important means of production in Bangladesh, it determines a household's
power and position, as well as providing an important base for upward
mobility, as noted earlier.

Table 11

Asset Acquisition Through Urban Incomes Earned by Migrants: Dacca Survey

Monthly Income	Urban land for house building	Agricultural land
< 400	–	0.50
401–600	0.19	1.65
601–800	0.11	2.35
801–1000	0.40	4.44
1001–1500	1.09	5.35
1500 +	1.29	8.39
F Values	1.98	14.11
Significance Level	0.08 level	.001

Table 11 shows that the higher income rural migrants increased their
rural land holdings with the help of the income earned in urban areas[14].
Agricultural land bought rises with income from half an acre (.50 acre)
for the lowest category to more than 8 acres for the highest income
migrants. The difference in mean 'acres' of land bought by different
income categories with the help of money earned in urban areas was found
to be statistically significant. Urban land is expensive and the mean
area of urban land bought also varies with the income of the migrants.
These findings clearly suggest that migration provides an important
vehicle for further strengthening the economic position of the 'pull
migrants' and their families, and its effect increases with the income
of the migrant prior to migration. These disproportionate economic benefits are expected to further accentuate the economic disparities between
the two groups. This hypothesis is supported by Table 12, which represents data on the total value of movable and immovable assets by current
income owned by the migrants in the rural areas before migration and in
movable and immovable assets by current income owned by the migrants in
the rural areas before migration and in the urban and rural areas after
migration to Dacca.

Examination of the above table reveals a skewed distribution of assets
by income groups. The migrants with lower income own a much smaller
share of total assets in relation to their size in the sample. On the
other hand, migrants in higher income categories own a greater share of
total assets in relation to their size. For example, if we confine our
analysis to distribution of assets before migration, we will find that
although the migrants with lower income (i.e., those earning less than
Taka 601) account for 51 percent of the total households, they hold only
36 percent of the total assets. The asset share of the middle income
groups (i.e., those earning Taka 601–1000 per month) is proportional to
their sizes. On the other hand, the migrants with higher incomes (i.e.,
those earning more than Taka 1001 per month) account for 16 percent of

Table 12

Total value of movable and immovable assets owned by the migrants in
rural areas before migration and in the urban and rural areas after
migration: Dacca

Income Categories (in Taka)	House-hold Numbers	House-hold %	Total Value of assets before migration (in Taka)	Distri-bution of assets before migration %	Total Value of assets after migration (in Taka)	Distri-bution of assets after migration %
< 400	99	14.43	1,444,700	6.78	1,834,050	5.13
401-600	251	36.58	6,323,026	29.70	7,805,600	21.86
601-800	146	21.28	4,769,099	22.40	5,326,149	14.92
801-1000	72	10.49	1,892,500	8.89	3,452,800	9.67
1001-1500	63	8.18	3,184,990	14.96	5,137,299	14.39
1500+	55	8.01	3,672,000	17.25	12,144,980	34.01

the households but they own 32 percent of the total assets, i.e., twice
their share. This unequal distribution of assets among the migrants is
further accentuated from pre to post migration periods. For example,
the highest income groups doubled their share of total assets from 17 to
34 percent, while the corresponding share of the lower income groups
decreased from 36 percent to 27 percent from pre to post migration periods.

Policy implications

Migration has been viewed in classical/neoclassical analysis as an equi-
librating mechanism. An important implication is the reduction in the
economic gap between rich and the poor that would be achieved through
the migration process, particularly through the removal of surplus
labour. The lower income households would benefit through a filter down
mechanism, alteration of the man/land ratio and increased productivity.
This study shows that the rewards to migration vary with and is positively associated with income, education oocupation and other 'endowments'.
The rural areas of Bangladesh are polarising among economic lines and
rural-urban migration aids this process. The majority of rural households are already desperately poor and increasing land acquisition by
larger land holding households implies increasing alienation of the land
from poorer households. In Bangladesh where the overwhelming mass is
poor, where occupational alternatives in rural areas are scarce, and
societies are rigidly stratified, this process can only be dehumanising
and destabilising in the long run. The current system of high rewards
to education and urban occupations in the formal sector (that are limited in a low income country) should be reevaluated.
The policy options should be discussed in the light of the patterns
discussed in this paper - particularly the disproportionate benefits of
migration to the 'pull' migrants. It is undesirable, even if possible,
to control migration, for as this study shows remittances also help the
poor migrant families. They can increase consumption and have been able
to increase their meagre land holdings, income and level of education.
However, the costs of migration are also much higher for these groups,
particularly in terms of health and life expectancy. Social and public
policy should aim at increasing the rewards of migration to these lower
income groups through aid to the sector - primarily the informal sector -
in which they find employment. Such aid could attempt to increase the

70

level of productivity, both in urban and rural areas, through technology
and institutional innovations - low income credit, marketing cooperatives, support of auxiliary industries and so on.

This study has documented the nature and magnitude of the higher rewards to pull migrants that accrue from education. Training geared toward improving the skill levels of the 'push' migrants, particularly
vocational training, would increase national and urban productivity.
Broad based increase in levels of productivity are required for efficient
and equitable growth of the country. Public intervention in favour of
'push' migrants is required - i.e., giving them more training, promul-
gating and enforcing minimum wage laws and removing the differential
access to the means of production.

The paper has demonstrated that current migration patterns and processes are income regressive, widens the income and productivity gap and
reinforces polarisation in rural areas. In the absence of progressive
intervention, migration will reinforce existing economic stratification
and its related negative human impacts - malnutrition, ill health, low
worker productivity and violence.

NOTES

[1] This hypothesis was developed by Connell, Gupta and Lipton (1977)
    after sifting evidence from various rural based studies and also
    analysing data from 40 villages in India.
[2] There exists close ties between rural and urban elites in Bangladesh.
    These ties are determined not only by blood connections but also by
    mutual economic and political interests (Khan 1980).
[3] This differential education mobility by education background of the
    migrants cannot be attributed to their differences in age. The
    median ages of the migrants both before (in rural areas) and after
    migration (in town at present) do not vary markedly by the level of
    education (see Appendix B). Even when we control for age at the time
    of migration, we find educational mobility is mostly concentrated
    among those who have had somewhat higher level of prior education.
    This finding holds true for almost every age group (see Appendix C).
[4] When adjusted for estimated average inflation between the time when
    the migrants first left the rural areas and the year they were sur-
    veyed in Dacca city, the increase in real income works out to be 123
    percent. The migrants have been living in Dacca city on an average
    for 12 years. The survey was conducted in 1980. Taking 1969-1970
    as 100, the value added price of 1980 was estimated to be 533.11
    (Ahmed 1983). The estimated rate of inflation remains unchanged even
    when we take the base of 1967-1968 as 100.
[5] One important explanation of this finding is that many of those who
    are now junior high or high school graduates were students and/or
    unemployed prior to migration.
[6] Dacca Survey:

Occupation Categories	Monthly average income (in Taka)
Higher level professional/executive	2047
Junior level professional/executive	1227
Business	1078
Sales and Clerical	710
Mill/Skilled workers	704
Service/Informal	539

(F = 18.95 df 6,697, Significant at .001 level)

[7] The independent effect of each variable was estimated through successive iterations, observing the variable decrease in the total explained sums of squares for each. This was 14.58 for education, 10.80 for occupation, 8.7 for marital status, 2.13 for family size, 1.15 for age, 4.2 for duration of stay, 1.26 for contact in town, .08 for both the number of make workers and residential status.

[8] Family size, followed by ownership of land, on the other hand are the important factors determining one's economic success in rural areas. Employing data of migrants' families in rural areas of the Faridpur Survey, we found family size and ownership of land explaining 26 percent and 4 percent respectively of log annual income of a rural household over and above which could be explained by all other variables together (see Appendix D).

[9] Only a handful of migrants (mainly the students) receive money from their kin in rural areas.

[10] While resource transfer can be 'in kind' and cash, in this analysis only cash transactions are examined.

[11] Those who have been working in government offices, private firms, mills and factories, ranging from the position of peons to high officials and executives.

[12] The median income of the migrant families is Taka 2597 exclusive of remittance and Taka 3264 inclusive of remittance. The corresponding figure for the study population is Taka 2354.

[13] 78 percent of the total remittance is received by the rich migrant families.

[14] The migrants originating from higher land holding classes also buy more land with the help of money earned in urban areas as is supported by data obtained from the Faridpur Survey.

Land holding status of migrants' households (in acres)	Mean land acquired by migrants (in acres)
Landless	0.40
less than or equal to 1.50	0.77
1.51 - 4.50	1.84
4.51 - 7.50	6.86
7.51 +	7.63

APPENDIX A

Data employed in this study are those collected from 68 villages in
Mymensingh district, two villages in Faridpur district of Central Bangladesh and also from the Dacca metropolitan area. For convenience, these
study areas are termed Mymensingh, Faridpur and Dacca studies.

Two villages of the Mymensingh district were selected from four
Thanas [1]. (Mukhtagacha, Fulbaria, Gaffargaon and Trisal). The sample
was drawn in two stages. First, the villages in the above mentioned
Thanas were stratified according to the land use pattern. Thereafter,
ten percent of the villages were randomly drawn from each stratum with
probability equal to the proportion of the households in the particular
stratum. This yielded 68 villages. Second, the households in each of
the selected villages were stratified into 36 groups on the basis of land
holding size and non-agricultural income. From each of the above strata,
10 percent of households were selected randomly with probability equal to
the proportion of the households in each stratum. This resulted in 1828
households. One hundred percent of these households were subsequently
surveyed to identify households from which at least one member had out-
migrated. An out migrant in this study was defined as one who had been
away from the household for at least six months. The information on
migrants was obtained from the head of the household. The study was
conducted in 1979.

The two villages containing 231 households in Faridpur district were
selected from Bhedorganj Thana. One hundred percent of these households
were surveyed to identify the out migrants. Using the same definition
of a migrant as in the Mymensingh study, we could identify 112 out migrants from the two villages. Migrants accounted for 18 percent of the
total population of the study villages. Information on migrants was obtained from the head of the households in rural areas. However, additional information was collected from 51 out migrants who could be contacted in Dacca city.

Data of the Dacca metropolitan study were drawn from four adjoining
areas of Dacca city, the capital of Bangladesh. These areas are: 1)
Dacca municipality; 2) Narayanganj municipality; 3) Mirpur municipality
and 4) Tongi municipality. Three stages sampling procedure was used to
collect data. First, the municipalities were stratified into wards/
blocks and 10 percent of the blocks/wards were selected randomly with
probability proportional to the total blocks in each municipal area.
This yielded 8 wards/blocks from four municipalities. Second, within a
municipality, blocks were selected from ecological zones [2] on the basis
of probability proportion to the size of an ecological zone. Third, one
hundred percent of the 44,800 households of 8 blocks were enumerated and
each head of household was classified on the basis of his/her occupation
and duration of stay. From each stratum, 2 percent of the households
were selected randomly with probability equal to the proportion of households in each stratum. This resulted in 896 households. Of these, 686
households were headed by male migrants from rural areas and were included in this study.

The Dacca Metropolitan study was conducted in 1980.

NOTES

[1] A Thana is an administrative unit which on an average consists of
    100,000 - 160,000 people.
[2] Each city was divided into a few ecological zones on the basis of ren-
    tal values of the buildings and the residential history of the area.

APPENDIX B

Median ages of the migrants in rural areas before migration and in urban areas after migration by their current level of education.

Level of education	Faridpur Study		Dacca Study	
Current	Before	After	Before	After
Illiterate	15.2	34.2	20.6	34.6
Below 5 grade	10.0	30.0	–	–
5 grade	16.4	34.6	–	–
1 - 5 grade	–	–	19.4	33.8
6 - 9 grade	17.4	34.5	19.5	36.0
10 grade	18.5	33.1	–	–
10 grade +	–	–	21.6	38.7
12 grade +	–	–	21.5	34.1

APPENDIX C. Education mobility of the migrants by their previous age and education (i.e., when they first moved from rural to urban areas)

Dacca Survey (N = 661*)

Level of Education (before migration)	Age-groups (before migration)																	
	1-9			10-14			15-19			20-24			25-29			30+		
	S	1+	Total	S	1+	Total	S	1+	Total	S	1+	Total	S	1+	Total	S	1+	Total
Illiterate	77.8 (14)	22.2 (4)	100.0 (18)	100.0 (25)	–	100.0 (25)	98.2 (55)	1.8 (1)	100.0 (56)	98.5 (66)	1.5 (1)	100.0 (67)	100.0 (26)	–	100.0 (26)	88.8 (32)	11.1 (4)	100.0 (36)
1-5 grade	80.0 (4)	20.0 (1)	100.0 (5)	83.3 (30)	16.7 (6)	100.0 (36)	96.6 (57)	3.4 (2)	100.0 (59)	100.0 (40)	–	100.0 (40)	96.5 (28)	3.5 (1)	100.0 (29)	100.0 (16)	–	100.0 (16)
6-9 grade				92.3 (12)	7.7 (1)	100.0 (13)	81.6 (31)	18.4 (7)	100.0 (38)	96.3 (26)	3.7 (1)	100.0 (27)	93.3 (14)	6.6 (1)	100.0 (15)	94.1 (16)	5.9 (1)	100.0 (17)
10 grade				100.0 (2)	–	100.0 (2)	53.8 (14)	46.1 (12)	100.0 (26)	83.9 (26)	16.1 (5)	100.0 (31)	93.3 (14)	6.7 (1)	100.0 (15)	100.0 (7)	–	100.0 (7)
11-12 grade							66.6 (4)	33.3 (2)	100.0 (6)	70.6 (12)	29.4 (5)	100.0 (17)	80.0 (4)	20.0 (1)	100.0 (5)	100.0 (2)	–	100.0 (2)
College							100.0 (1)	–	100.0 (1)	100.0 (8)	–	100.0 (8)	100.0 (11)	–	100.0 (11)	100.0 (7)	–	100.0 (7)

Note : S = remained the same

1+ = advanced education level at least one step ahead of the previous level.

*The table excluded 25 cases who have had non-institutional/religious education.

APPENDIX D

Stepwise regression of log yearly household income (in Taka) on age and education of head of the household and family size, total number of adult male workers and ownership of land of the household in a village in Faridpur district.

Independent Variable	R^2 change	Regression coefficient	S-E of B	t	Significance of t
V6C1 (F. size)	.2633	.0774	.0112	6.89	.0000
V64C1 (Land)	.0413	.0002	.00005	3.38	.0008
V38C1 (Education)	.0130	.0477	.0194	2.45	.014
V63C1 (No.Adult Workers)	.0101	.0720	.0340	2.11	.0353
V36C1 (Age)*	–	–	–	–	–
Constant		2.8		50.95	.0000

R^2 = 32.77, F = 36.20, (df 4,297) significant at beyond .0000 level.

*Age did not enter into the equation because it failed to meet the minimum significance level criterion (i.e., P value .10) to be an explanatory variable.

Note: V6C1 = Family size. Measured in terms of total numbers of household members who normally eat and sleep under the same roof and have family ties.

V64C1 = Total ownership of land by members of the household. Measured in terms of decimal.

V38C1 = Education level of head of the household. Determined in terms of highest grade completed.

V63C1 = Total number of adult male working members in the household.

REFERENCES

Ahmed, Sadiq, 'An Analysis of Inflation in Bangladesh', Boston University, Boston, 1983 (mimeo).

Alamgir, M., 'Some Analysis of Distribution of Income, Consumption,
Saving and Poverty in Bangladesh', Bangladesh Development Studies,
Vol. 11, No. 4, October 1974.

Bangladesh Bureau of Statistics, 1974 Bangladesh Population Census
Report: National Volume, Government Printing Press, Dacca, 1977.

Bose, S.R., 'The Price Situation in Bangladesh - Preliminary Analysis',
The Bangladesh Development Review, Vol. 1, No. 3, July 1973.

Chaudhury, R.H. and Curlin, G., 'Dynamics of Migration in a Rural Area
of Bangladesh', Bangladesh Development Studies, Vol.111, No. 2,
April 1975, pp. 182-230.

Chaudhury, R.H., 'Determinants and Consequences of Rural-Urban Migration'
(forthcoming).

Connell, J. et al, Migration from Rural Areas: The Evidence from Village
Studies, Oxford University Press, Delhi, 1977.

Das Gupta, B., 'Migration from Villages', Economic and Political Weekly,
Vo. X, No. 42, October 1982, pp. 1652-1662.

Feldstein, M.S., 'A Binary Variable Multiple Regression Model of Analy-
zing Factors Affecting Prenatal Mortality and Other Outcomes of
Pregnancy', Journal of the Royal Statistical Society, Series A, 129,
Part 1, 1966, pp. 61-63.

IRDP, Integrated Rural Development Programme, 1977, Bangladesh Rural
Development Project No. 1: Bench Mark Survey Mymensingh, November,
1977, pp. 66-69.

Khan, M.R., 'Comment on Target Groups and Regional Development: Case
for More Comprehensive Social Policy', in Regional Development
Dialogue, Vol. 1, No.1, spring 1980.

Lipton, M., 1976, 'Migration from Rural Areas of Poor Countries: The
Impact on Rural Productivity and Income Distribution', Paper presented
at the Research Workshop on Rural-Urban Labour Market Interactions,
IBRD, Washington D.C., February 5-7, 1976.

Suits, D., 'The Use of Dummy Variable Regression Equation', Journal of
the American Statistical Association, No. 52, 1957, pp. 548-555.

Todaro, M., 'A Model of Labour Migration and Urban Unemployment in LDCs',
American Economic Review, Vol. 59, 1969, pp. 138-148.

Tomasson, J., et al., 'Summary Report of the 1977 Land Occupancy Survey
of Rural Bangladesh', Bureau of Statistics, Dacca, 1977.

6 A System Approach to Housing Delivery

L. CHATTERJEE

1. INTRODUCTION

There is a great need in most developing countries to increase housing investment and to use it with greater efficiency. Explosive population growth, high rates of rural-urban migration, lagging infrastructure investment and changes in socio-cultural attitudes – particularly towards family formation – has increased the gap between housing needs and supply. The consequent deterioration in housing conditions has fuelled concerns for poverty eradication and the adoption of a basic needs approach to housing planning, for adequate shelter is a fundamental human need and probably second only to food. Active concern with housing, as contrasted with prior neglect, has brought the issue of housing investment and planning to the forefront.

Development of effective strategies for increasing housing investment and improving housing conditions, for currently deprived households, are constrained in three basic ways. First, there is a lack of coherent and consistent housing policy in most developing countries. Contradictions exist between several objectives of national and regional housing policies, such as equity versus growth or the centralised versus local autonomy issues in housing delivery. A second difficulty lies in the determination of appropriate procedures, required institutional changes and selection of instruments that can assure the effective execution of the objectives. Particularly, internal and external bottlenecks to successful delivery must be identified and mitigated. Third, establishment of housing goals implies measurement – of needs, economic feasibility and performance. Yet, there is a lack of sufficient data to support accurate measurement. Analytical procedures have to be developed in the light of these data restrictions.

If the basic needs approach is to become more than a change in development thinking and become standard development practice, then these constraints have to be addressed. Since there are tradeoffs between the numerous objectives of a housing policy (with a direct attack on housing poverty and provision of minimum consumption thresholds as only one of the objectives), prior determination of the relative importance of each objective is essential, if strategies to provide basic housing needs are to be successfully implemented. This paper presents a framework to analyse the housing delivery system, identify its structural components and highlight the contradictions that must be addressed so that housing strategies for poverty alleviation can be meaningfully implemented. In the next section the components of the housing delivery system and the processes that sustain the system are identified. Clearly, the processes that sustain a socialist housing system will differ from those sustaining a liberal modification of the market system. Nevertheless, all housing

systems are composed of internal components, particular to that ideolo-
gical framework, and strategies can only be successful if they are cog-
nizant of and analysed within the existing institutional and organisational framework.

In the second section this framework is applied to housing finance
systems, and low income financial intervention for meeting basic housing
needs is discussed. In the final section the data and analytic issues
are highlighted.

2. A MODEL OF A HOUSING DELIVERY SYSTEM

Housing strategies will be realistic and effective only if their design
and implementation are consistent with the overall organisational institutional and fiscal framework of individual regions. Two illustrations are provided. If a better distribution of housing services across
different income groups or neighbourhoods of a metropolitan area is the
objective, it cannot succeed if there is an inegalitarian distribution
of economic and political power. Socio-economic transformation, through
mobilisation of power by lower income groups, is a necessary accompani-
ment and public sector support for community organisation, through technical assistance, is a prerequisite for successful redistribution. If
the objective is to increase local autonomy and support decentralised
housing delivery systems (for greater equity and to reduce costs) the
use of housing cooperatives could be an instrument. However, such an
organisational instrument is unlikely to be effective if collective incentives are not provided. If only private incentives exist in the
housing system then cooperation among households within the collective
is likely to break down as competition rather than cooperation will generate the highest payoffs. Similarly cross subsidies, however desirable
and efficient, are unlikely to occur unless incentives for cross subsidies are built into the housing delivery system.

Considerable attempts to decrease housing poverty through the adoption
of more equity oriented instruments such as sites and services, public
provision of housing, or encouragement of low income finance systems has
led to disillusionment, in many instances, due to the high cost of implementation and inability to reach target groups. These actions, however well meaning, have been ineffective not because of their logic or
project design characteristics but because of the inconsistencies between
their internal attributes and the organisation, institutional, and asset
distribution system in which they were implemented. Low cost, self help
and grass roots participation strategies have degenerated when control
over resource mobilisation and allocation decisions were not vested in
these groups. Thus, the limited access of the poor to the benefits of
public sector urban and housing investment results from the mismatch between the existing housing delivery system and intervention instruments.

However, there are numerous experiments and examples of successful intervention where leakages have been minimal and the poor have fully benefitted from the investment. These experiments have been described in
case studies - for example in Ahmedabad, India (deSouza 1980) or Ismalia
(Sudra 1979). However, for replicability and generalisability, a general
model has to be derived from these case studies. A schematic diagram of
the general model is provided in Figure 1.

The model suggests that the various external and internal preconditions
required to effectively improve the housing conditions of low and moderate income groups should be viewed in a systems framework. A set of
elements are endogenous to the housing sector within a region and they

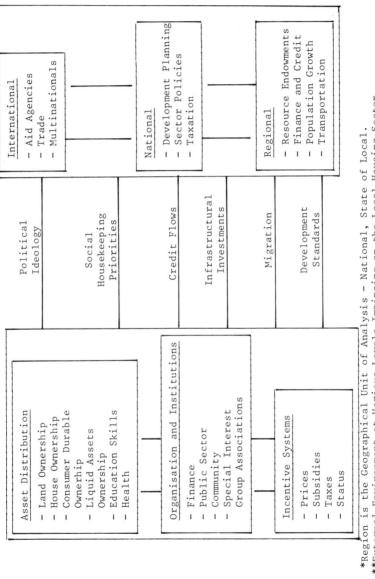

HOUSING SECTOR WITHIN A REGION *

NON HOUSING SECTOR: **
THE EXTERNAL ENVIRONMENT

International
 – Aid Agencies
 – Trade
 – Multinationals

National
 – Development Planning
 – Sector Policies
 – Taxation

Regional
 – Resource Endowments
 – Finance and Credit
 – Population Growth
 – Transportation

Political Ideology

Social Housekeeping Priorities

Credit Flows

Infrastructural Investments

Migration

Development Standards

Asset Distribution
 – Land Ownership
 – House Ownership
 – Consumer Durable Ownerhip
 – Liquid Assets Ownership
 – Education Skills
 – Health

Organisation and Institutions
 – Finance
 – Public Sector
 – Community
 – Special Interest Group Associations

Incentive Systems
 – Prices
 – Subsidies
 – Taxes
 – Status

*Region is the Geographical Unit of Analysis – National, State of Local.
**External Environment at Various Levels Impinging on the Local Housing Sector

Figure 1. A Model of a Housing Delivery System.

can be broadly classified into three categories. Policies taken to modify these internal system components - such as increase house ownership
or improve housing consumption standards of the poor - will be influenced
by the characteristics of the non housing sector impinging on it at various levels. The dialectical relationship between these two system components - the endogenous and the exogenous - have to be considered, for
the external environment provides opportunities. Since this environment
is outside the control of the sector - it also provides the fixed constraints. These external attributes will determine the overall feasibility of the intervention, the actual cost of modification of the internal
components, the desirable and undesirable outcomes of intervention.

Attempts to modify asset distribution or housing incentive systems
have been less effective than projected because the external world attributes and its linkages have been ignored. Most project objectives
and design has focussed on the internal components of the housing sector.
A better match between the two sectors would reduce the costs of delivery
to low and moderate income groups.

Four elements in the housing delivery system are recognised: Asset
Distribution, Organisations and Institutions, Incentives and External
linkages. The first three components define the 'inside' of the system.
As in any system, it is the interaction between the inside components
and the external environment that determines the output of the system.
Although the relative importance of each component will vary from region
to region, together they provide a common description of the housing
system.

Assets are viewed as embracing not only land and physical capital but
also the variety of human skills termed human capital. This definition
of assets derives from the notion that a household's income flows from
the ownership of all these sectors. Assets allow households to acquire
access to various production inputs and skills acquisitions that augment
their initial ownership (therefore has a reinforcement effect). Initial
advantages in asset ownership above some threhold level, widens disparities over time due to intergenerational transfers and difference in access
to skill and credit acquisition.

The leading role of asset distribution in determining the organisational and institutional structure is evident in most developing countries,
for the characteristics of organisations and institutions are consistent
with the degree of asset concentration. In highly inegalitarian market
oriented societies, effective demand is exercised by the well off who
make the relevant choices and they determine minimum lot size, infrastructure standards and credit policies i.e. institutional policies.
Limited supplies of high quality construction material - such as cement,
iron and glass - are subsidised or encouraged through building codes,
while abundant indigenous construction materials are ignored (Chatterjee 1980). These widen asset and housing consumption inequalities, and
scarce inputs of capital and energy get inappropriately applied.

If asset distribution is inegalitarian there is likely to be a few
house owners and predominance of renters and tenement dwellers. If
asset distribution is made more egalitarian there is likely to be more
owner occupier and tenant associations. Therefore, any policy in a market society, desiring a more egalitarian distribution, will have to
design instruments and incentive systems that can broaden ownership.
Over time the organisational and institutional subsystem can influence
asset ownership through external linkages, e.g. Changes in ideology can
bring about land reform and a more widespread ownership of land as in
Egypt, Korea and Tawain. However, this redistribution to be effective
has to be accompanied by changes in institutions, and incentive systems

that can set in motion new processes that can sustain it in the long run. Otherwise the goods, services and production technologies used by existing organisations and institutions will reinforce the given asset distribution and bring about reconcentration of assets, i.e. make the policy ineffective. External linkages that can modify the three 'inside' components are development standards, flows of ideas, capital and people. These linkages and flows can change asset distributions, organisational patterns and incentive systems.

The organisational structure has a spatial dimension which pertains to the geographic arrangement of service facilities, transport and utility networks, and open spaces. A spatial organisation that efficiently links homes with production and consumption facilities reduces the real cost of production and consumption and thereby increases real incomes.

Incentives fall into two broad groups. Individual incentives provide differential rewards to individuals of different skills and productivity. These incentives are well developed in market systems. Collective incentives can be found in housing cooperatives, informal finance systems and community development organisations. Change in political ideology can bring about an emphasis on collective incentives and more participatory delivery systems. The function of housing intervention is to modify the existing structure through changing the incentives in order to achieve the desired development objectives (e.g. provision of basic shelter needs or increase local participation).

To sum up, the four components - asset distribution, organisations and institutions, incentive subsystems and external linkages - are interlocking parts of a housing delivery system. If a housing program is introduced in the region in the form of sites and services or through an institutional innovation such as a housing cooperative - the effectiveness of the program or the distributional impacts will be determined by these systemic relationships. These ideas are explored through a concrete application to low income housing finance.

3. LOW INCOME URBAN HOUSING FINANCE: AN APPLICATION

The major characteristic of this model is that housing development is viewed as a systemic process. It suggests that effective modification of current housing consumption patterns will require more than piecemeal changes in any one of the components - asset distribution, organisation or incentive systems. Coherent, consistent and mutually supporting interventions in all the system components will be required for effective targetting. This argument is pursued further in the context of Low Income Housing Finance. Past interventions illustrate the effectiveness of strategies that have ignored the broader institutional - organisational - incentive - relational milieu sketched above. Examples drawn from Brazil, Nigeria and Egypt demonstrate the weakness of adhoc strategies. Policy interventions, more consistent with the theoretical framewor sketched earlier, are suggested.

Characteristics of low income housing finance

Housing finance is a crucial element for increasing housing supply. A house is a lumpy investment and its value is several times the current income of the average house owner. If the owner is entirely dependent on internal resources for total funds, then the process of construction will be slow and there will be a limited expansion of the stock. The level of consumption and the pace of construction can be increased

through credit availability at various stages - for land acquisition,
purchase of building materials, payment of labour and contractor services. Table 1 shows the impact of finance on affordable house prices
for the bottom 40% in selected states of Nigeria. Financing that is
accessible to the poor, and tailored to their housing expenditure behaviour, can expand the supply of low cost housing and improve housing
consumption standards consistent with basic needs approach.

In order to improve the quality of the housing stock and to increase
home ownership, a broad based housing finance policy is required. The
finance function calls for the transfer of funds from savings surplus
units to savings deficit units. To do this efficiently there must be
institutions that can mobilise funds from savings surplus households and
transfer them, through short, medium and long term loans to household/
organisations in need of these funds. Consequently, resource mobilisation has become a major issue for developing countries and there has
been a growing interest in ways and means to structure and help housing
capital markets in developing countries (UN 1968, 1978).

Housing finance is characterised by a number of attributes which distinguish it from industrial and commercial finance and negatively affect
its competitiveness in the overall finance market. These attributes
affect the borrower, the lender and the competitiveness of the mortgages
vis à vis other financial instruments. Consequently, housing finance in
its conventional form benefits only a few - generally the upper income
groups.

Table 1
Impact of Housing Finance on Affordability:
Selected States of Nigeria: 1975

Region	Mean [1] Household Income of Bottom 40%	Estimated Affordable House Prices	
		Capitalisation of Expenditures[2]	Market Convention[3]
Nigeria	686	863	1715
Bauchi	432	642	1080
Kano	432	667	1080
Lagos	1196	1454	2990
Ondo	541	645	1353
Rivers	380	479	950
Bennie	374	591	935

1) Average Household Size - 5.2 members
2) Based on current housing expenditures patterns and 15 year loan
   maturity
3) Price is 2.5 times annual income. Conventional rule of thumb.
Source: Chatterjee 1980.

The characteristics are:
1) The size of the loan is likely to be large relative to the income of
   the borrower or the annual income from the asset - thus a large debt
   to value ratio.
2) Large debt ratios imply long repayment schedules. Therefore, the
   employment record, potential earnings and yield from the asset assume
   critical importance. (These conventional requirements are ill suited
   to the income earning patterns of the majority in developing countries.)
3) The actual or perceived risks associated with long repayment sched-

ules mandates possession of 'legal' titles and sizeable collateral.

In addition to these problems derived from the character of housing investment, a special set of problems results from the character of earnings of lower income groups. The poor have a greater diversity in the sources and patterns of earning than middle and upper income groups. They depend on self employment or multiple jobs to augment their incomes from the low wage formal sector. While their overall income may be adequate for low cost housing, the pattern of these earnings may be irregular. In addition, many belong to the informal sector. The flow of net income from trading, operating small shops, driving taxis and like activities may be sufficient for servicing payments on modest dwelling units but conventional criteria disqualifies them from formal sector institutions because it is difficult to verify their incomes and determine credit worthiness. In most developing countries these groups have to depend on self financing (equity financing) in contrast to the debt financing received by higher income groups.

The urban areas, where the low and moderate income groups are locating, are witnessing rapid growth. Due to the constraints posed by lack of finance, housing is built through an incremental process in largely unserviced peripheral areas. For example in Cairo, such informal housing accounts for 70% of the new growth and the loteamentos of Rio de Janeiro account for 45% of the housing market (Vetter 1977, PADCO 1981). In these large and expanding low income housing submarkets low income households are mobilising monetary and nonmonetary resources to finance their houses. Low income finance can help governments to efficiently capitalise on these self help efforts for meeting basic housing needs.

The efforts of the Brazilian Government in low income finance provides an interesting illustration of the difficulties associated with the application of conventional approaches. The Brazilian government gave an important place to housing in its development agenda. This commitment to housing was in recognition of its key role in income generation, labour absorption and multiplier effects on the economy - particularly on industrial production (Schulman 1977). In 1964, it created an apex housing finance institution - the National Housing Bank (BNH) - allocated the funds from the compulsory saving scheme of the payroll tax for a Social Security Fund (FGTS) and gave it sweeping powers to use this large, long term resource base to create and supervise a complex institutional structure for housing finance (Carpenter 1975). In addition to supporting a variety of instruments for the mobilisation of capital for housing and urban infrastructure (in which it was remarkably successful), the BNH designed favourable finance terms for low income borrowers through its Low Income Housing Finance Program (SIFHAP), as shown in Table 2 (Anderson Lessard 1976). The BNH designed low income finance programs with concessionary interest rates and required lenders to allocate funds to 'popular' (lowest income group), 'economic' and 'intermediate' groups. The BNH effort in aiding the housing sector became a model for several Latin American countries e.g. the INFONAVIT in Mexico. For example, the INFONAVIT's resources were mobilised through a 5% mandatory payroll tax on employers. Similar mandatory savings forms the core of the Philippines housing finance system (USAID 1979). The practice of differential rates of interest, progressive in favour of the economically weaker groups of society, has also been adopted by other countries e.g. India's HUDCO.

While the program design in Brazil showed a sensivivity to the conditions of low income groups, an analysis of the allocation of BNH funds in 1975 is revealing (Table 3). In the 1966-1975 period the BNH attempted to provide finance and invest in programs to help those with 'lower ac-

quisitive powers'. Nevertheless, the share of the lower income groups
consistently declined, during this period (Figure 2). This figure moni-
tors the lending activity trends and shows that the participation of
households with less than 10 minimum salaries decreased from 70% to 5%,
and those with incomes more than 10 minimum salaries increased from 25%
to 68% of total activity (Novaes 1976). Nevertheless, in 1975, 80% of
BNH resources were derived from the working classes through the 8% FGTS
payroll deductions (Anderson Lessard 1976). BNH's emphasis on creating
specialised programs for low income groups and the adoption of concessionary interest rates, not withstanding, was ineffective in meeting the
objectives. Since 1976, the BNH has been increasingly functioning as a
comprehensive urban development bank and has channelled its resources to
sanitation projects, highway construction and utility provision. The
allocation of funds to such public goods does not permit estimation of
the incidence received by different income groups. Much of the benefits
accrue to owners of land (through price increases). This consistent
shift toward middle and upper income target groups and urban infrastructure investments reflects the lack of absorption of funds by economically weaker members of society.

The limitations of existing low income housing finance systems

Surveys indicate that low income households generate high rates of
savings for purchase of consumer durables (UN 1978, Chatterjee 1981).
Conventional instruments fail because they ignore the existing asset
distributions, savings incentives and patterns, and existing credit
mechanisms of the target groups. Given the inegalitarian income and
asset distributions, low per capita incomes and wealth, high levels of
illiteracy and lack of formal education, these subsidised opportunities
are inaccessible to the majority in spite of progressive interest rates.
Other criteria for access - eligibility standards, collateral and rigid
repayment schedules with the threat of foreclosure - work against the
household. To sum up, families are unable to take advantage of the
programs of formal institutions as their policies do not address their
financing needs.
    Current strategies adopted by this group can provide clues for the
evolution of instruments adapted to the repayment capacity of lower income households. Credit management is not alien to the low income
households who are accustomed to meeting their credit needs from a variety of sources - money lenders, loans from building material suppliers,
relatives, friends and informal rotating credit associations - loosely
termed the informal system. It represents the unorganised capital market and from its prevalence and vitality it appears to be sizeable. Yet
its attributes are ignored by public policy. A financing scheme that
can address the needs of these target groups and supplement current
'self help' efforts, must be built up from this existing base.
    The unorganised capital market has been hitherto ignored because of the
oppressive domination by usurious money lenders and inefficient use of
credit for social purposes such as marriage, births and deaths. Money
lenders represent only one type of supply sector response to the credit
needs of low income households. Informal saving mechanisms, such as
rotating credit associations that exist in a variety of countries represent an adaptive mechanism that warrants further exploration. Ardener
(1974) notes the existence of such associations in Taiwan, Japan, India,
Malaysia, Vietnam, Ghana, Cameroon, Sierra Leone, South Africa, Zambia,
Sudan and West Indies. They have been analysed in Mexico (Lewis 1959),
barrios of California (Kurtz 1973), Nigeria (Bascom 1952, Chatterjee

Table 2
Concessionary Finance for Low Income Groups
in Brazil: 1975

Loan Size in UPC	Maximum Interest Rate %	Maximum Payment - Income Ratio %
0- 100	1.0	18
100- 300	2.6	20
300- 400	3.3	25
400- 600	6.0-6.6	25
600- 800	7.3-7.9	25
800- 1000	8.6-9.3	25
1000- 3500	10.0	25-40

Source: Compiled from Anderson Lessard (1975).

Table 3
Incidence of Loans Received for Urban Housing
in Brazil: 1975

Level of Income (in cruzerios)	Percent of Total Loans Received %	Percent of Total Urban Households %	Percent of Total Income Received by Households %
Below 825	5	81.1	46.8
825-1650	30	11.7	25.4
1650	50	7.2	27.8
Urban infrastructure	20	-	-

Source: Compiled from Novaes (1976).

1980), Tonga (Morten 1978), and Egypt (Abt Associates 1981, Chatterjee 1981).

In Egypt they are called Gamiyas and in Nigeria, Essusus. Gamiyas and Essusus are voluntary associations of individuals who agree to contribute a prefixed sum at fixed intervals (daily, weekly or monthly). The periodicity is based on the households earnings schedule. The pooled funds of each interval is allocated to each member once during the cycle and the association is terminated at the end of each cycle. They function as temporary savings associations in which mutual support, community management and control, and goal directed savings are crucial features.

The widespread prevalence of these mechanisms result from their consistency with the asset and income attributes of the target group and the incentive systems. These organisations are adapted to the divertity in sources and patterns of earnings. Credit worthiness of an individual (therefore eligibility to participate in the savings association) is a function of past credit performance and trustworthiness, and not a function of their levels of income. In this organisation form riskiness is derived from personal attributes - i.e. attitudes, behaviour and past credit performance. Income is not used as a proxy measure as in formal institutions. The savings period is determined by the individual's assessment of his/her financial situation and earnings expectation; it is not determined by the institution. Moreover, the terminating rela-

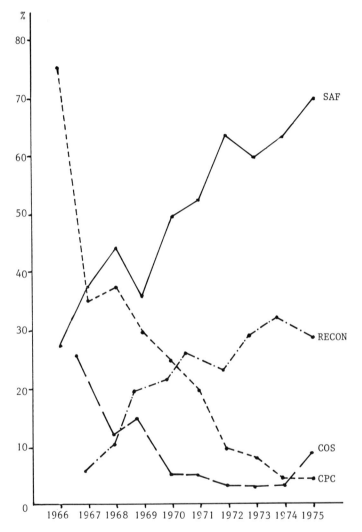

Figure 2.   Allocation of Credit by Income Group: Brazil, 1966-1975.

Source: Novaes 1976.
Legend:
COS: Cartera de Operaciones de Naturaliza Social (below 5 minimum salaries)
CPC: Cartera de Projectos Cooperativos (below 10 minimum salaries)
SAF: Superintendencia de Agentes Financieros (higher than 10 minimum
      salaries)

tionship of a savings cycle is consistent with the low income household's ability to predict its future earnings and claim on it only for the short run.

The incentive systems are also adapted to the attributes of the target group. As noted the savings are goals directed. Individuals join a savings group to raise funds for a specific purpose. It allows the aggregation of a small amount of savings, made over an extended period into a more economic lump sum. Community based control mechanisms (and particularly the fear of loss of credit worthiness) are important when the marginal propensity to save is low and there is less 'surplus' available from meeting the consumption needs. Without collective support and incentives it is unlikely that the savings could be aggregated over the period. It is the 'commitment to the personalised' community of peers that acts as both a control mechanism and an incentive. Surveys indicate that delinquency is rare and in cases where they occur due to severe illness, death or other catastrophic events, there is a social insurance mechanism. Members equally divide the loss caused by the default payment.

Rotating credit associations provide examples of organisational mechanisms reflective of the asset distribution and incentive systems characteristic of low income households in developing countries. Its widespread occurrence and popularity derives from its consistency with systemic attributes emphasised earlier in the general model. When integrated with the external environment - e.g. the formal sector - through credit and information flows, they can be used to mobilise savings from and promote improved housing opportunities for low income groups. Their strengths in meeting the small scale and frequent credit requirements of a large number of individuals is complementary to the formal sector. For example, administration of small loans is a deterrent to formal sector institutions with their high administrative costs. Determination of credit eligibility based on personality traits is infeasible due to the high cost of information. Substitution of formal but impersonal delinquency control mechanisms such as legal notices and foreclosure with 'moral and social' pressures is also impractical for formal institutions as these mechanisms are inconsistent with the systemic attributes of formal institutions. Yet, loans have to be small, frequent and geared to the household capacity for servicing the payments if low income groups are to receive the benefits of finance. As these credit mechanisms promote savings among low income (particularly among those unfamiliar with or fearful of banks), help collect small savings streams into economic sums and provides interest free credit (as there are no administrative costs) in a highly personalised community based context, they provide a potential institutional adjunct to the formal system.

Implications for housing finance policy

A major objective of housing finance policy should be to link viable rotating credit associations (RCA) with private sector financial institutions in a joint effort to mobilise funds, improve housing conditions, expand ownership opportunities and channel savings into asset formation. In such an endeavour the national housing mortgage association or the Housing Bank (the apex housing finance institution) should act as a catalytic agency. The Neighbourhood Housing Services program in the United States, under the sponsorship of the Federal Home Loan Bank Board provides an illustration of a working model of a vertically linked but community based institution that specialises in neighbourhood housing development through the provision of small, numerous 'high risk' loans - risk defined by conventional banking criteria.

The Neighbourhood Housing Service program is a local, self help, non governmental program that has addressed itself to the revitalisation of low income and declining neighbourhoods in major American cities (Action 1975). It does this by a) raising capital for a high risk revolving loan fund, b) providing finance to individuals whose insufficient income makes them ineligible for conventional loans (non bankable), c) administers loans and determines amortisation payments using affordability criteria. Thus credit terms are flexible and varies with client attributes. The credit devision is based on personal knowledge of the applicant and accompanied with counselling. The key to the successful implementation of the N.H.S. program has been its small scale neighbourhood approach, social interest and commitments, and careful selection of participants.

While each N.H.S. is nongovernmental and community based, national agencies such as the F.H.L.B.B. and HUD have been essential for its development (Action 1975). Their involvement has focussed on technical assistance, through a series of mandatory training workshops, ensuring the participation of private financial institutions and dissemination of information among individual N.H.S. on a continuing basis. A small amount of seed money is provided for the high risk loan fund, and the N.H.S. can draw on the commitment based on demonstrated efficiency.

While the N.H.S. model should not be transplanted to developing countries (for N.H.S. programs vary between neighbourhoods in the US), the key features of the linkage between community based, minimally bureaucratic, local programs and high level 'formal' sector agencies is worth replicating. Several important administrative and policy issues such as centering on size of the N.H.S. neighbourhood, complementary local government activities, effective mechanisms for fund raising, have been assessed and have parallels for the incorporation of RCA's into the housing finance sector in developing countries. A broad based program requires the break down of the current dual system in the 'capital market'.

4. CONCLUDING COMMENTS: IMPLICATIONS FOR ANALYTICAL TECHNIQUES

Formulation of housing policies consistent with the analytical framework delineated here requires simultaneous attention to be paid to the behaviour of a number of actors, institutions and linkages in and among the two sectors - housing and non housing. While numerous quantitative techniques for housing analysis have been developed in recent years in statistics, econo-socio-psychometrics, operations research, decision theory or financial analysis, two problems need to be addressed if quantitative techniques are to be effectively integrated with housing policy analysis. First, the traditional distinction between normative and positive analysis has to be minimised. Second, analytic fragmentation of housing issues has to be reduced.

In social science methods there has been a tradition of distinguishing between normative and positive statements. Normative statements devolve from cultural and moral values and are thus untestable. Scientific method (and quantitative analysis is rooted in scientific method) has been deemed inapplicable and recourse has been made to the humanities - logic, religion, ethics and law - for guidance. Scientists - social or natural, pure or applied - deal with positive statements. Postive statements, however inexactly, describe the world as it is. Consequently, facts, hypotheses, testing procedures, reliability and validity have been its key methodological concerns. The distinction between humanities and sciences loses its validity in planning and applied science - social or natural - as scientific knowledge is used to steer society in desired directions. The moment objectives are selected and pursued the normative and positive elements become so intertwined that we have to treat quantitatively that which is basically qualitative. Just as the distinction between pure and applied science became blurred with the scientific development of technology in the 19th and 20th centuries, so the distinction between humanities and sciences is becoming blurred with the development of planning and decision sciences. Currently, questions to which answers are sought are as important as how they are answered through the process of scientific enquiry. Thus methods that allow the incorporation of qualitative 'humanistic' information with quantitative and observable facts will become increasingly important in analytic procedures.

Numerous quantitative techniques have already been developed for and are used in housing analysis. However, disparate and diverse techniques are used to analyse the same housing problem as they are viewed from the limited perspective of each actor or institution. For example, in analysing the issue of housing finance for low income households, the perspective of the planner, government administrator, financial institution, community organiser and social analyst will vary. So will their analytical framework and quantitative technique. For example, the financial institution will analyse its fiduciary viability and use actuarial and accounting methods, whereas an administrator is likely to be interested in its fiscal and political impacts and is likely to use an evaluation methodology. This variation reflects their different norms and objectives. If quantitative methods are to address the policy questions then the diverse concerns of these actors and institutions have to be reflected in the analysis and hybrid techniques will have to replace the simple elegance of earlier procedures. This volume discusses a few of these newer and exploratory techniques in later chapters.

To sum up, our ability to improve living conditions of low income groups is constrained by our framework of analysis (which is fragmented and not systemic) and an inappropriate use of techniques whose assumptions violate the basic attributes of the phenomena being analysed. Current developments of 'nontraditional' techniques more consistent with the data and the system attributes can bring about more effective relationships between the housing practitioner and the analyst.

REFERENCES

Abt Associates, Informal Housing in Egypt, USAID, 1981.

Action Housing, Inc., The Neighborhood Housing Services Model, HUD, 1975.

Anderson, A. and Lessard, D.R., 'Price Level Adjusted Mortgages in Brazil', in Modigliani F. and Lessard, D.R. (eds), New Mortgage Designs for an Inflationary Environment, Cambridge, Mass., 1975.

Ardener, S., 'The comparative study of rotating credit associations', Journal of the Royal Anthropological Institute 94, 1964, pp. 201-229.

Bascom, W., 'The Esusu: a credit association of the Yoruba', Journal of the Royal Anthropological Institute 82, 1952, pp. 63-70.

Chatterjee, L., 'Appropriate Financial Institutions for Meeting Basic Shelter Needs', in Lasker, G. (ed), Human Systems, Ecology and the Social Sciences, Pergamon Press, New York, 1980.

Chatterjee, L., 'Effective Targeting for Basic Shelter Provision', Economic Geography, Vol. 57, No. 1, 1981.

Souza, Alfred de, The Indian City, South Asia Books, Delhi, 1978.

Kurtz, D.V., 'The rotating credit association: an adaptation to poverty', Human Organization, 32, 1972, pp. 49-58.

Lakshmanan, T.R. and Chatterjee, L., 'The Urban Built Environmental System: Performance and Policies for the Poor', in Misra, R.P. (ed), Humanizing Development, Maruzen Asia, Tokyo, 1982.

Lakshmanan, T.R., 'A Systems Model of Rural Development', World Development, Vol. 10, No. 10, 1982, pp. 885-898.

Lewis, O., Five Families, Basic Books, New York, 1958.

Morten, K., 'Mobilizing money in a commercial economy: a Tongan example', Human Organization, 37, 1, 1978.

Novaes, E.S., La Vivienda de Interes Social Dentro del Sistema Financiero de la Vivienda en el. Brazil, Rio de Janeiro, 1976.

Padco Inc., The National Urban Policy Study, USAID, Egypt, 1980, (mimeo).

Reynolds, C.W. and Carpenter, R.T., 'Housing Finance in Brazil: Towards a New Distribution of Wealth', in, Cornelius W.A. and Trueblood, F.M. (eds), Latin American Urban Research Vol. 5, Sage Publications, Beverly Hills, California, 1975.

Sudra, Tomasz, 'The Case of Ismalia - can architect and planner usefully participate in the housing process?', Open House, Vol. 5, 1980.

United Nations, Finance for Housing and Community Facilities, E. 68, IV 4, New York, 1968.

United Nations, Non Conventional Financing of Housing for Low Income Households, New York, 1978.

USAID, General Summary of the Housing Finance Systems of Selected Nations in the Asian and Pacific Regions, Washington, D.C., 1979.

Vetter, D.M., Low Income Housing Policy for Development: An Evaluation of the Brazilian Experience, Berkeley, California, 1977.

7 Public Expenditure and the Performance of Regional Production Enterprises: Analytical and Policy Issues

T. R. LAKSHMANAN AND A. ELHANCE

1. INTRODUCTION

The extensive literature on sources of economic growth has identified
the crucial role of public expenditures in physical and social overhead
– transportation facilities, power, water and sewer facilities, education, health, nutrition, recreation, etc. (Schultz 1961, Denison 1967,
Maddisson 1970, Correa 1970, Robinson 1971, Nadiri 1970, Saxonhouse
1977, Selowsky 1981). There is a two-fold return to regional resources
from the provision of these physical and social amenities. First, the
delivery of improved education, health care and recreation directly improves welfare of the regional human resources or individuals demanding
these amenities – in the form of better skills, reduced absenteeism, etc.
Similarly the provision of roads, airports and utilities improves the
productivity of producer capital (machinery, equipment, livestock, etc.)
and consumer capital (housing and residential structures, etc.). In the
long run, all this improves the productivity of regional physical and
human resources, output and income. This income effect resulting from
the effective demand for amenities is the amenity-demand effect (Klaassen
1968). The second income effect, termed the amenity-supply effect, derives from the attractiveness the provision of regional amenities poses
for industries outside the region, especially the more productive activities that demand superior facilities.

High levels of these amenities are enjoyed in the more affluent societies, which can mobilise the considerable level of public expenditures
necessary to support the amenities. In developing societies, with far
more limited resources, the levels of amenities resulting from transportation, utilities, health, education and nutrition investments are lower;
perhaps, in some cases, below the threshold levels where their effects on
output are negligible, i.e., a sort of low level equilibrium trap. In
regions whose residents must endure widespread epidemics, nutritional
inadequacies, inadequate power and poor accessibility, it is likely that
productivity is below the potential level possible, with existing stocks
of capital and effective labour.

As a consequence, a major thrust of development policy in backward
regions of developing countries is to increase the provision of these
capital goods in transportation, power, education, health, etc. so as to
increase the productive potential and income of these regions. Since
these investments are either provided in the public sector or under public sector control. the critical analytical questions are: How much and
what types of public investment should be made at what locations and when
in order to promote regional development?

Since physical and social overhead investments are large and lumpy, it
is important, especially in developing countries with scarce resources,

to understand the nature of contributions such investments made to regional income. The objective of this paper is to present and discuss the policy contributions that public investments of different types make to the productivity of enterprises in a region. It is conceivable that only some kinds of public capital effect the output in some industries. Some investments may augment labour, improving its skills and productivity. Others may improve the productivity of physical capital. Again, some types of public investnemts may play a greater role in output determination in the earlier stages of regional growth while others may come into play later. Some investments may even have an adverse effect on some sectors. The model we present here is capable of providing ex ante assessment of regional public investments so that scarce public resources can be optimally employed to improve the performance of regional enterprises and to encourage development in backward regions.

In the next sections of the paper, we review the literature on the interdependence between public expenditures and the growth of productive enterprises in order to elucidate major analytical and policy issues in stimulating regional development. We proceed in the following section to outline a model capable of describing the interdependence between public investment and regional growth, and identifying its analytical properties. We conclude the paper with a discussion of the potential of this model for regional policy analysis.

2. INTERDEPENDENCE BETWEEN PUBLIC EXPENDITURES AND REGIONAL GROWTH

A review of interdependences

Although a mix varies from country to country, the greater part of all resources is in private ownership – in the hands of farmers, small traders and businessmen, who, acting independently and with flexibility, provide a vital source of entrepreneurship and economic growth. The fundamental public policy issue in most developing countries, thus, is one of how best to utilise scarce available resources – natural endowments, capital stock and labour skills – to promote economic development. Where there is a viable private sector, the role of the public sector (in most cases) is to stimulate or sustain economic growth. Conversely, the private sector is unlikely to contribute effectively to economic development without a public sector capable of providing – at a manageable cost – the requisite infrastructure and an overall conducive environment.

If public investment in electricity, transport, water, education, vocational training, health, etc. is inefficient – its costs excessive and its output low – the economic returns from the country's total available investments will drop and overall growth impaired. If public services such as transportation, power or training are weak and unreliable, the enterprises will be less efficient. This interdependence between the quality of public investments and the performance of regional enterprises can be illustrated in the case of transportation and education.

In transportation-poor regions, supply and demand are restricted by the high cost of moving and by ignorance of where goods can be sold and for how much. In the case of farm products, high cost of transport and long delays, with consequent damage to perishable produce have been powerful deterrents to increasing food supplies. Produced food rots because transport is not available. Isolated communities remain ignorant of market opportunities or of new ideas and new techniques since information, like everything else, travels slowly on primitive roads.

Industrial activity is also severely hampered in terms of difficulty of accessing production inputs and markets. Poor transportation necessi-tates excessive inventories at high cost to compensate for unreliable deliveries. Thus, a good case can be made that appropriate transport facilities are an important necessary condition for regional development. Indeed, illustrations of this link in both developed and developing countries are legion.

There is an extensive literature on the relation between economic growth and education (or including health, human capital). Investments in education come in many forms - formally organised training, study programmes and training, on-the-job and institutional training and re-training. Such educational investments can overcome many of the defic-iencies of workers that impede their productivity, e.g., illiteracy, fear of change and new knowledge, immobility, etc. Further the acquisi-tion of newer skills permits the introduction of newer production tech-nologies.

A variety of empirical studies illustrates this connection between education and growth. Schultz (1961) was one of the first to suggest that growth in the US, 'unexplained' by conventional factor imputs, is due to the rapid increase in the quality of labour through education. Noting that the stock of education in the US rose by approximately 850 per cent between 1900 and 1956 as compared with an increase in reproduc-able capital of 450 per cent (in 1956 dollars) he argued that the return to investment in education is at least as high as, if not higher than, that to non-human capital. Denison (1967) also reaches a similar con-clusion. He estimates the contribution of education to the growth of per capital income between 1929-1957 as 42 per cent (as compared with Schultz's estimate of 25-45 per cent for the same period).

Several production-function studies on sources of growth in developing countries are noteworthy in this regard. While these aggregate models are rough tools using sometimes shaky data, they provide an important idea of the likely quantitative significance of different factors in growth.

In a study of 22 developing countries over the period 1950-1965, Maddison noted that, on average, policy-induced growth in the form of investments in improving health and education accounted for 40 per cent of measured growth (Maddison 1970). Nadiri, who has brought together and surveyed a number of production function studies by others, con-cludes that except for fast growing countries like Japan, Israel and Mexico, the contribution to measured growth of total labour input growth is greater than the contribution of capital input growth (Nadiri 1972). Further, Nadiri disaggregates the labour input contribution into various components. From Table 1 (and the background work by Correa) it can be noted that education is responsible for about one-third-of-one-half of labour's contribution to the growth of output. The contribution of education is very large in slow growing economies such as the UK and Belgium while in some fast growing economies such as Germany it is also low. In developing countries, except for Argentina the contribution of education is smaller. Indeed the smaller contribution of education in developing countries may be due to the low rate of return on education as compared to that in physical capital [1].

However, the (potential) importance of education in developing coun-tries is clear in the work of Kruger (1968) who shows that unless the stock of human capital in these countries is improved first they would not equal per capita income of the US even if they were endowed with exactly the same labour and capital quantities as the US. Hayami and Rutton (1971) show that both general and technical education contributes

one third to narrowing the differential between agricultural productivity in the developing countries and the US. General education is the
most important type of education.

Table 1

The Contribution of Labour Input Components to Economic Growth

Country	Period	Contributions of Labour Input Type			
		Education	Health and Nutrition	Employment Growth	Total Labour Input
Argentina	1950-62	0.53	0.12	0.93	1.58
Brazil	1950-62	0.18	0.43	1.83	2.44
Chile	1950-62	0.20	0.20	0.65	1.05
Colombia	1950-62	0.20	0.49	1.66	2.35
Ecuador	1950-62	0.23	0.32	0.92	1.47
Honduras	1950-62	0.29	0.82	1.06	2.17
Mexico	1950-62	0.05	0.93	1.43	2.41
Peru	1950-62	0.14	0.57	0.67	1.40
Venezuela	1950-62	0.19	0.21	2.19	2.59
India	1950-62				1.86
Philippines	1947-65				2.24
Netherlands		0.24	0.04	0.78	1.06
USA	1950-62	0.49	0.02	0.90	1.41
W. Germany	1950-62	0.11	0.28	1.49	1.88
France	1950-62	0.29	0.15	0.07	0.51
Belgium	1950-62	0.43	0.09	0.40	0.92
UK	1950-62	0.19	-0.03	0.50	0.76
Japan	1950-62	0.31	n.a.	2.48	

Source: Correa 1970, Nadiri 1972.

A framework for analysing interdependencies

It is to take advantage of the beneficial effects (discussed above) of
infrastructure that public sector in many developing countries attempts
to provide, directly, goods and services (mainly capital) goods designed
both to supplement and to induce a favourable response from the productive enterprises. In the case of private enterprise, economic theory
would suggest that perfect capital markets will result in an efficient
allocation of capital, regionally and sectorally, given tastes, technology and the 'state of the environment'. The state of the environment
to which the private enterprises in a region are adjusting includes the
prior level of spatial distribution of economic activities and the extant
stock of physical and social capital in the region (Figure 1). The scale
of the regional public capital stock - transport, the urban built environment, health, education facilities, etc. - have an important impact,
in this view, on subsequent private investment decisions and on the location decisions made by firms. Since the initial distribution of public
infrastructure is partly predetermined by the level of spatial array of
firms and households, there is an interdependent system as shown in
Figure 1.
A number of efforts have been made to empirically test the interdependence outlined in Figure 1 (Lakshmanan and Lo 1970, Mera 1973). Since
public goods are available to all firms in a region, these approaches
view public capital as entering all firms' production functions. How-

96

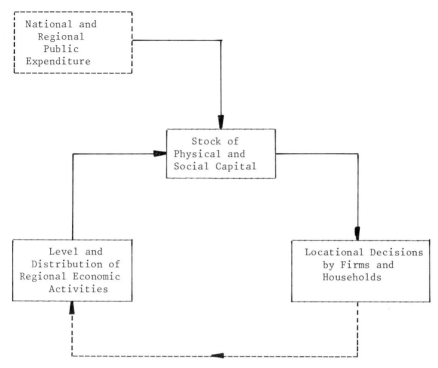

Figure 1. Interdependence of Private and Public Investment Decisions.

ever, while available to all, total use must be equal to or less than
the physical capacity. Hence public capital is viewed as a stock and
often in physical terms (Leven, Legler and Shapiro 1970) [2].

Lakshmanan and Lo attempted to estimate the effects of 17 different
types of physical and social overhead capital over a twenty-year period
in the municipios of Puerto Rico through the use of a Cobb-Douglas production function:

$$X_{ij} = f[L_{ij}(t), K_{ij}(t), S_j(t)] \qquad (1)$$

where

$X_{ij}(t)$ = Output in sector i, municipio j, at time t
$L_{ij}(t)$ = Employeers in sector i, municipio j, at time t
$K_{ij}(t)$ = Stock of physical capital, sector i, municipio, time t
$S_j(t)$ = Vector of social overhead capital stock, in j, at t.

A similar formulation was used by Koichi Mera for Japanese data. In
addition to the traditional factors of production- capital and labour -
Mera used an environmental factor (V) in the production function.

Thus, Y = Y(K,L,V) where Y = income produced in the sector.

The environmental factor V is specified as an additive combination of
three types of private capital stocks

K_1 - private capital for primary sector
K_2 - private capital for secondary sector
K_3 - private capital for tertiary sector
and, four types of social capital

G_1 - government provided improvements for primary sector
G_2 - public utilities
G_3 - transportation and communication facilities
G_4 - social welfare facilities - health, education, etc.

Five environmental factors are formed by different <u>additive</u> combinations of these seven types of capital i.e.

$$V_1 = G_2 + G_3$$
$$V_2 = G_2 + G_3 + G_4$$
$$V_3 = G_1 + G_2 + G_3 + G_4$$
$$V_4 = G_2 + G_3 + K_1 + K_2 + K_3$$
and $$V_5 = G_1 + G_2 + G_3 + K_1 + K_2 + K_3$$

Thus, G_2 and G_3 - the two social capital stocks related to public utilities, transportation and communication - are hypothesised as the core of the environmental factor. In the most extensive form of the hypothesis, all kinds of capital stocks are considered to form the environmental factor V_5.

The estimating equations for this model are :

$$\ln \frac{Y_i}{E_i} = a + b \ln \frac{K_i}{E_i} + c \ln \frac{G_i}{E_i} + d \ln \frac{V_i}{E_i} \qquad (2)$$

where

$Y_i \equiv$ output (income from sector i)
$K_i \equiv$ private capital stock in sector i
$G_i \equiv$ relevant social capital for sector i
$V_i \equiv$ relevant environmental factor for sector i
$E_i \equiv$ employment in sector i

In estimating these equations, alternative combinations of other inputs are included in logarithmic forms for each sector, e.g. cultivated land area for primary sector; G_2 and G_3 for secondary sector; and G_3 and G_4 for tertiary sector. Some estimations are done by combining private and social capital in an additive manner rather than multiplicatively. Further, technological changes are introduced through a time variable and a spatial density variable is included in further estimation.

To elicit the elasticity of subsitution between the private and social capital stocks, a modified CES production function is formulated where:

$$Y_i = c \, e^{\lambda t} \, e_i^{\alpha} \, [dK_i^{-p} + (1 - d) \, g_i^{-p}]^{-B/p} \qquad (3)$$

Both Lakshmanan and Lo and Koichi Mera use essentially a Cobb-Douglas function in which social overhead capital is introduced in what turns out to be a reduced-form specification posing problems for interpreting the results (Greene 1981).

Another 'factor-augmenting' approach for <u>indirectly</u> incorporating social overhead capital into regional growth theories has essentially concentrated on the 'labour-augmenting' role of such capital through increases in labour productivity. One example of this work is provided by Wheeler (1980):

$$Q_{it} = Q_{it} \, [K_{it}, \, L_{it} \, *(L_{it}, \, H_{it}, \, N_{it}, \, E_{it}), \, A_t] \qquad (4)$$

Country i, time period t
$A_t \equiv$ some measure of general state of technology
$Q_{it} \equiv$ output; K_{it}, $L_{it} \equiv$ use levels of capital and labour

H_{it}, E_{it}, N_{it} ≡ measures of general levels of health, education and nutrition, respectively.

By further specifying the supply functions for N_{it}, E_{it}, H_{it} based on per capita production and capacity variables, a simultaneous systems of equations is obtained:

$$N_{it} = N_{it} \, (^{Q_{it}/}P_{it})$$

$$E_{it} = E_{it} \, (^{Q_{it}/}P_{it}, \, G_{E_{it}})$$

$$H_{it} = H_{it} \, (^{Q_{it}/}P_{it}, \, N_{it}, \, E_{it}, \, G_{H_{it}})$$

where

P_{it} ≡ population

$G_{E_{it}}$ and $G_{H_{it}}$ ≡ measure of capacity levels for the provision of public education and health services.

By specifying a functional form for 'augmented labour' in the following manner :

$$L^*_{it} = L_{it} \, H_{it}^{\Theta_1} \, {}_{N_{it}}^{\Theta_2} \, N_{it}^{\Theta_2} \, E_{it}^{\Theta_3} \tag{3}$$

and after eliminating an augmented CES production function in favour of an augmented Cobb-Douglas, the final production function is obtained

$$Q_t = A_t \, K_t^{r_1} \, (L_t \, H_t^{\Theta_1} \, {}_{N_t}^{\Theta_2} \, E_t^{\Theta_3})^{r_2} \tag{6}$$

Thus, unitary elasticities of substitution are assumed for both the augmented labour and production functions.

The essential argument underlying Wheeler's model is that output is determined not only by the predetermined levels of capital and labour, but also by the labour augmenting role of education, nutrition and health. The latter three variables are themselves determined, simultaneously, by the level of per capita output and exogenously determined measures of capacity levels for education and health services.

While Wheeler's model is a definite advance over the earlier unidirectional causality static models, it still remains in the tradition of single factor augmentation models. In addition, social amenities enter the production functions as cariable inputs implying instantaneous adjustments (albeit in percentages) without any internal or external augmented labour functions also implies stringent a priori restrictions in parameters. Also, since Wheeler is mainly interested in the overall production implications, factor demand equations in the presence of augmenting social welfare capital are not worked out.

Next we present our model which takes advantage of recent theoretical developments to overcome the major deficiencies described in the previous work and to incorporate social overhead capital in an explicit structural fashion.

3. A MODEL FOR ASSESSING REGIONAL PUBLIC INVESTMENT

Based on recent advances in the specification of flexible production (cost) functions and in duality theory – specifically restricted profit (cost) functions with dynamic adjustments (Lucas 1976), we specify an econometric model which <u>explicitly</u> incorporates social overhead capital into regional production behaviour without imposing unnecessary <u>a priori</u> restrictions on substitution possibilities or model parameters. The proposed model also improves on the partial 'single factor' augmentation approaches of earlier research (Section II) based on only two factors of production – capital (K) and labour (L), by extending the analysis to include two additional factors – materials (M) and energy (E) – within a more comprehensive framework [3].

In this model, while the four factors – private capital (K), labour (L), energy (E) and materials (M) – enter the production process as variable inputs, S is a vector of <u>quasi</u>-fixed inputs with fixed levels in the short run. The <u>quasi</u>-fixed inputs S are provided by the public sector (governments), while production takes place in the private sector. Thus, changes in the level of S do not have a tradeoff effect on the output. Firms do not face an internal cost of adjustment for investments in social overhead capital. Given assumptions of profit maximising firms and no uncertainties, we assume that the production process combines:

(a) variable inputs $x = \{x_i\}$, $i=1, \ldots, M$ which are perfectly competitive with prices $w = \{\hat{W}_j\}$, $j=1, \ldots, M$ which are known with uncertainty and remain stationary over time,

and

(b) <u>quasi</u>-fixed input $S = \{s_i\}$, $i=1, \ldots, N$ which can be varied at a cost $c_i(\dot{s}_i)$ where $\dot{s}_i = \frac{dS_i}{dt}$ is the change in the ith <u>quasi</u>-fixed input with respect to time and where

$c_i(0) = 0$, $c_i'(\dot{s}_i) > 0$, $c_i''(\dot{s}_i) > i, o = 1, \ldots, N$

(the primes ' and '' represent first and second derivatives). This implies positive, increasing marginal costs of adjustments for the <u>quasi</u>-fixed inputs.

into

(c) a concave production function $F = F[x(t), s(t)]$ to produce the output.

In our model, x = K, L, E, M Variable Inputs
and s = S_1, S_2 Quasi-fixed Inputs
where S_1 = some measure of social physical capital stock.
and S_2 = some measure of social welfare capital stock.
Assuming that there exists a production function

$$Q = f(K, L, E, M, S_1, S_2) \tag{7}$$

then, theory of duality between profit and production (Shepherd 1953) implies that, given short run profit maximisation behaviour, the characteristics of production implied by (7) can be <u>uniquely</u> represented by a <u>normalised profit function</u> of the form

$$N = N(P_K, P_L, P_E, P_M, S_1, S_2) \tag{8}$$

where p_i, $i=K, L, E, M$ are <u>normalised</u> (by output price, P) factor prices.

A number of flexible functional forms can be chosen for N – generalised Leontieff, transcendental logarithmic, Box-Cox – but we have chosen a quadratic approximation to N, such that:

$$N = \alpha_0 + \sum_i \alpha_i p_i + \sum_j \alpha_j s_j + 1/2 \sum_i \sum_k r_{ik} \, p_i \, p_k + 1/2 \sum_i r_{ii} \, p_i^2$$

$$+ \sum_i \sum_j r_{ij} \, p_i \, s_j + 1/2 \sum_j r_{jj} \, s_j^2 + r_{12} \, s_1 \, s_2 \qquad (9)$$

where

i , $k \equiv K, L, E, M$

$j \equiv s_1, s_2$

Utilising the property that $\dfrac{\partial N}{\partial p_i} = -x_i$

i.e., the short run profit maximising quality demanded of the <u>ith</u> variable input, we obtain:

$$- K = \alpha_K + r_{KK} \, P_K + r_{KL} \, P_L + r_{KM} \, P_M + r_{KE} \, P_E + r_{Ks_1} \, s_1 + r_{Ks_2} \, s_2$$

$$- E = \alpha_E + r_{EE} \, P_E + r_{EK} \, P_K + r_{EL} \, P_L + r_{EM} \, P_M + r_E \quad s_1 + r_{Es_2} \, s_2$$

$$\qquad (10)$$

$$- L = \alpha_L + r_{LL} \, P_L + r_{LK} \, P_K + r_{LE} \, P_E + r_{LM} \, P_M + r_{Ls_1} \, s_1 + r_{Ls_2} \, s_2$$

$$- M = \alpha_M + r_{MM} \, P_M + r_{ME} \, P_K + r_{ME} \, P_M + r_{ML} \, P_L + r_{Ms_1} \, s_1 + r_{Ms_2} \, s_2$$

The condition of symmetry of the matrix of second order partial derivatives $\partial x_i / \partial p_j$ leads to the following parameter restrictions:

$$r_{KE} = r_{EK}; \; r_{KL} = r_{LK}; \; r_{KM} = r_{MK}; \; r_{EL} = r_{LE}; \; r_{EM} = r_{ME}; \; r_{LM} = r_{ML} \quad (11)$$

Thus the system of equations (9) and (10) subject to parameter constraints (11) constitutes the means of estimating the <u>short run</u> demands for the variable inputs K, L, E and M.

A more valid assumption regarding the available stock of social overhead capital and its impact on production seems to be that current production is <u>not</u> affected by the changes in the stock of social overhead capital during the current time period, but only by the available stock at the beginning of the current period. Thus, output in current period $Q(t)$ is a function not of $s_1(t)$ and $s_2(t)$ but of $s_1(t-1)$ and $s_2(t-1)$.

Under the postulates of our model, this assumption seems much more valid since producing units are assumed to take into account the <u>available</u> stock of social overhead capital in making their production decisions for the current period. Within this framework, it would seem more reasonable that these decisions are based on the available stock of s_1 and s_2 at the beginning of the current period rather than possible additions and deletions to these stocks over the current period.

In this situation, we need to respecify $Q(t)$ for the profit maximisation model

$$Q(t) = Q[K(t), L(t), M(T), E(T), s_1(t-1), s_2(t-2)] \qquad (12)$$

This modifies the estimating equations in the following way.

Profit maximisation model

Normalised Variable Profit $= Q - P_K K - P_L L - P_M M - P_E E$

$$= \alpha_0 + \alpha_E \, P_E + \alpha_K \, P_K + \alpha_M \, P_M + \alpha_L \, P_L + \alpha_1 \, s_{1_{-1}} + \alpha_2 \, s_{2_{-1}}$$

$$+ 1/2 \left[r_{KK} \ P_K^2 + r_{EE} \ P_E^2 + r_{LL} \ P_L^2 + r_{MM} \ P_M^2 + r_{11} \ s_{-1}^2 + r_{22} \ s_{2_{-1}}^2 \right]$$

$$+ r_{KL} \ P_K \ P_L + r_{KE} \ P_K \ P_E + r_{KM} \ P_K \ P_M + r_{LE} \ P_L \ P_E + r_{LM} \ P_L \ P_M + r_{EM} \ P_E \ P_M \quad (13)$$

$$+ r_{Ks_1} \ P_K \ s_{1_{-1}} + r_{Ls_1} \ P_L \ s_{1_{-1}} + r_{Es_1} \ P_E \ s_{1_{-1}} + r_{Ms_1} \ P_M \ s_{1_{-1}}$$

$$+ r_{Ks_2} \ P_K \ s_{2_{-1}} + r_{Ks_2} \ P_L \ s_{2_{-1}} + r_{Es_2} \ P_E \ s_{2_{-1}} + r_{Ms_2} \ P_M \ s_{2_{-1}}$$

$$- K = \alpha_K + r_{KK} \ P_K + r_{KE} \ P_E + r_{KM} \ P_M + r_{KL} \ P_L + r_{Ks_1} \ s_{1_{-1}} + r_{Ks_2} \ s_{2_{-1}}$$

$$- L = \ldots \ldots \ldots$$
$$- E = \ldots \ldots \ldots$$
$$- M = \ldots \ldots \ldots \ldots \ldots, \text{ with restrictions } (11)$$

Adjustment paths for quasi-fixed inputs

The Lucas (1976) model of dynamic external cost of adjustment postulates that changes in quasi-fixed input levels (accumulation or deaccumulation) during any period do not have any tradeoff effect on the level of current output. Applying the same reasoning to regional production behaviour, it can be assumed that since cost of adjusting levels of social overhead capital does not directly fall on the producing firms, these adjustments do not affect (i.e., subtract from) the current output levels.
    Lucas (1976) has shown that the short run demand for the quasi-fixed factors can be generated as:

$$\dot{s}(t) = B^*[s^*(t) - s(t)] \quad (14)$$

where B^* is a matrix of adjustment parameters which depend on the exogenous variables, production technology, and the cost of adjustment functions.
    Assuming that the stock of each quasi-fixed factor s_i depreciates exponentially at rate δ_i and the z_i is the gross addition to the stock of s_i, we have

$$\dot{s}_i = x_i - \delta_i \ s_i \quad (15)$$

If the cost of adjustment function is specified as:

$$c_i(\dot{s}_i) = \hat{q}_i \ z_i + \hat{q}_i \ D_i \ (s_i) \quad (16)$$

where

$$\hat{q}_i \equiv \text{asset purchase price of quasi-factor } s_i \ .$$

It can be shown that

$$N_{s_i} - u_i - rq_i \ D_i'(\dot{s}_i) + q_i \ D_i'' \ (\dot{s}_i) \ \ddot{s}_i = 0, \ i=1, \ \ldots, \ N \quad (17)$$

where $u_i \equiv (\hat{q}_{i/p})(r + \delta_i)$ is the normalised user cost associated with the service flow from quasi-fixed factor i when marginal costs of adjustments are constant, and $q_i = \hat{q}_{i/p}$.
    The short run demand equation for quasi-fixed factors s_1 and s_2 can then be obtained as:

$$s_1 - s_{1_{-1}} = -1/2[r - \{r^2 - \frac{4r_{s_1 s_1}}{q_{s_1} d_{s_1 s_1}}\}^{1/2}].[-\frac{1}{r_{s_1 s_1}}\{\alpha_{s_1} + r_{ks_1} P_K + r_{Es_1} P_E$$

$$+ r_{Ms_1} P_M + r_{Ls_1} P_L - U_{s_1}\} - s_{1_{-1}}] \qquad (18)$$

and

$$s_2 - s_{2_{-1}} = -1/2[r - \{r^2 - \frac{4r_{s_2 s_2}}{q_{s_2} d_{s_2 s_2}}\}^{1/2}].[-\frac{1}{r_{s_2 s_2}}\{\alpha_{s_2} + r_{Ks_2} P_K + r_{Es_2} P_E$$

$$+ r_{Ms_1} P_M + r_{Ls_1} P_L - U_{s_2}\} - s_{2_{-1}}] \qquad (19)$$

where $D(\dot{s}_i) = 1/2\ d_{s_i s_i}\ \dot{s}_i^2$ is a quadratic approximation to the cost of

adjustment function $D(\dot{s}_i)$ in equation (17).

The assumptions - especially the positive second derivative $c''(\dot{s}_i)>0$ - imply that as the addition to any quasi-fixed input at a particular time increases, it become marginally more costly. In the case of quasi-fixed social overhead capital, this condition can be shown to prevail for a number of reasons. For example, the region may face upward sloping supply functions for social overhead capital due to higher costs of borrowing, congestion costs affecting the provision of physical infra-structure, increasing installation and start-up costs in addition to market price leading to diseconomies of scale, etc. It is necessary that these conditions hold in order to reflect the reality of quasi-fixed nature of social overhead capital for otherwise, the region could adjust to its desired level of these inputs without incurring any addi-tional costs, a situation contrary to reality.

Equations (13,18,19) form a system of 6 equations, the parameters of which completely specify the dynamic demand functions. This system of equations can also be used for eliciting various elasticity - short run price, long run price, cost price and user cost elasticities.

4. ANALYTICAL AND POLICY IMPLICATIONS

We have presented above a theoretically rigorously specified model that can be econometrically estimated to analyse the effects of different kinds of social and physical overhead capital on factor productivities and factor demands within regional production systems. The requisite data base is available at the national level of a few developing coun-tries. In India, preliminary enquiries suggest that data on regional production, factor input and public expenditures are available at the regional level.

Since the adjustment paths of quasi-fixed inputs (public capital) are nonlinear, the use of nonlinear maximum likelihood techniques (MLE) is necessary. This can be done by appending classical, independent and multivariate normally distributed disturbance terms, reflecting errors in profit maximisation to the factor demand equation.

What can be learned from the implementation of this model? First, as a set of structurally specified equations, this model is an improvement over previous production function studies and permits unambiguous policy interpretations. Thus, the econometric analysis envisaged for a number of countries could generate the following types of information.

- the output elasticities of public investment, i.e., the effects of different types of public investment on the outputs of different sectors in a region.
- the effects of public capital on factor demands by sector.
- the complementarities between different types of public investments in a region. This is important since the full effects of a particular type of public investment (e.g., road network) may not be realised until complementary developments (water supply, housing, industries, etc.) have also taken place.
- information on all the above types of impacts at different stages of development. By analyzing these effects across countries and regions that have experienced different levels of development, information of this type can be obtained. The review of Section II identified such variables between developed and developing countries in the impacts of education on development. Our model could help identify such differences, if any, among developing countries differentiated by per capita income.

However, the issues of infrastructure development policy analysis are broader in many respects than the scope of the model. For instance, while it is possible to develop an infrastructure policy for particular regions with the help of this model the development of the same regions can be affected as much or more by improvement in the national infra-structure which may require improvement elsewhere. In the long run the completion of a national network of roads, an electricity grid or certain ports may bring more benefits to peripheral backward regions than preferential measures within the region itself. Diversion of national needs may cometimes work to the disadvantage of the regions which are given preferential treatment.

For example, in the case of India, where some underdeveloped regions (like Orissa and Bihar) exist in close geographical proximity to a developed region (like West Bengal) with strong interconnections through labour migration, raw material and product markets and trade, it is quite conceivable that investments in infrastructures in the developed regions may have more beneficial, long-lasting effects on development of the target backward regions. These considerations acquire increased significance especially in the case of resource-deficient developing countries.

It is possible to take into consideration spillover effects of public investments in one region on others. For that purpose, our model must be embedded as part of a multiregional model in the national economy. Such an expanded model would include besides the production model, a labour market block, income block and interregional transport blocks (Lakshmanan 1981, 1983).

In such a multiregional model interrelated production and transportation models would be the core (Figure 2). A labour market block, income determination block and a block for regional government expenditures round out the model. The regional facilities and amenities block is determined by the level of regional government expenditures and, in turn, affects the comparative advantage of the region for production activities and hence the next cycle of regional production. A variety of specifications exist for such interlinked models (Issaev et al. 1982, Bolton 1982, Lakshmanan 1981, 1983).

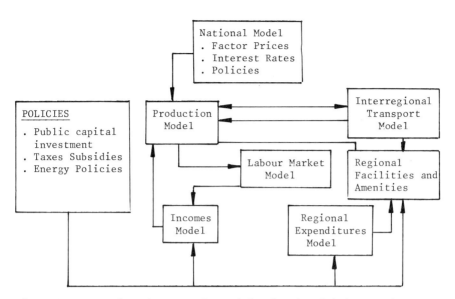

Figure 2. The Major Elements of a Multiregional model for Development.

NOTES

[1] In India, the rate of return for education varies from 7 percent
    (for higher education) to 17 percent (for primary education), while
    they range between 17.2 to 26.1 percent for physical capital. This
    could result from the government policy of overinvesting in education
    regardless of demand and by the type of education that is emphasised
    (Nadiri 1972).
[2] Leven et al. argue that the stock of physical capital in the public
    sector activities mainly establishes the capacity of the service
    (e.g., traffic lane capacity, sewage pipe diameter, etc.), while it
    is the variable inputs which determine the quality of service. For
    example, good education depends on the quality of teaching materials,
    somewhat independently of the quality of the school building, pro-
    vided minimal space requirements for holding a training activity are
    available.
[3] For a more detailed presentation see Elhance (1981).

REFERENCES

Bolton, R., 'The Development of Multiregional Economic Modeling in North America', in Issaev, B., Nijkamp, P,, Rietveld and Snickars, F. (eds), Practice and Prospect of Multiregional Economic Modeling, North-Holland Publ. Co., Amsterdam, 1982, pp. 157-170.

Corea, H., 'Sources of Economic Growth in Latin America', Southern Economic Journal, July 1970, pp. 17-31.

Denison, E., Why Growth Rates Differ: Postwar Experience in Nine Western Countries, Brookings Institution, Washington, DC, 1967.

Elhance, A. Impact of Social Overhead Capital on Production Activities: Regional Dimensions, PhD Dissertation Proposal, Department of Geography, Boston University, Boston, 1981.

Greene, D., 'Comment on Koichi Mera's Paper on "City Size Distribution and Income Distribution in Space'", Regional Development Dialogue, spring 1981, pp. 124-126.

Hayami, Y. and Ruttan, V.W., Agricultural Development: An International Perspective, The Johns Hopkins University Press, Baltimore, 1971.

Issaev, B., Nijkamp, P., Rietveld, P. and Snickars, F. (eds), Practice and Prospect of Multiregional Economic Modeling, North-Holland Publ. Co., Amsterdam, 1982.

Klaassen, L.H., Social Amenities on Area Economic Growth, OECD, Paris, 1968.

Kruger, A., 'Factor Endowments and Per Capita Income Differences Among Countries', Economic Journal, September 1968, pp. 641-659.

Lakshmanan, T.R. and Fu Chen Lo, A Regional Growth Model for Puerto Rico: Analysis of Municipal Growth Patterns and Public Investment, CONSAD Research Corporation, Pittsburgh, 1970.

Lakshmanan, T.R., A Multiregional Model of the Economy, Environment and Energy Demand, Paper prepared for presentation at the 51st Conference of the Southern Economic Association, New Orleans, LA, November 1981, and revised for publication.

Lakshmanan, T.R.,'Information Systems for Regional Development with Special Emphasis on Developing Countries', in Nijkamp, P. and Rietveld, P. (eds), Information Systems for Integrated Regional Planning, North-Holland Publ. Co., forthcoming.

Leven, C., Legler, J.B. and Shapiro, P., An Analytical Framework for Regional Development Policy, MIT Press, Cambridge, 1970.

Lucas, R., 'Adjustment Costs and the Theory of Supply', Journal of Political Economy, August 1976, pp. 331-334.

Maddison, A., Economic Progress and Policy in Developing Countries, Allen and Unwin, London, 1970.

Mera, K., 'Regional Production Functions and Social Overhead Capital: An Analysis of the Japanese Case', Regional Science and Urban Economics, Vol. 3, No. 2, 1973, pp. 157-186.

Nadiri, M. Ishaq, 'Some Approaches to the Theory and Measurement of Total Factor Productivity: A Survey', Journal of Economic Literature, Vol. 8, No. 4, 1970, pp. 1137-1177.

Nadiri, M. Ishaq, 'International Studies of Factor Inputs and Total Factor Productivity: A Brief Survey', Review of Income and Wealth, 18, 1972, pp. 129-148.

Robinson, S., 'The Sources of Growth in Less Developed Countries', Quarterly Journal of Economics, August 1971.

Saxonhouse, G.R., 'The Productivity Change and Labor Absorption in Japanese Cotton Spinning 1891-1935', Quarterly Journal of Economics, 91, 1977, pp. 195-219.

Schultz, T., 'Investment in Human Capital', <u>American Economic Review</u>,
    March 1961.
Selowsky, M., 'Nutrition, Health and Education: The Economic Signifi-
    cance of Complementarities at Early Age', <u>Journal of Development
    Economics</u>, 9, 1981, pp. 331-346.
Shepard, R.W., <u>Cost and Production Functions</u>, Princeton University
    Press, New Jersey, 1953.
Vóigh, F.,'The Task of Modern Transport Science', <u>International Journal
    of Transportation Science</u>, Vol. 1, 1974, pp. 255-262.
Wheeler, D., 'Basic Needs Fulfilment and Economic Growth: A Simultaneous
    Model', <u>Journal of Development Economics</u>, 1980.

PART C: ANALYTICAL METHODS

8 Methods for Urban and Regional Policy Analysis in Developing Countries: An Introduction

P. NIJKAMP

The widespread acceptance by the less developed countries (LDCs) of goals
that seek to mobilise societal resources for promoting sustained development, has fostered, over the last century, a large development literature that is rich in policy prescriptions. These presciptions link goals
and objectives with policy instruments so as to marshall existing resources more efficiently, and to use these resources more effectively.
With greater planning experience, formal procedures are being increasingly substituted for intuitive judgements. The aim of this greater form-
ality and sophistication is to promote consistency and increase implementation potential of development planning. Policy makers are confront-
ed with many uncertainties when they draw up their plans, and formal procedures permit the analyst to trace and quantify the impact of alternative policy instruments on the economy and society.

Two problems relating to this increasing formalisation are of importance. First, there is the set of institutional constraints that are
associated with the design of politically viable organisations that can
successfully define and translate goals and objectives into appropriate
planning procedures. The frictions and prospects regarding such policy
issues have been highlighted in part A of this book. Second, there is a
set of analytical issues that are associated with inadequate data bases
characteristic of 'statistically underdeveloped' countries. Therefore
there is an increasing need to address a) the issue of appropriate institutions and of analytical methods that are consistent with developing
country attributes, and b) obtain more interaction between policy makers
and analysts. Part B of this book addresses these issues in the context
of urban and regional policy analysis with a particular view to methods
and techniques that can assist and guide policy makers and planners in
their search for effective development strategies.

Although mathematical and statistical theory, econometric and socio-
metric methods have done an impressive job of filtering quantitative data
in the advanced economies, they have been of less use in the developing
world. These methods have had limited applicability in developing countries, for they place extremely severe restrictions on the data. Consequently, the results of these methods have been generally mediocre when
applied to planning purposes.

Consequently, it is a very important task to critically judge the kinds
of models that can be meaningfully applied in developing countries. In
regard to this one needs a careful review of spatial interaction models,
programming models, system dynamics models, regional and urban planning
models, and the like. In particular, it is a challenge to envisage situations where the data base required to design and calibrate these
models is insufficient.

However, in recent years there has been a development of several non-

traditional methods that are likely to be more appropriate for information processing in 'poor data' situations. These methods, regardless of
their inherent applicability, have not found their way from scholarly
journals to general use. They are relatively unused in policy development and modelling.

The major purpose of Part B of this book will be to acquaint social
and policy scientists with a selected set of techniques that may be potentially powerful. It seeks to address this lacunae by providing insights into the perspectives and constraints of these new techniques and
their appropriateness for meeting policy planning information needs for
specific urban and regional problems.

In the first contribution to Part B of this book, Marcial Echenique
reviews a wide variety of specific applications of models for urban and
regional policy analysis in developing countries. These models are used
as a vehicle to illustrate major difficulties and advantages of using
advanced mathematical techniques in planning. The author also pays extensive attention to common misconceptions about the use of models in
planning and decision making. Some of these issues are also taken up
more extensively by other authors in subsequent chapters of Part B.
Especially the various case studies employed by Marcial Echenique illustrate the pros and cons of mathematical models in development planning.

The design of relevant policy models and the use of quantitative
methods in policy analysis require adequate information systems. The
production of information for policy making and planning also needs an
analysis of the modularity, flexibility and versatility of the necessary
data and models for specific planning issues. In Peter Nijkamp's article
particular attention is paid to structured data systems, with a special
view to a systematic description of an integrated impact analysis and a
multidimensional evaluation by means of information systems for urban
and regional planning.

In a subsequent article, Peter Nijkamp and Michiel van Pelt discuss
spatial impact analysis in development planning. The drastic urban and
regional changes in the Third World - emerging inter alia from the endogenous dynamics, exogenous impulses and policy measures - requires an
accurate assessment of all anticipated and foreseeable consequences of
public policies and programs. In regard to this, a systematic, coherent
and multidimensional systems approach is proposed that is also applicable
to 'poor data' situations. Various subsystems linked in a logical way
may be dealt with in such a spatial impact analysis.

Next, Geoff Hewings focusses attention on a specific type of impact
analysis, viz. an interregional accounting system for development planning under conditions of limited information. The work he reports on
concerns model building and its application in countries with limited
information on the spatial disaggregation of a social accounting matrix
system for a country. He also states that this approach provides a unifying framework for project selection, project monitoring and project
evaluation.

In the next chapter, Piet Rietveld provides a survey of 'soft data
analysis', a set of methods that aims at dealing with variables measured
in a qualitative (e.g. ordinal or nominal) sense. Special attention is
paid to contingency table analysis, rank correlation methods (such as
ordinal principal components analysis, multidimensional scaling analysis
and ordinal cluster analysis). The author also introduces an operational
way of including qualitative information in explanatory models. He con-
cludes that qualitative data methods have reached a stage of maturity
that warrants a wide variety of applications in case of imprecise data.

The problem of less reliable and/or multidimensional information in a planning context is taken up further by Peter Nijkamp and Henk Voogd. The authors provide a brief survey of various types of multiple criteria analyses that have demonstrated their potential and applicability in recent years. A typological description of the most relevant techniques based on hard versus soft data and on discrete versus continuous choice problems is presented. The authors conclude that such multiple criteria evaluation methods may play multiple roles in development planning.

The next author, Yee Leung also pays attention to the weak data base of urban and regional planning in developing countries. In his view, imprecision of the decision making processes necessitates the development of a methodological basis by which weak information can be analysed and decisions can be formally derived. Fuzzy sets theory in general and fuzzy mathematical programming in particular are proposed as plausible analytical methods for urban and regional programming in such an environment. This article is pedagogical in nature. To familiarise researchers or practitioners with the theory, some basic notions of fuzzy sets theory are first reviewed. The fundamental ideas of fuzzy linear programming and its application to urban and regional programming are then examined. The flexibility of the framework appears to be pertinent for realistic planning. Though the methods are mainly designed to solve planning problems in developing countries, they are also developed to analyse similar situations in developed countries.

Finally, Irma Adelman and Jairus Hihn address the problem of discontinuous changes that cannot be modelled in the usual sense. The analysis of systems that incorporate discontinuous change and multiple equilibria has been hanpered by the inability to use formal estimation techniques for models with the above properties that satisfy the condition that the observed values of the state variables are at or near their respective equilibria values. These models are generated by bifurcating processes or catastrophe theory. Under this condition, many of the manifolds that arise in bifurcation and catastrophe theory can be estimated by using either least squares, the method of moments, or maximum likelihood. As a first step, the authors also suggest a statistical method for identifying the properties of discontinuities inherent in a data set and which of the basic catastrophe manifolds is likely to yield the best representation of the data.

The abovementioned analytical issues indicate that a major problem with traditional development theory is its neglect of uncertainty regarding spatial choice behaviour, structural parameters and external changes. Especially in developing countries, systematic and appropriate information systems are mostly lacking, so that conventional statistical and econometric techniques must fail. In regard to this, recent developments in the field of soft econometrics, qualitative statistics and multiple criteria analysis may be extremely helpful. A closer orientation of analytical methods and techniques toward the actual decision problem at hand, the institutional basis of development policies, and the available information systems would no doubt lead to an enrichment of both development planning and policy analysis.

In this respect, qualitative multiple criteria evaluation methods, fuzzy set methods and also methods based on bifurcation and catastrophe theory may highlight our insights into the complex mechanism of development processes in less developed areas. These categories of analytical methods may also be more appropriate for taking account of structural changes in developing countries, including distributional issues. Altogether, we may once more emphasise that development problems require an adjusted and specific development oriented spatial research methodology.

9 The Use of Planning Models in Developing Countries: Some Case Studies

M. ECHENIQUE

1. INTRODUCTION

The objective of this paper is to review some specific applications of mathematical models in developing countries. In fact the review is limited to a set of applications in which the author had a direct involvement. In no way can this paper be considered either as a comprehensive review of models or as a review of typical applications of models. Instead the cases presented here are used as a vehicle to illustrate, in the author's opinion, the most common difficulties and advantages of using advanced mathematical techniques in planning. The case studies presented here range in geographic scale from metropolitan planning to regional and even international planning. The countries where these studies took place belong to a group which are in an intermediate development process. They cannot be classed poor developing countries, and one of the cases presented, Spain, can hardly be called a developing country. But, the utilisation of advanced mathematical techniques is most useful precisely in this group of countries: fast growing industrialising, with large urbanisation and development problems. At both ends of the development scale, either the very poor countries with very little development or the very rich countries with stable population or even declining population, the issues of urbanisation do not occur with the same urgency.

The countries considered in this paper range from oil-rich countries like Iran and Venezuela, to fast growing industrialised countries like Brazil and Spain.

2. SOME COMMON MISCONCEPTIONS ABOUT THE USE OF MODELS

Before entering into the subject of the paper properly, it is useful to discuss some of the most common criticisms of the use of models in developed or developing countries. It is common to hear statements like: 'I do not believe in models'. This is equivalent to saying: 'I do not believe in thinking'. Models are always used, no matter what, whether explicitly or implicitly stated. It is impossible to plan something without the use of models. Models are a representation of the problem and as such as an absolute prerequisite for the understanding of what is and therefore what can be if a given action is implemented. It is however another matter to say: 'I do not believe in this particular model' giving some reasons and proposing an alternative one. This is quite acceptable.

Another common statement which is heard is: 'I do not believe in quantitative models'. There are good reasons behind such a statement as in

many cases the numerical values utilised by the models are more the
product of the imagination of the model builders than what is going on
in reality. However, this is still better than no explicit hypothesis
at all. At least if a logically consistent model is employed and some
numerical values are hypothesised for initial input variables, it is
possible to derive some output values which can be compared with the observed reality. If that output resembles reality, while it is is not
possible to prove that the model is correct, at least it would have been
established that the model may represent the situation and a rational
discussion can proceed for establishing the merits of a given course of
action.

Of course, experienced planners may have good models in their heads
which could be superior to explicitly stated models. But this situation
is rare in developing countries. The staggering rate of growth of urban
areas and the difficulties encountered are not easily transferable from
one country to another. Each city may have peculiar topography, or a
historical development of their transport network different from others,
or the production and distribution of wealth among the population very
different from another city. While it is possible to establish certain
causal structures in general which can be transferred in time and space,
it is necessary to relate them to the particular place under consideration. Anyway, it is difficult to find planners who have experience in
the implementation of large scale investment such as, for example, a
rapid transit system. It may be that in one city a rapid transit was
successful due to the peculiarities of the geography, density of development or to the lack of competing modes. But there is no guarantee
that a solution which was successful in one place will be successful in
another. In order to proceed rationally an analytical study should be
made which necessarily demands the use of quantitative models.

Another criticism of the use of models in developing countries is the
lack of data available. Sometimes it seems that the critics imply that
data must exist prior to the models. That is putting the cart before
the horse. Data is the product of models. As Hesse (1963) says:
'Observations are not written in the face of events to be transferred
directly into language, but there are already interpretations of events'.
This interpretation depends on the framework of reference or model of
reality which specifies which is the relevant fact, and if it is collected how this is to be used. Naturally if there is no data at all in a
given situation, it will be an immense task to develop a sophisticated
model. The only alternative would be to develop very simple, robust
models, and collect the essential data for them.

Another typical criticism which is heard is that the models are too
simplistic and do not reflect the situation accurately. Of course
models, by definition, are a simplification of reality. If they were
not, they would be reality itself and not a model. The art of model
making is to simplify to the maximum the elements and relationships in
the model, without losing the essential interactions which may render
the predictions useless. The dilemma is that the models must be simple
enough for those who use them, yet comprehensive enough for the purpose
for which they are proposed. 'To refuse to consider simple models, because after all the world is a complicated place, is sheer nihilism
which could bring any development to a standstill' (Stone 1963).

Most of the criticisms levelled against models are more often criticisms of the shortcomings of the theoretical foundations of the models.
This does not call for their abandonment, but for their improvement.
Equally, the failures of certain applications of models have been more
often than not, failures of the planning process, that is to say the

institutions and their specification of the problem.

Finally, another common criticism of the use of sophisticated analytical techniques in developing countries is the unavailability of properly trained personnel. This can be a real problem in particular cases, and proper care should be exercised in setting up training programmes to ensure that the knowledge is transmitted from the consultants to the permanent staff. It is, however, not reasonable to use techniques which though simple, do not give the full range of implications of a given decision.

Planning departments are usually very vulnerable to the formidable combination of the sellers of high technology solutions and ambitious politicians. The foreign firms which sell solutions to transport problems, such as undergrounds, or sewerage disposal units or whatever technological novelty may in vogue, have an impressive backup composed of the latest models and, more powerful still, the necessary financial arrangements which make their system very attractive. These firms usually offer studies at no cost to the city. Sometimes the studies are financed by the country which sells the technology, through their development aid programmes and easy loans are arranged to finance the building of the projects. In their effort to sell the large scale system, the international firms engage commissioned agents locally who usually have important political connections. The planning agencies must therefore be able to analyse their proposals with the latest models if they are not to be dismissed for not having taken an 'important' factor into consideration.

3. THE CASE STUDIES

There are eight case studies presented in this paper. Each one of them has been selected to illustrate some aspects of the use of models. The following list presents the case studies in chronological order of commencement.
1) The SISTRAN Study (1974). This study was concerned with the development of a coordinated programme for the passenger transport within metropolitan area of Sao Paulo in Brazil.
2) The Teheran Development Plan (1976). This study was concerned with the evaluation of the impact of major urban development and transportation projects in the region of Teheran in Iran.
3) The SPT Study (1977). This study was concerned with the development of a transport planning system for the State of Sao Paulo in Brazil.
4) The Bilbao Study (1977). This study was concerned with the development of a land use and transport model for the revision of the Bilbao metropolitan area structure plan in Spain.
5) The TAV Study (1978). This study was concerned with the feasibility of developing a high speed train for the corridor of Rio de Janeiro – Sao Paulo – Campinas in Brazil.
6) The MUT Study (1979). This study was concerned with the development of a land use and transport model for the city of Sao Paulo in Brazil.
7) The Guasare New Town Study (1981). This study was concerned with the location and programme of a new town to support coal mining activities in the region of Zulia in Venezuela.
8) The Gibraltar Study (1982). This study was concerned with the forecasting of usage of a new fixed crossing (tunnel or bridge) linking Europe to Africa through the Straits of Gibraltar.
Each of the cases selected are illustrative to some extent of the

issues concerning the use of models. In fact these issues can be classed
into three dimensions. The first dimension refers to how well the problems are understood by decision makers, and hence how well specified was
the question put forward. Two classes can be distinguished within this
dimensions: well specified and vaguely specified problems. However, it
is not implied here that a vaguely specified problem is something undesirable. It may mean that the causes are not identified and therefore
the possible solution has not been formulated. This latter case imposes
an added burden to the analyst as there are a lot of initial investigations into understanding problems.

Four case studies can be classed as well-specified problems. The
Gibraltar study question was: how many passengers and freight will use
the fixed crossing if it were built in a given time horizon and with
varying assumptions in connection with prices. The Guasare New Town
study question was: is it justifiable to develop a new town to support
the new coal mines? Where should it be located and what size should be
planned for? The TAV study question was: is the development of a high
speed train in the corridor justifiable? Finally, the SPT Study did not
have a single main question, but a range of questions related to the
efficiency of the transport sector and the more balanced distribution of
economic activity in the State of Sao Paulo.

The other four cases can be classed as vaguely specified problems.
In fact the SISTRAN study was clearly specified at the outset but it
became clear that the solutions to be decided upon were not necessarily
the most suitable.

The Teheran Development Plan, the Bilbao Study and the MUT Study were
more to do with the preparation of an instrument, i.e. the model to
tackle a range of issues. This would assist in the understanding of the
problems of each city, propose alternative solutions and evaluate them
for recommendations to the political authorities.

The second dimension relates to the ability of the models to give
reasonable answers to the issues studied. Some of the models utilised
can be classed as having a strong theoretical basis for answering the
question. Others are weaker and some of the issues could only be answered partially or with strong assumptions. Again, it is not implied
here that if there is no good theory the issues cannot be tackled. The
world cannot stop until a good theory is developed. In reality it may
be necessary to use deficient models until a better one is developed.
However, the analyst must make clear to the decision makers the shortcomings of the instrument utilised, and point out the assumptions made.

Four cases presented here had a good theoretical basis to answer, at
least in a reasonable time horizon, the issues posed. The TAV Study,
which used a combination of a direct demand model (Quandt-Baumol 1969)
with a hierarchical multinomial logit model (Daly and Zachary 1976).
This allowed the modelling of modal choices to be represented reasonably
well, as well as taking into consideration the added trip generation
caused by the introduction of a new mode. The Guasare Study, the Bilbao
and Teheran Studies used similar models which simulate the interaction
between land use and transport. The models represented explicitly the
workings of both markets: land and transport. Therefore these prices
were determined endogenously as a result of policy interventions. The
theoretical basis of the models used can be described as random utility
models.

The other four cases had shortcomings in the theoretical basis for the
purpose at hand. In fact the Gibraltar Study used a similar model as
the TAV Study. The difference here was that the inputs to the model of
Gibraltar were subject to considerable uncertainty depending on north-

118

south (i.e. Europe-Africa) trading relations and rates of growth of African economies. The SISTRAN Study could not predict the impact on land values of different transport options. This shortcoming was subsequently overcome by the MUT Study, but this latter model was too detailed and cumbersome to be of real use. The SPT study used a spatial input-output model with fixed technical coefficients but variable trade coefficients depending on transport and other locational prices. The fixed technical coefficient had limitations in terms of measuring the impact of policies in terms of overall economic growth in the state.

The final dimension relates to the institutions themselves. Four case studies are presented in which the commissioning institution had a stable arrangement and clear demarcation of responsibilities. These are the SISTRAN Study, which was done for the Mayor of Sao Paulo and the conclusions adopted by the implementation agencies of the municipality. The Bilbao Study done for the Greater Bilbao Metropolitan Area, which though later absorbed by the new Basque Regional Government, had a continuity of staff and responsibilities which ensured the implementation of results. The TAV Study was done for the Federal Ministry of Transport of Brazil and the recommendations implemented. The Gibraltar Study is in the process of being concluded, and the institution has the clear governmental responsibility to study the problem.

The other four studies were commissioned by weaker institutions. In two cases, the SPT and MUT studies, some of the commissioned institutions disappeared altogether due to changes in the political direction resulting from the reactions to the conclusions and the recommendations of the studies. The Teheran case was similar and also showed the difficulties encountered by advisory-only groups without the financial muscle to implement the conclusions. The case of Guasare New Town is still uncertain. While the commissioning institution has a good track record on the implementation of regional development programmes, it is not clear who will be the authority which will implement the recommendations. There are difficulties in demarcation of responsibilities between the regional corporation, the mining corporation and the potential municipal authorities.

Figure 1 shows that classification of the case studies in these three dimensions.

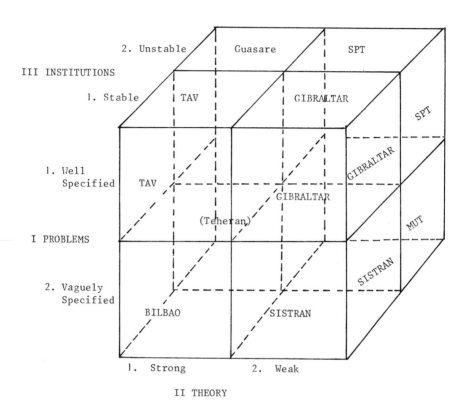

Figure 1.

4. THE SISTRAN STUDY: PASSENGER TRANSPORT STUDY FOR THE CITY OF SAO PAULO, BRAZIL

4.1 The objectives of the study

The SISTRAN study was designed with two basic objectives in mind:
i) to formulate a coordinated programme for passenger transport within the metropolitan area of Sao Paulo
ii) to create the technical and operational capabilities essential to the maintenance of a continuous and comprehensive transport planning system.

The project was commissioned in 1974, at a time when the local authorities in Sao Paulo were considering which of two development strategies to abandon in the fact of increasing financial pressures to cut back on the intended metropolitan transport programme. The first alternative under consideration involved curtailing the construction of an urban motorway complex, whilst continuing with plans to complete a proposed underground network.

The second involved sustaining the motorway building programme but bringing work on the underground to a halt. A fundamental concern of SISTRAN was to investigate these two alternatives.

The client was SMT (Sao Paulo Municipal Transport Authority) and EMPLASA (Sao Paulo Metropolitan Planning Agency).

4.2 Details of the study

The approach adopted in SISTRAN was centred upon the development of a three-part planning system. This comprised: an information system which handled the available data describing activities, networks and traffic flows; a simulation system which modelled the operation of the transport and land markets and an evaluation system which enabled the costs and benefits of alternative policies to be assessed within the model (see figure 2).

The basic data source employed was the 1968 Sao Paulo Origin – Destination-Survey which provided information on car- and non-car-owning households and on non-residential activities. For the purposes of the study the metropolitan area was divided into 78 zones and for each the number of car/non-car trip origins plus the number of non-residential destinations was measured. Traffic flows stratified by time of day and mode of travel were available from the survey. Supplementary building stock data were obtained from the 1968 and 1975 cadastres, and network data were collected from transport operators.

4.3 The model

In view of the paucity of existing data a fairly simple model framework was developed. Within the model trips were allocated between zones for car and non-car owning households, according to mode and route of travel. Several modes including car, bus, train, metro, trolley bus and combination-mode travel were used. The allocations were made on the basis of transport costs (money and time) and the location of activities and land uses as measured by the number of origins and destinations in a zone. Initial estimates of costs and times were modified to take account of congestion and the model was then iterated until equilibrium was reached between supply and demand. Having obtained the equilibrium price, changes in land use and activities were calculated by re-allocating trip origins and destinations in the next time period, taking account of the regional

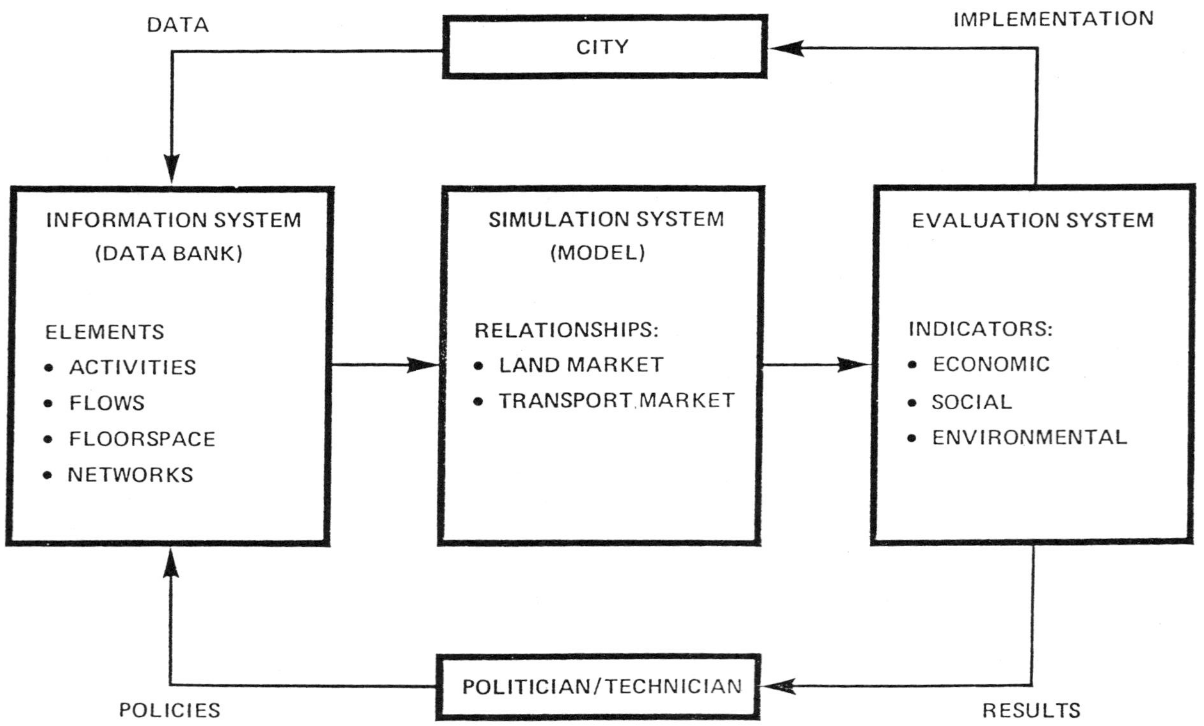

Figure 2: PLANNING SYSTEM

growth in trips expected on the basis of increases in population and income. The allocation of activities (and trips) to each zone was carried
out as a function of the predicted price of transport plus the availability of land and infrastructure (see figure 3).

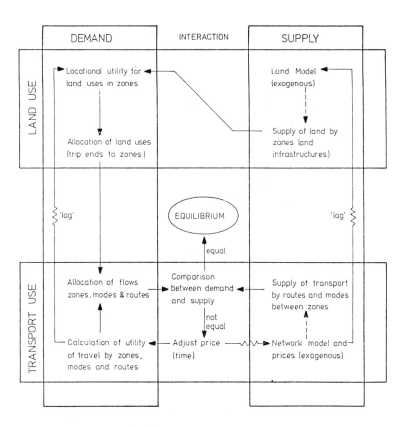

Figure 3. Simulation System - Model of the Transport Market

4.4 The Policies

From the outset it was clear that the complementary nature of the underground and motorway systems necessitated some form of continued investment in both. Drastic revisions to the proposed programmes were required. Two less costly alternatives to the proposed motorway systems
were devised:
(i) A reduced network based upon current motorway projects and comprising
    internal and external area programmes costed respectively at 16,384
    million cruzeiros and 11,684 million cruzeiros by 1985.
(ii)A substitute network, based upon arterial highways with controlled
    intersections, involving a reduction in capacity from 2000 to 1200
    vehicles per land per hour and costed at 6,284 million cruzeiros by
    1985.
  With regard to the underground, early tests with the model indicated a
poor performance of the first (north-south) line. Simulations performed
showed that at best the proposed project would absorb only a fraction of
public transport journeys. The possibility of a complementary public
transport network was therefore investigated, aimed at increasing utilisation of the metro by suppression of competing bus lines and introduction of a feeder service which would deliver travellers to metro stations. Three basic alternatives were investigated with regard to the
underground:
(i) A low cost investment policy involving the development of a basic
    public transport network, based initially upon conventional buses
    operating in bus-only corridors to provide the necessary public ser-
    vices. Tests of alternative public systems including express and
    conventional bus, light rail, trolley bus and train, indicated that
    the trolley bus option should eventually be pursued to replace the
    conventional buses and operate on a fully integrated basis with metro
    and suburban rail. The low investment option was costed at 6,786
    million cruzeiros by 1985, in addition to the cost of committed in-
    vestment in the suburban railways and north-south/east-west under-
    ground lines.
(ii)A medium level investment alternative including a third south-east/
    south-west underground line together with the basic network in a re-
    duced form. This was costed at 13,014 million cruzeiros by 1985.
(iii) A high level investment option involving the construction of third
    and fourth underground lines, in addition to the basic network. This
    was costed at 20,836 million cruzeiros by 1985.
This model was used to test over 30 combinations of projects through time
and basic policy packages were finally compared to a base case representing committed investment only up to 1985.
1. High investment in public transport: basic network plus metro lines
    3 and 4.
2. Medium investment in public transport: basic network plus metro line
    3.
3. Low investment in public transport: basic network only.
4. High inner area road investment: internal urban motorway programme.
5. Low road investment in external and internal areas: arterial high-
    ways.
6. High outer area road investment: external urban motorway programme.

4.5 The findings

The results of the policy tests are presented in the evaluation table
(see table 1).

Table 1

Example of Evaluation of Packages against the Basic Run (i.e. committed investment only) – 1985

		Public Transport Investment			Road Investment		
		A. High: Basic Network & 2 Metro Lines	B. Medium: Basic Network & 1 Metro Line	C. Low: Basic Network only (Trolley)	D. High: Internal Motorway	E. Low: Arterials	F. High: External Motorways
I Economic Efficiency (millions of Cruz)	Cost (discounted)	20,836	13,014	6,786	16,384	6,284	11,684
	Annual Benefits:						
	Consumer (Traveller)	1,828	1,370	673	1,553	940	601
	Operators & Government	- 184	77	259	333	355	112
	Total	1,664	1,447	932	1,886	1,295	713
	Rate of Return %	7.89	11.12	13.75	11.51	20.60	6.10
II Social Distribution (%)	Low Income % of Total Benefits	52	57	44	44	48	50
	High Income % of Total Benefits	48	43	56	56	52	50
	Peripheral Area % of Total Benefits	34	43	31	42	63	60
	Core Area % of Total Benefits	66	57	69	58	37	40
III Other Criteria (Environmental)	Pollution % Change	- 19.47	- 15.95	- 10.73	3.89	7.80	- 1.90
	Petrol Cons.Change %	- 14.57	- 12.31	- 8.59	8.76	7.82	2.10
(% Change over base)	Accessibility for:						
	Car Users	- 1.9	- 1.7	- 1.8	13.8	10.4	5.4
	Public Users	13.1	11.1	3.4	4.3	2.8	1.9
	Development in						
	Preferred Areas (East)	- 4.15	- 3.39	- 3.19	3.75	0.68	5.50
	Unsuitable Areas (South)	- 5.74	- 5.45	- 6.63	3.33	2.10	5.33
	Use of Public Transport	29.6	24.9	17.5	- 8	- 7.6	0

Source: SISTRAN: Alternativas Estudadas (Vol. II, 1975 – Secretaria do Estado dos Negocios Metropolitanos – EMPLASA & Prefeitura do Sao Paulo)

Following consultations with local planning staff and politicians a final package was formulated based upon medium investment in public transport and low investment in roads. In addition, a central area car restraint policy, in the form of a parking tax, was tested for 1980. This was found to provide additional benefits of 48 million cruzeiros (mainly due to increases in government and transport operators revenues) and also to benefit low income groups and peripheral areas. Tests of this policy also indicated reductions in pollution and petrol consumption together with increases in public transport accessibility and use. In addition car restraint was found to encourage decentralisation and to produce a striking effect with regard to reducing congestion.

4.6 Recommendations

In the light of the evaluation results a number of recommendations were made to the planning authorities.
   In the short term:
(i) the basic public transport network should be established, based upon bus-only lanes and streets, to be replaced eventually by trolley buses which could be manufactured locally and would provide an efficient non-polluting alternative
(ii)a metropolitan urban transport authority should be formed to operate the public transport network and to exercise control over licensing private bus operators and fares
(iii)a road investment programme centred upon arterial highways should be implemented
(iv)the east-west suburban rail link should be improved
(v) a central area car restraint policy should be implemented.
   In the medium term:
(i) the basic public transport network should be expanded through the construction of the third metro line and expansion of the trolley bus system
(ii)a number of road investment programmes should be introduced including external motorways and a number of arterial highways

4.7 Conclusions

SISTRAN was completed within 12 months. The system was installed on the clients' computer in Sao Paulo and the necessary staff training required for its maintenance provided. As recommended a new metropolitan transport authority (EMTU) was established, the development of the basic network is well underway and increases in parking charges, though below the suggested level, have been implemented. The only major departure from the recommendations is that a high level of investment has been made in the suburban state railway.
   In 1978 time provided the real test of SISTRAN. The completion of a new O-D survey provided the means of comparing the model predictions with observations made on the ground in Sao Paulo. Despite some shortcomings anticipated on the basis of such a simple model the accompanying table demonstrates a remarkable degree of correspondence between predicted and real-world observations (see table 2).
   The success of SISTRAN and subsequent compilation of a more detailed data base led to the new Sao Paulo Metropolitan Transport Authority (EMTU) together with the municipal (COGEP) and metropolitan (EMPLASA) planning authorities to commission a further study (MUT) with the intent of refining and extending the model and testing the effects of a whole new range of policies.

Table 2

Comparison between predictions of SISTRAN model and Survey

	Survey	SISTRAN	% difference
Socio-Economic			
Total population	10,382,000	10,650,000	+ 2.6%
Number of households	2,433,000	2,500,000	+ 2.3%
Average monthly income	$ 7,747 cr	$ 7,634 cr	- 1.5%
Car owning households	1,091,000	1,240,000	+13.6%
Non-car owning households	1,352,000	1,260,000	- 7 %
Transport			
Total car & taxi trips	6,029,000	6,098,000	+ 1.1%
Bus trips	8,542,000	8,710,000	+ 2.0%
Metro trips	548,000	529,000	- 3.5%
Train trips	493,000	462,000	- 6.3%
Total Public	9,583,000	9,701,000	+ 1.2%
Other	180,000	-	-
Total all modes	15,792,000	15,799,000	0.04%

This case study illustrates a number of interesting issues. First, the client thought that the problem was identified and the study should produce a precise answer to it. In reality, the basic alternative solutions (i.e. motorways versus underground) were discovered to be faulty, and a major rethinking of the alternatives took place. This produced a more subtle utilisation of all modes of transport in coordination and a program of improvements on a small scale but of great effectiveness.

The institutions involved with the study had clear leadership from the mayor of the city who was himself personally involved in the details of the study. This produced, after a few months, a consensus of opinion on the options which should be discarded and the alternatives which, although not very glamorous, were effective in tackling the city's transport problems. Once the results were analysed and absorbed by the different agencies, an immediate implementation programme was devised which was successfully carried through.

The model was, of course, too simple and this was its strength. Everybody understood the basic ideas and results. But it also had its weaknesses, especially with respect to the land use component. The city's finance was based on the rates charged to buildings, which in turn relates to their market value. As the model was rather aggregate, it was not possible to estimate the impact of different transport policies in the market value of the properties. The subsequent mayor of the city was particularly keen on taxing the increases of property values through a betterment levy tax. The model could not answer these issues and a new model was developed, five years later, which is described below: the MUT study.

5. THE TEHRAN DEVELOPMENT PLAN

5.1 The objectives of the study

The Tehran study was designed to meet three basic objectives:
(i) To evaluate the impact and interactions of major urban development and transportation projects in the Tehran region of Iran
(ii)To assess the effectiveness, equity effects and desirability of alternative urban policy options'

127

(iii)To train local professionals in the use of advanced analytical planning techniques.
The client was the Tehran Development Council Secretariat (TDCS).

5.2 Details of the study

The objectives of the study were met through the development of a comprehensive model designed to estimate and evaluate the effects of different policies on regional growth, land use and travel demand. This
model was applied to the study area subdivided into 30 zones with 24
city zones. The area included a population of 4,179,000 responsible for
7,117,000 daily trips.
A major development in this project was the treatment of regional
growth, land use and travel demand within one carefully integrated model
framework. In particular, the formulation of a submodel capable of simulating the operation of the land use market is especially worthy of
note. This submodel provided a means of representing the competition for
land from all sectors of the Tehran economy, drawing upon output from the
transport submodel to calculate the locational costs so central to this
problem.

5.3 The model

The model used for the purpose of predicting the outcome of alternative
policy options was developed in the form of three interconnected submodels (see figure 4).
(i) A Regional Growth Model - This was designed to estimate the future
    growth of activities throughout the region, taking into account
    demographic characteristics, investment policies and the distribu-
    tion of income. The activities were categorised into 12 types:
    employment in agriculture, industry, government and services and 8
    residential activities grouped by household income.
(ii)A Land Use Model - The purpose of this model was to allocate activi-
    ties to the land available in zones, taking account of the accessi-
    bility, the rent, the building costs and the attractiveness of each
    zone to each activity type. The rent pattern was adjusted until the
    competition between different activities for location was in balance
    throughout the city (i.e. the demand for land was equilibrium with
    the supply of land in each zone).
(iii)A Transport Model - The transport model established travel patterns
    by mode (car, bus, walk, metro, shared taxi) taking account of the
    spatial distribution of activities predicted by the land use model.
    The trips were loaded into the appropriate network and compared with
    the available capacity. The travel costs and times were adjusted to
    take account of congestion and the process was iterated until trans-
    port equilibrium loadings were achieved. The resulting transport
    costs were fed back into the land use allocation procedure.
The model was installed in the client's computer in Tehran. The cali-
bration of the model's parameters was carried out. The precision of the
model was tested by using the model as calibrated on 1971 data to predict the 1976 situation. A comparison of these results with the actual
1976 data demonstrates a high level of accuracy.

5.4 The policies

Thirteen policy packages comprising different combinations of the land
use and transport policy elements shown below, were evaluated for a hori-

zon period until 1991.

Parking	no change/low increase/high increase
Fares	not integrated/integrated, flat rate fares/integrated, graduated
Metro	no metro/small metro/large metro
Roads	small network improvement/large network improvement
Employment	no tax/tax on employment location
Housing	no subsidies/subsidies
Land	restrictive/extensive controls/market
New Towns	market/planned development

The evaluation system was designed to compare through time the relative benefits of pairs of plans incorporating various future transport
and land use strategies. The resulting measures of net benefits were
output separately for land use and for transport effects. The distribution of benefits between different income groups and between various
other groups in society was displayed. The evaluation was developed for
use in conjunction with expert local opinion. In this respect the procedures adopted proved particularly useful in highlighting inconsistencies in proposed policy combinations, pinpointing unrealistic policy
options and showing the effects of time upon the simultaneous operation
of economically complex policy combinations (see figure 5).

5.5 The findings

Evaluation of the thirteen packages suggested:
(i) Trip restraint could be achieved by imposing a parking tax, though
    too high a tax would produce an undesirable degree of decentralisation
    to areas with inferior public transport accessibility.
(ii)Increases in fare levels could provide the much-needed improvement
    in bus supply but in the absence of a corrective social policy, total
    benefits would accrue at the expense of lower and middle income
    groups. As Tehran grows so too will the case for graduated fares.
(iii)A large metro would rapidly bring benefits to wealthier travellers
    and would benefit all income groups in the long term. In contrast,
    the rate of return on a large road network though substantial in the
    short term, would decline in the long term to an insignificant level.
(iv)Land release policies, particularly the more far-reaching, would
    create benefits for all land users.
(v) Employment tax would be undesirable since revenue would be consider-
    ably outweighed by losses to land users.
(vi)Housing subsidies could achieve only limited re-distribution and
    would operate with a large deficit.

5.6 Conclusions

Despite a tight time schedule and restriction imposed by data limitations, the project was successfully completed. The model and evaluation
programs were installed and made operational at the computer centre of
the Plan and Budget Organisation, the proposed policies were analysed
and the training of the local staff was completed satisfactorily. In
the final report it was suggested that in the light of results from
primary tests certain policy alternatives should be redesigned and
better combinations of certain time varying options selected. In terms
of the project's objective of assessing the desirability of alternative
urban policy options, it was concluded that any plan should incorporate
(i) A policy of land release

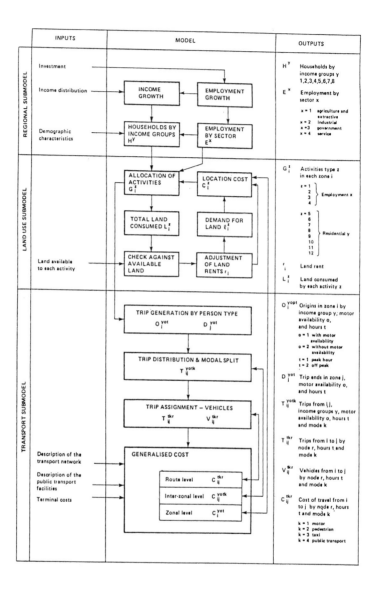

	INPUTS	MODEL	OUTPUTS

REGIONAL SUBMODEL

Investment

Income distribution

Demographic characteristics

INCOME GROWTH

EMPLOYMENT GROWTH

HOUSEHOLDS BY INCOME GROUPS H^y

EMPLOYMENT BY SECTOR E^x

H^y Households by income groups y 1,2,3,4,5,6,7,8

E^x Employment by sector x

  x = 1 agriculture and extractive
  x = 2 Industrial
  x = 3 government
  x = 4 service

LAND USE SUBMODEL

ALLOCATION OF ACTIVITIES G_i^z

LOCATION COST C_i^z

TOTAL LAND CONSUMED L_i^z

DEMAND FOR LAND ℓ_i^z

CHECK AGAINST AVAILABLE LAND

ADJUSTMENT OF LAND RENTS r_i

Land available to each activity

G_i^z Activities type z in each zone i

  z = 1
  2
  3 } Employment x
  4

  z = 5
  6
  7
  8 } Residential y
  9
  10
  11
  12

r_i Land rent

L_i^z Land consumed by each activity z

TRANSPORT SUBMODEL

TRIP GENERATION BY PERSON TYPE O_i^{yot} D_j^{yot}

TRIP DISTRIBUTION & MODAL SPLIT T_{ij}^{yotk}

TRIP ASSIGNMENT – VEHICLES T_{ij}^{tkr} V_{ij}^{tkr}

GENERALISED COST

  Route level C_{ij}^{tkr}
  Inter-zonal level C_{ij}^{yotk}
  Zonal level C_i^{yot}

Description of the transport network

Description of the public transport facilities

Terminal costs

O_i^{yopt} Origins in zone i by income group y; motor availability o, and hours t

  o = 1 with motor availability
  o = 2 without motor availability
  t = 1 peak hour
  t = 2 off peak

D_j^{yot} Trip ends in zone j, motor availability o, and hours t

T_{ij}^{yotk} Trips from i,j, income groups y, motor availability o, hours t and mode k

T_{ij}^{tkr} Trips from i to j by node r, hours t and mode k

V_{ij}^{tkr} Vehicles from i to j by node r, hours t and mode k

C_{ij}^{tkr} Cost of travel from i to j by node r, hours t and mode k

  k = 1 motor
  k = 2 pedestrian
  k = 3 taxi
  k = 4 public transport

Figure 4. Detailed structure of the model

(ii) Control over central area car usage
(iii) A policy geared towards improved bus profitability.

The Municipality accepted the recommendations put forward concerning land release and transport priorities and initiated procedures to achieve the desired results.

The subsequent political events in Iran have, presumably, impeded progress along the lines suggested by the study. But before this situation took place a number of difficulties arose on demarcation of the line of responsibilities between different agencies. The Tehran Development Council could only coordinate policies at the metropolitan level, but their role was only advisory. The municipal authorities did have the power of investing in development projects. In particular, the Mayor of Tehran went his own way contracting works independently from the guidelines established by the TDCS, which created many problems.

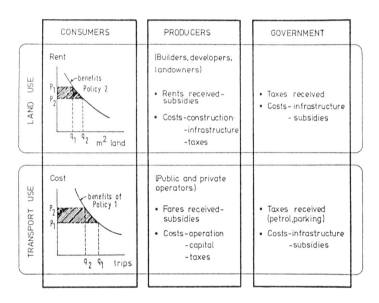

Figure 5. Economic Evaluation System

Similarly, the national ministries, in their haste to spend money on grandiose projects, committed the city to badly thought out projects.

The case study showed that the model was able to cope quite well with the vaguely specified policies. The actual development of the data base and of the model was useful for the staff in TDCS to learn about the causal relationships between different factors affecting the city's development.

It was also useful to be able to test and understand the full range of implications of some of the policies and projects proposed by different agencies. Some of them, and in particular the proposals for the road network (parts of which were under construction), were so incoherent that, with the information provided by the model, it was possible to stop their further implementation and redesign portions.

The case study also showed that with weak institutions, such as TDCS, whose role was only advisory, the utilisation of the model gave some of the necessary support for their arguments, which needed to be much more persuasive than institutions which controlled investment money.

6. THE SPT STUDY: TRANSPORT PLANNING SYSTEM FOR THE STATE OF SAO PAULO, BRAZIL

6.1 The objectives of the study

The Sao Paulo Transport study (SPT) was concerned with state transport policy and regional development problems. It was commissioned with three major objectives in mind:
(i) To improve the economic efficiency of the Sao Paulo state transport sector, placing particular emphasis upon the railways as part of an attempt to reduce state dependency on imported oil.
(ii) To improve the distribution of benefits arising from transport policy in favour of the poorest regions of the state.
(iii) To reduce the rate of growth in the metropolitan region of Sao Paulo.
SPT was instigated at a time when each of the state transport authorities was seeking additional financial resources, either to expand or simply to maintain operations at the existing level. The project was geared to testing and evaluating a wide range of alternative policies reflecting a host of controversial issues which surrounded proposals for transport investment and regional development in Sao Paulo at the time.

The client was the State Secretariat for Transport, the state railway (FESPASA), state highways (DERSA) and the state office for transport planning (TRANSESP). The World Bank contributed to the financing of the project.

6.2 Details of the study

A three-part information-simulation-evaluation system was developed to meet the needs of the SPT study. The focal point of this system was a regional commodity flow model, designed to treat transport demand within an economic development context by relating flows of passengers and goods to patterns of production and consumption throughout the state. Data for the study were stored and analysed using the information system and policy testing was carried out within the evaluation system. Census data provided the primary source of information describing economic activity and for the purpose of the study these were aggregated into groups having common transport requirements. Information on land use, including actual and potential production, were added to these and data describing the existing transport networks were collected from the respective operators, together with information on interzonal freight and passenger movement classified by mode, route, season and time of day.

A novel feature of the SPT study was the development of a commodity flow model to capture the fundamental relationships between the transport and economic system of Sao Paulo. The model was built within the input-output framework originally proposed by Leontief, but different from conventional input-output models in its use of physical (goods and passengers) as opposed to monetary flows. Use of this type of model ensured consistency between zonal production and consumption and interzonal commodity flows. Given the regional development aspects of SPT the model presented a particularly attractive proposition since estimation of production and consumption automatically took account of zonal developments in terms of sectoral specialisation, employment and population.

6.3 The model

The model used for simulating the effects of alternative policy options actually comprised two interconnected submodels (see figure 6).
(i)   Annual Transport Demand Submodel (ATDS) - Taking estimates of population and income levels by zone ATDS was used to estimate final demand in tonnes for each zone and each commodity. Using the 1975 industrial and household consumption surveys input-output tables were constructed in order to establish the relationship between commodity groups. The procedure handled the household consumption of different commodities and trip generation for different purposes. The sub-model was built within an iterative structure so that during the process of final demand projection sets of intermediate demands were generated for each zone.
     Interzonal flows of goods and passengers were then simulated using a singly-constrained gravity type model. This distributed tonnages and trips as a function of both transport costs and times and the 'attractiveness' of the zones in terms of its potential for the production of any given product.
(ii) Transport Assignment Submodel (TAS) - This converted annual commodity flows into weekly figures using an adjustment factor to reflect time-varying flows of goods with a seasonal production cycle. These weekly flows were then assigned to particular modes and routes as a function of transport costs, times and route capacity. Following the initial loadings onto the various networks, travel and costs and times were adjusted to reflect congestion. The process was then iterated until equilibrium was reached in terms of supply and demand. The final set of costs and times was aggregated for different commodity groups and fed back into ATDS in order to estimate flows in the succeeding time period.

6.4 The policies

The model was used to simulate the effects of alternative policies and the advantages/disadvantages of these were compared using the evaluation system. The predicted outcomes of each policy were evaluated using a number of social, environmental and economic indicators, paying particular attention to any differential impact in the four main regions of Sao Paulo (see figure 7). Each policy was compared to a base case reflecting current trends and committed development only for the years 1980, 1985 and 1990. Three main sets of policies were examined:

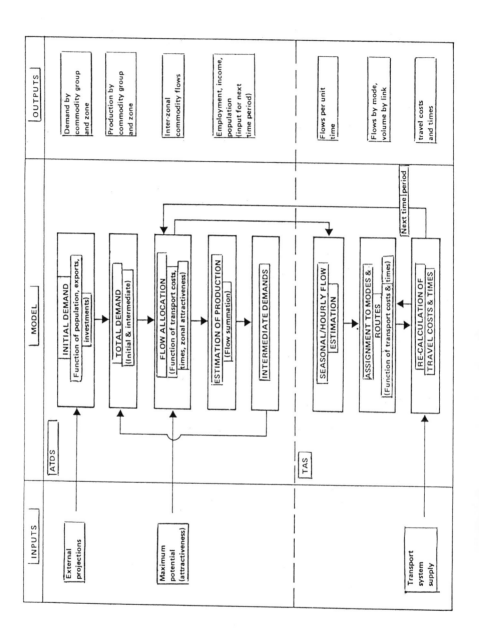

Figure 6.   Structure of SPT model

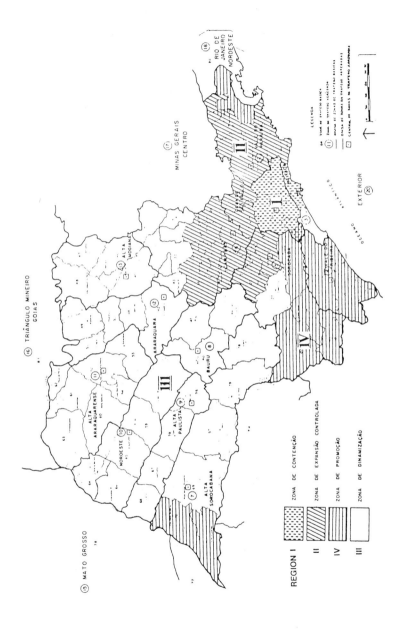

Figure 7. Regions of Sao Paulo State

(i) Regulatory   - forced rail transport for certain commodities
                    - industrial decentralisation through controlled metro-
                      politan area development
(ii)Pricing   - implementation of rail tariffs equal to long-run
                      marginal costs
                    - increased road tolls
(iii) Investment   - medium level highway investment
                    - low level highway investment
                    - development of the River Tiete waterway.

The results of the policy tests are presented in the evaluation table
(see Table 3).

6.5 The findings

The results of the evaluation indicated:
(i) Forced modal split could increase the railways share of goods traffic
    with little additional investment in infrastructure
(ii)Controlled metropolitan area industrial development could reduce
    Region 1 growth beyond 1975 more than 3 percent to below 1 percent
    per annum. As a consequence industrial production in Regional II
    and III would double and triple respectively and the dispersion of
    establishments would bring about an increase in road traffic, neces-
    sitating extra investment to maintain the level of service.
(iii)Rail tariffs would need to be increased on most products by a factor
    ranging between 1.0 and 1.78. The simulation suggested a resulting
    loss in traffic of about 5.0 percent but a very substantial increase
    in revenue.
(iv)The provision of 50 road toll posts in addition to the 4 existing
    ones could reduce highway freight traffic, reduce congestion and
    produce a 5.5 percent increase in public transport utilisation by
    1980.
(v) A medium level of highway investment, based upon improvement of
    capacity in links with a volume/capacity ratio in excess of 0.5
    could increase the level of service over the network as a whole.
    A lower level of highway investment, allowing certain links to op-
    erate at more than 75 percent of capacity, had a similar though less
    pronounced effect but tended to benefit only the inner areas.
(vi)Development of the Tiete waterway to connect the River Parana with
    the rail terminal close to Sao Paulo city would provide the capacity
    for up to 20 million tonnes of freight per annum. The simulation
    results indicated that the waterway could capture 13 percent of the
    total grain traffic going to the port of Santos from other Brazilian
    states each year.

6.6 Conclusions

Following close consultations with the political authorities a final
policy package was put together. This comprised regulatory policies to
enforce the rail transportation of specific commodities in certain areas
and to encourage industrial decentralisation. It was recommended that
rail tariffs equal to long-run marginal costs should be adopted and that
the road toll system should be extended to a limited extent. Development of the Tiete waterway was strongly recommended and it was suggested
that the medium level highway investment policy should be pursued. Evaluation of the final policy package indicated a total annual benefit of
1,979 million cruzeiros by 1985, increasing to 5,345 million cruzeiros
by 1990. The package was costed at 8,985 million by 1985 and 16,456

Table 3

Example of Evaluation of Policies Against Bank Run (committed investments only).

		A:Forced Model Split (1985)	B:Industrial Permits	C:Rail Tariffs (1980)	D:Toll Charges	E:Highway Level D	F:Highway Level E	G:Waterway
I Economic efficiency (Millions of cruz)	Cost (Discounted)	24	375	1	125	3,225	1,806	2,668
	Benefits:Freight	-81	10	-433	-1,952	-8	-98	-40
	Passengers	260	-727	68	-1,694	368	284	20
	Road	379	338	28	583	403	368	-94
	Rail	204	-439	469	-199	301	240	280
	Waterways	24	0	-1	0	0	0	26
	Ports	62	0	-19	4	1	0	0
	Government	-152	343	5	3,244	-225	-165	19
	TOTAL	696	-475	-19	-14	840	629	211
	Rate of Return %	*	*	*	*	26.0	34.8	7.9
II Social distribution (%)	Region I:Sao Paulo	58	-27	-24	-37	34	47	-97
	II: Control	-1	-49	-31	-24	32	36	-17
	III: Dimani-sation	44	22	-29	-34	22	12	8
	IV:Promotion	2	-2	-16	-5	92	5	6
	Passenger car owners	96	-97	-100	-100	8	93	130
	Non-owners	4	-3	0	0		7	-30
III Other criteria	Energy: Petrol	-.6	4.9	-.3	-3.7	1.3	.9	0
	Diesel	-3.2	1.4	-.8	-.5	-1.0	-.8	0.2
	Electricity	22.3	1.7	-3.9	9.4	-4.2	-2.7	-12.2
	Containment of Sao Paulo	no	yes	no	no	no	no	no
	Development of Interior	yes	yes	no	no	no	no	no

* Not significant as the policy does not involve capital cost or have negative benefits.

Source: SPT.

137

million by 1990, giving annual rates of return of 22 percent and 32.5 percent respectively.

The final recommendations, together with a financial analysis of their costs and the necessary management and organisational requirement for policy implementation, were presented as the basis on which to formulate the first transport plan for the state of Sao Paulo.

Unfortunately, the commissioning institution, TRANSESP, being a new organ developed by the State Secretariat for the coordination of the state transport policy, was continuously under attack from the larger and longer established institutions such as railways, ports, airlines, etc. The fact that the model provided a more objective estimation of the likely outcomes of policies and investment programmes created difficulties. The transport operators saw this more as a threat than as a help. The FEPASA (state railways) complained bitterly about the curtailment of some of their investment programmes as they were found to be necessary. This also occurred with the port authority.

The political muscle of such large enterprises was sufficiently strong to convince the incoming governor of the state to dissolve the planning office TRANSESP and transfer the model to a technical research institute, IPT, for its upkeep. The model was therefore 'safely' put aside as a consultative tool, but not as a central policy making tool.

This case study shows that well specified problems, which give 'wrong' political answers are likely to be dismissed. Well-established institutions with clear political leadership are required for the implementation of policies which are necessary but unpopular. The weight of powerful institutions are stronger when their interests are affected than any rational evaluation of the needs of the society at large. This case study did have some shortcomings on the theoretical basis of the model as the long term productions using the model relied on fixed technological coefficients, that is to say that factor prices would not affect the input quantities required for any given output. The model was only responsive to variations in locational costs.

7. THE BILBAO STUDY: THE DEVELOPMENT OF AN INTEGRATED LAND USE AND TRANSPORT MODEL FOR THE METROPOLITAN AREA OF BILBAO, SPAIN

7.1 The objectives of the study

In 1977 the planning authorities of Greater Bilbao commissioned the development of a simulation model which could be used in the revision of the Metropolitan Area Structure Plan. The objectives of the modelling project were threefold:
(i) To provide a means of forecasting the future demand for land and floorspace needed for housing, industry and services in Bilbao.
(ii)To enable the requirements for the road network to be estimated.
(iii)To assess the impact of major public transport projects – such as the relocation of the airport and the intended expansion of the harbour and port facilities of the city.
The client was the Administrative Corporation of Greater Bilbao.

7.2 Details of the study

The aims of the study were realised through the development of a land use and transport model designed to focus on the major policy issues of relevance to the Bilbao situation. In addition to transportation problems these included land zoning for different activities, plot ratios,

138

public services provision and location, and taxation and subsidies in the housing sector. The model was applied to an area subdivided into 27 internal plus 6 external zones and was calibrated using data from O-D and industrial surveys conducted in the city during 1972 and 1975.

An important feature of this model was the introduction of an explicit treatment of the stock of buildings or floorspace. An incremental model estimated the volume of new construction and of demolition of floorspace. This was done on the basis of the supply of land and the difference between the rents for floorspace predicted by the model and the total costs of building new floorspace in each zone.

Also a unified account of locational expenditure allowed an explicit tradeoff between the costs of transport and the costs of housing for a household.

7.3 The model

The model developed for use in Bilbao comprised four main modules: regional growth, land use, transport and economic evaluation (see figure 8).
(i) Regional Growth Model - the function of this module was to estimate future growth of employment in light and heavy industry across the region. This was then used as the basis for generating residential (household) activities and services.
(ii)Land Use model - the purpose of this model was to allocate the various activities to the model zones, taking into account the attractiveness of the zone, the locational utility for each activity and any restrictions on capacity. For each time period this model was also used to estimate the demand and supply of floorspace in each zone. Floorspace per unit activity was estimated as a function of zonal rent for competing residential and service activities and the estimated rent pattern was then adjusted across the area until supply and demand were balanced in each zone.
(iii)Transport Model - the submodels of this module were used to perform trip generation, model split, distribution and assignment to the network. The number of trips generated to work, shopping, education and other services were estimated for car and non-car owners. These were then split between public and private transport modes and assigned to the network using a multi-path assignment technique based upon a cascade algorithm. The resulting costs and times were then fed back into the land use module to affect the location of activities in the subsequent time period.
(iv)Evaluation - an essential component of the Bilbao project was the development of an evaluation model designed to process and place an economic and social interpretation on the output of the land use and transport simulations. The evaluation thus provided a means of measuring the desirability or otherwise of the planning policies simulated through the model, and a basis on which to make decisions.

7.4 The policies

Since the implementation of the model, the planning authorities in Bilbao have simulated and evaluated a number of land use and transport policy packages. Numerous improvement/expansion alternatives for the public and private transport network have been tested, together with some major employment and land use policies. Important policies have been implemented as a result of the model such as the access to the Rontegui bridge, the exit of Ugaldebieta and planning of the arterial

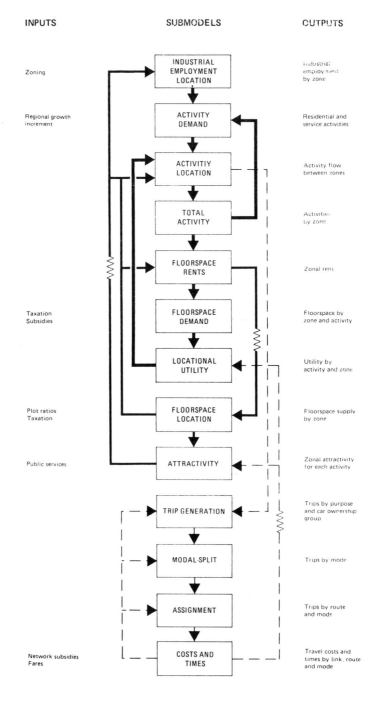

INPUTS	SUBMODELS	OUTPUTS
Zoning	INDUSTRIAL EMPLOYMENT LOCATION	Industrial employment by zone
Regional growth increment	ACTIVITY DEMAND	Residential and service activities
	ACTIVITIY LOCATION	Activity flow between zones
	TOTAL ACTIVITY	Activities by zone
	FLOORSPACE RENTS	Zonal rent
Taxation Subsidies	FLOORSPACE DEMAND	Floorspace by zone and activity
	LOCATIONAL UTILITY	Utility by activity and zone
Plot ratios Taxation	FLOORSPACE LOCATION	Floorspace supply by zone
Public services	ATTRACTIVITY	Zonal attractivity for each activity
	TRIP GENERATION	Trips by purpose and car ownership group
	MODAL-SPLIT	Trips by mode
	ASSIGNMENT	Trips by route and mode
Network subsidies Fares	COSTS AND TIMES	Travel costs and times by link, route and mode

Figure 8.   Land use and transport submodel structure

140

highway network for the area right of the river.

7.5 Conclusions

In terms of the basic objectives of the project the modelling and evaluation exercise has been a success. The model was used as an objective
aid to policy making in connection with the structure plan and has continued to function as a practical aid in the day-to-day planning process
of the metropolitan authority.

In 1979 the completion of a further traffic survey in Bilbao enabled
the predictions of the model to be verified against real-world observations. The results of this comparison indicated that on the major routes
in and out of the city the forecast traffic flows were within 5 percent
of actual vehicle counts. The accuracy of predictions such as this,
combined with the overall success of the project, led to a commission
for a further modelling study in 1981.

This case study illustrates that if the institutional setting of the
work has continuity, it is possible to succeed, despite vaguely formulated problems.

In fact, the Corporation of Greater Bilbao has now been absorbed by
the recently formed Basque Government, but all the technical staff and
the model have been transferred to the Ministry of Public Works.
This group has become an essential element in the government decision
making process as it is consulted about any major decision affecting the
metropolitan area. The case study shows that it is not necessary to
have well-formulated problems. The fact that a model with a good theoretical basis is implemented which simulates the situation, and therefore reproduces the problems, is in itself a very useful tool. It allows
the causes of the problems to be understood, and the alternative courses
of actions to be identified and evaluated.

8.   THE TAV STUDY: THE FEASIBILITY OF A HIGH SPEED TRAIN IN THE CORRIDOR
     RIO DE JANEIRO - SAO PAULO - CAMPINAS, BRAZIL

8.1 The objectives of the study

This study was designed to investigate various alternative options available for meeting inter-urban travel demand along the Rio de Janeiro -
Sao Paulo - Campinas corridor. In particular the project was concerned
with examining the possibility of introducing a high speed train service
(TAV). The work commissioned was divided into five sub-studies which
dealt with aspects of land use, passenger and freight demand, the availability and costs of high speed rail technology and route location. The
aims of the project were:
(i) To estimate existing and future patterns of passenger and freight
    demand for different modes within the study area.
(ii)To forecast the future modal split of passenger travel resulting
    from alternative transport development strategies.
(iii)To examine the costs and benefits of alternative investment options
    and to present a financial analysis for the optimum strategy.
The client was the federal Ministry of Transport of Brazil, which oper-
ated through its agency GEIPOT. The results of the study were received
by the agency and accepted.

8.2 The model

The development of a transport model was central to meeting the requirements of the passenger and freight demand sub-studies and this was complemented by the development of an evaluation module. A three-tier zoning system was adopted for the study. This comprised 12 relatively small zones within the corridor proper, eight larger, adjacent zones and four external zones. Population data and forecasts were obtained largely from the land use sub-study. Traffic data were obtained from earlier studies in Sao Paulo (SPT) and Rio (PRD), supplemented by operating statistics. The model dealt separately with internal area interzonal passenger traffic, interzonal freight traffic and other traffic deemed to be unaffected by the options under consideration. In addition, to reflect variations in trip-making and mode choice passenger demand was further divided into business travel and non-business travel stratified by car ownership and income group of the traveller.

In view of the basic problem of simulating mode split and trip generation, travel demand was modelled using a direct demand type formulation (Quandt and Baumol 1969) based upon a multilevel, multinomial logit model (Daly and Zachary 1976). This differed from earlier similar models in two important ways. Firstly, the treatment of mode split allowed clustering into sub-groups comprising modes which provided reasonable substitutes for one another. The multilevel formulation avoided the 'red bus/blue bus' paradox by providing almost constant estimates of the relative utility of similar choices but did not require that predictions of an attitude of one mode be governed by attitudes to other quite different modes. Secondly, a method was devised for linking modal split and trip generation via a composite utility measure ensuring that the cross-elasticities of the model were always positive.

A major consideration in model development was that demand should be responsive to supply in terms of travel costs, speed and service. The model selected was built within an iterative structure in which demand was stimulated as a function of system supply and level of service became a function of the demand for travel. Two interacting submodels (see figure 9) were employed to model supply and demand.

(i) Demand Submodel – This was used to estimate the number of peron trips between zones by different modes for the forecast years. The procedure commenced by calculating interzonal flows in the base year, using a cross-sectional interaction model. Taking the existing network, exogenously determined changes in population and income were then used to estimate the growth in trip-making for the forecast year. Generation/suppression of trips was determined as a function of the utilities in the network supplied and mode split was handled within the utility maximisation framework of the logit model. Corresponding forecasts of demand for freight travel were taken from the SPT study.

(ii) Supply Submodel – This provided a means of simulating the transport networks for the various options and years considered in the study. Car and truck submodes plus bus, train, high speed train and air modes were modelled. Travel times and speeds were calculated for links subject to capacity restraint, and following the networks for each mode interzonal minimum paths were defined on the basis of generalised costs. Taking interzonal flows output from the demand submodel assignment to each of the modal networks was performed using a minimum path algorithm chosen because of the simplicity of the network. The costs and times output were fed into the demand model and the process was iterated several times until equilibrium was obtained

Table 4

Evaluation Table

Change over base case	Discounted Benefits (Cr\$ 1979 x 10^6)			
	Freight transfer	Passenger transfer	TAV (high attraction)	TAV (low attraction)
User Benefits				
Net utility of trip (A—B)	3280	109150	375606	133710
Car operating cost (C)	899	−7970	42701	13909
Consumer taxes/subsidies (D)	346	−4699	−40030	−29873
Fares (E)	−1510	−5558	153325	79386
Total	3545	127377	219610	70388
Operator Benefits				
Passenger fares (F)	−1510	−5558	153325	79386
Operating costs (G)	−1086	20268	−10563	−3739
Taxes (H)	−40	695	−989	−479
Total	−384	−26521	164887	83604
Freight				
Operating costs (G)	83988	−1264	−1375	2331
Taxes (H)	−7723	—		
Total	−76265	1264	1375	2331
Government Benefits				
Taxes/subsidies (I)	−7417	−4004	−41019	−30352
Road maintenance costs (J)	−5733	−1471	−83	−688
Total	−1684	−2533	−40936	−29664
Capital costs (K)	—	—	163835	163835
Grand Total (A—B C—D—E+F—G—H+I—J—K)	−74788	−99587	181091	−41838

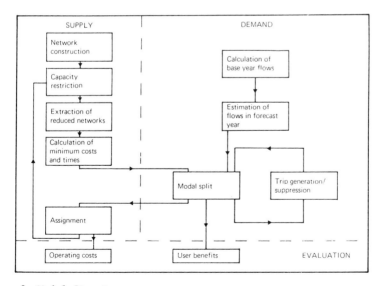

Figure 9. Model Structure

143

in terms of demand and supply.

8.3 The policies

The terms of reference of the project required the consideration of
three basic policy options:
(i) transfer of freight from road to rail, using the existing rail sys-
    tem more intensively in order to free the road system for passenger
    use
(ii) transfer of passengers from road to the existing rail system by im-
     proving passenger train services without prejudice to freight ser-
     vices
(iii) construction of a high speed passenger train (TAV) link between Rio
      - Sao Paulo - Campinas.
An evaluation system was developed to compare each alternative with a
base case representing the minimum investment required to maintain traffic flow at the lowest acceptable level. Each option was simulated using
the model and the effects evaluated from 1975 to the year 2000. The results, based upon a per capita income growth of 4 percent per annum are
summarised in the evaluation table (see table 4). The TAV option was
examined assuming both high and low attraction factors, representing
respectively cases in which high speed trains provided a more or equally
attractive proposition than a competing air service with identical costs
and times. Changes in areal accessibility (as measured by changes in
composite utility) for the base case in 1975 and 2000 and TAV in 2000
were investigated by plotting contour maps of disutilities.

8.4 The results

The model runs and evaluation revealed a number of interesting effects
of the different policy options:
(i) Forced freight transfer would constitute a poor alternative in the
    corridor. In terms of passenger travel and government receipts the
    effects of this policy proved small. The major impact arose in terms
    of increased operators' costs following the shift to rail of non-
    bulk items which have relatively high handling and distribution
    costs. The results of the study also indicated that by the mid
    1990's the Sao Paulo - Rio link of the rail line would have reached
    capacity with iron ore and cement anyway.
(ii) Improvement of passenger train services would generate major user
     benefits, largely due to an increase in the attractiveness of rail
     over bus in terms of frequency, reliability and punctuality. The
     level of improvement needed would however require large injections
     of capital. Towards the turn of the century this option would be-
     come more desirable as road congestion increased.
(iii) The TAV would draw passengers from all modes excluding cars, with the
      effect of increasing car traffic of feeder links and decreasing it
      on competing links. Although providing a healthy contribution to
      overhead costs, the increased volume of subsidised business travel
      would cause a sharp fall in government receipts. Spatially, 43% of
      benefits could be attributed to the Sao Paulo - Campinas section of
      the link, 10% to the Rio - Resende section, 44% to the Valley of the
      Paraiba and others sections and, as a result of competition in air
      travel, only 3% to the Rio - Sao Paulo section. As a consequence
      the viability of the section through the sparsely populated area be-
      tween Rio and Cruzeiro (44% of the total track length) was questioned
      under both hypotheses, and the viability of the Cruzeiro - Sao Paulo

section questioned under the lower attraction hypothesis. Using the assumption of a per capita income growth of only 2 percent per annum however, the construction of the Sao Paulo — Campinas section still appeared to be just warranted.

(iv) Accessibility was found to deteriorate between 1975 and 2000, as the cost of travel and travelling times by road increased. In 1975 when car provided a strong competitor with air, a steady decline in accessibility emerged between Sao Paulo and Rio.

The Sao Paulo corridor study was successfully completed within five months. The demand forecasts and estimates of modal split were passed to the client and a set of recommendations based upon the findings of the project were made. In particular, the client was advised of the doubtful utility/viability of the implementation of the TAV option in the Rio — Sao Paulo corridor given the presence of an air link between the cities which was highly competitive.

The study illustrates the case where the problem was clearly specified; there was a reasonably strong theoretical basis for the model and finally the institution which commissioned the work had sufficient continuity to receive the results of it and implement its conclusions. In this case the conclusions were negative as it was clear that the high speed train TAV was unlikely to compete in the main part of the corridor (Sao Paulo — Rio de Janeiro) with existing facilities and the small benefits which it would produce did not justify the large cost of implementing it.

9. THE MUT STUDY: A LAND USE AND TRANSPORT MODEL FOR THE CITY OF SAO PAULO

9.1 The objectives of the study

The purpose of this study was to produce a comprehensive system for monitoring and planning the pattern of future growth of the Sao Paulo Metropolitan Area in Brazil. The emphasis in the study was equally divided between the transport and the land use sectors since the major policies to be tested usually had implications for both of these sectors. The study was a follow-up to the SISTRAN study discussed above.

The principal objectives of the study were:

(i) To design and implement an information system which would be regularly updated and which would contain information on the supply and characteristics of the stock of land and buildings and on the supply and characteristics of the public and private transport system.

(ii) To design and implement a simulation system which would quantify the implications of future growth trends or planning policy decisions for both the land use and transport sectors.

(iii) To design and implement an evaluation system which would assess the quantified outcome of specific strategic planning policies in terms of their economic and financial implications for the Sao Paulo Metropolitan Area.

(iv) To train the counterpart staff in the underlying theory and in the use of the whole system to allow them to test a wide range of policy issues of relevance to Sao Paulo.

The client was a consortium of three municipal and state authorities:

COGEP — General Planning Council of the Municipality of Sao Paulo

EMTU/SP — Metropolitan Authority for Urban Public Transport for the State of Sao Paulo

EMPLASA — Metropolitan Authority for Planning in Greater Sao Paulo.

9.2 Details of the study

The Greater Sao Paulo Metropolitan Area has a population of approximately 13 million inhabitants and is growing at the very high rate of about one million people every two years through migration and natural growth. This area was divided into 633 zones for the storage of data in the information system. A suite of aggregation programs was developed which allowed the basic zonal and network information to be aggregated to less detailed user specified zone systems suitable for use in the simulation system. To make efficient use of computer resources, a hierarchical structure was developed such that different parts of the simulation system could be run at different levels of spatial detail as appropriate.

Because of the rapid rate of growth in the demand for floorspace and for transport it was crucial that the system developed should have dynamics adequate to represent the interaction between land use and transport factors in determining the spatial pattern of these changes.

The major innovations on the land use side of the study included: an explicit treatment of zoning laws to allow precision in testing their effects both on the construction of new buildings and on the uses to which existing buildings are put; an explicit treatment of the availability of water and sewage; and a separation of the stock of buildings into different types and qualities to represent more accurately the different patterns of usage and of rents they give rise to.

The major innovations on the transport side of the study included an elastic trip generation model responsive to changes in trip costs; a multilevel logit modal split model which included walk trips explicitly; the inclusion of trips comprised of combinations of modes (i.e. walks to bus to metro to train to walk) with the optional inclusion of integrated fares for specific mode combinations; the use of a composite travel utility carried through the transport model in a consistent fashion to the evaluation (see figure 10).

9.3 The land use model

The land use model can be separated into four component parts which interact with each other and with the transport model:

(i) The metropolitan growth submodel contains the interface between the other three parts of the land use model and the rest of Brazil outside the study area. It operates non-spatially and provides estimates for the study area as a whole of the growth in population by income group of employment-by-employment type and of the net increase in the supply of floorspace by type of building.

(ii) The floorspace supply allocation submodel allocates the total study-wide net increase in floorspace (by type) to individual zones on the basis of expected rents and construction costs and taking due account of the zoning laws. It also estimates the amount of demolition of existing floorspace that is created by redevelopment in already built-up zones.

(iii) The basic industry allocation submodel allocates the study-wide net increase in industrial employment to individual zones on the basis of past trends, accessibility, rents and zoning laws.

(iv) The activity allocation submodel allocates resident households by income group, and non-industrial employment by type to the existing stock of floorspace. This allocation process takes account of accessibility, the suitability and the rent of the different types of floorspace available, and the different abilities of households to pay for location. For subsequent use in the transport model this

146

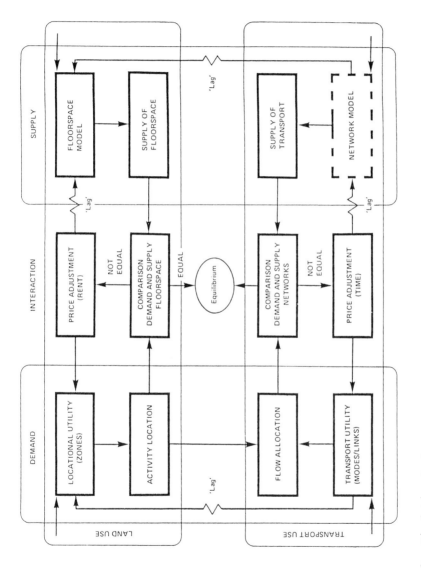

Figure 10.   Simulation System

147

submodel also calculates the flows of transport between homes and workplaces, shops and schools.

The main outputs from the land use model are: the volume of new buildings and demolition disaggregated by zoning law and water and sewage availability; the location of employment by type; the location of residents by income groups; and the floorspace rent. Each of these outputs is disaggregated by type of building and by zone.

9.4 The transport model

The transport model contains the four standard stages of: generation, distribution; modal split and assignment. The distribution is the first stage to be carried out. It is a part of the activity allocation submodel and gives the pattern of location of the workplaces, schools and shops used by the residents in each zone. The trip generation then estimates the number of trips made by residents for each of these purposes. The number of trips generated between a pair of zones is elastic to the generalised cost of travel between the zones.

The matrix of trips for households in each income group is then divided into the trips on the four main modes considered: auto; bus; train/metro; and walk. The modal split model used is a multilevel logit model. The trips on each main mode are assigned to the links of their transport network using a multipath assignment model. At this stage the trips were separated also into their component submodes on the network such as access trips by bus for the main mode train/metro.

The main outputs from the transport model are: matrices of the flows of people by each income group and main mode between all zone pairs; and the flows of vehicles by submode on each link of the transport network.

9.5 The evaluation system

A simulation system is of little use for practical planning studies unless it is linked to an evaluation system. The evaluation system developed here compares the simulated outcomes of two policies and provides information on the relative merits of various aspects of these policies to guide in eventual decision making.

The economic benefits from a policy are divided into those resulting from transport changes and from land use changes. The sectional breakdown of costs and benefits shows the impact of a policy on different income groups, different parts of the city and on users of services as well as on operators of services and on government. Non-economic indicators of performance such as levels of crowding and of social segregation are also included.

9.6 The policies

Although the initial phase of the study did not require tests of actual policies to be carried out, to check the robustness of the system some sample policies were tested. The impact of the second metro line currently under construction was assessed both in terms of its effect on the reduction of the demands for other transport modes and its neighbourhood and on the demand for higher density developments close to the stations. The effects were evaluated of changes in the existing zoning laws to ensure that fast-growing areas of the city did not reach intolerably high levels of congestion. A policy of restriction on the extension of the city into the surrounding rural areas was also run.

9.7 Conclusions

The combined information, simulation and evaluation system was demonstrated to be an effective aid to monitoring and planning the pattern of
growth in a large metropolis. In the implementation of the system, the
understanding gained of the processes influencing development patterns
has already proved valuable to the planners and the system illustrates
the probable outcomes of specific strategic policy measures to an extent
hitherto unavailable.

However, a number of difficulties arose from such an ambitious programme. Firstly, there was no clear appreciation of the problems of the
city, nor was there any direction of possible instruments to be used for
the guidance of their development. Secondly, the major institutions
which commissioned the work suffered substantial political changes during
the course of the study. In fact one of them, EMTU, disappeared altogether. Once trained, the staff of the project were immediately con-
tracted by consulting engineering firms for much higher salaries, which
removed them from the government agencies. No effort was made to train
replacement staff when this situation arose.

Finally, the model was too ambitious. The data base contained over 4
million property records aggregated into 633 zones. The transport network had over 16,000 links. Too many classes of buildings, of activities, of transport types, etc. were used, which made the model too cumbersome to use. In fact, during the development process of the model,
enormous resistance was made by the consultants to increasing the detail
of the model, but the advisors to the political authorities insisted on
the need of the model to answer minute issues.

The result was that the model was too close to reality, but without
being it! Models must be simple to be of any use if they are not to be
like the example of a 1:1 scale map which was perfect but impossible to
use as it could not be extended. However, the model is still in operation at the city's planning agency COGEP, but with little utilisation.

10. THE GUASARE NEW TOWN STUDY

10.1 The objectives of the study

The main objective of the study was to determine the best alternative
for the urban support of coal mining activities in the region of Zulia,
Venezuela. This could be the expansion of an existing settlement or the
development of a New Town. Additional questions were asked about the
size of the development, its timing and investment strategies.

There were also additional subsidiary objectives concerned with increasing the distribution of benefits of the alternative chosen to the
region as well as avoiding the dependency on coal mining as the only
source of economic activity.

The client was the Regional Development Coroporation of the Region of
Culia (CORPOZULIA).

10.2 Details of the study

The region of Zulia has a population of almost 2 million people centred
around the metropolitan area of Maracaibo with over 1 million inhabitants. The region is responsible for the majority of the oil production
in Venezuela, which is extracted on the east shore of the Lake of Maracaibo. The city of Maracaibo, on the west shore of the Lake, acts as

149

the main service centre for the oil industry. The stated intention of
CORPOZULIA was to increase the development of the region and to reduce
its dependency on oil extraction. The oil will run out in the not too
distant duture. Investment in coal and other resources was considered
as a priority. The study divided the region into 20 zones, which represented the main activity centres of the region with a more detailed
subdivision of the area around the mines of Guasare. This detail provided the basis for the locational studies.

The study took as a base the year 1981, collecting information on the
socio-economic characteristics of the population of the region as well
as the land and transport utilisation. The forecasts were for the years
1986, 1991 and 1996.

10.3 The model

A model similar to the one used in the Bilbao study was utilised here.
However, the scale of operations was sub-regional rather than urban.
The model contained a Regional Growth Model which forecast the growth of
economic activities and household formation. The Land Use model allocated the activities to the zones and the Transport model allocated
trips to networks. These two models forecast the prices of land and
buildings as well as transport. An Evaluation model, similar to that
used in Bilbao, was used to test the alternative policy options.

An innovation in this application was the development of detailed
financial model for the study which was attached to the evaluation model.

10.4 The policies

This aspect was the most innovative of the study. A substantial part of
the study was devoted to a detailed design and testing of alternative
policy options. The options can be described in relation to the areas
affected:
(i) Regional Policies, which investigated the impact on the region of
    Zulia of the different investment programmes of coal mining, rail-
    way development, new town building, road expansion, steel plant, port
    development, new industrial park, thermo-electric plant and develop-
    ment of agro-industrial enterprises. The different policies at this
    level produced different forecasts of employment, income, services
    and population growth.
(ii)Sub-regional Policies, which investigated the alternatives within
    the micro-region of Guasare in relation to the creation of a New
    Town as opposed to the expansion of an existing one and to the small
    expansion of many settlements. Within the alternative of the New
    Town development several locations were studied. Also at this level
    policies concerned with diversification of the economic base of the
    city were studied.
(iii)Urban Policies, which investigated alternative urban policies such as
    different levels of the provision of public housing; levels of sub-
    sidies in land acquisition and building materials for different
    income groups; alternative levels of service provision for infra-
    structure and social services.

10.5 The findings

The policies at regional levels established the framework within which
the rest of the study could develop. The annual growth of the industrial
sector fluctuated between 2.5% and 3.65% in different periods and accor-

ding to different policies. The agricultural sector declined and sta-
bilised with some of the alternative policy options. The population
forecast did not vary all that much according to the alternative policies, forecasting an extra one million people in the region by the year
1996.

The biggest differences in the impact of policies were obtained at sub-
regional scale. Each policy produced different development and growth
of incomes in each zone. The main findings are summarised below.
(i) The development of a New Town is difficult in the next 15 years. It
is only possible by a substantial level of public investment. In
fact the social rates of return on the investment were negative in
the policies of low investment, only one of the locational options
gave positive values in the medium level of investment and the majority of the options produced a long term benefit in the large investment programmes.
(ii)It is very difficult to diversify the economic base of the city beyond a small increase in agro-industry. It is however, worthwhile
investing money in the diversification programme but only to a
limited extent.
(iii)From the locational point of view the expansion of an existing town
(Carrasquero) produced the least cost option, but the benefits are
not high in the large investment option, while an alternative location (La Estrella) produced, in the high investment option, the
largest benefit. In the medium investment option a location close
to the mine (Mannelote) produced the best return, but was more a
support camp to the mining activities than a sub-regional centre.
At the urban level some interesting conclusions were obtained:
(i) It is necessary to subsidise land and transport in order to attract
the population and diversify the economic activities of the settlement and micro-region.
(ii)It is difficult to attract medium and high income groups, which tend
to gravitate towards Maracaibo. If those groups are highly subsidised in their housing, they are attracted to the new town in a
limited way, but these groups increased the land and property values,
repelling low income groups which tended to settle in villages outside the town without infrastructure.
(iii)It is probable that the new town will contain mainly medium and low
income groups, if both transport and land are subsidised for those
groups and not higher income groups. This policy produced the largest population in the town and accrues positive returns on the investments.
(iv)Land parcels influence the location of medium and low income groups.
Those groups which are attracted to the new development are mainly
employed in the service sector. Self-building is their main form of
housing which demands more land per family than public housing, due
to the slower rate of building and the materials used.

10.6 Conclusions

The details of each alternative policy were presented to the regional
authorities with the recommendations in terms of size of development,
location, investment levels, subsidies, etc.

The options are, at this stage, being evaluated further at the physical design level. The final decision will take place within a year to
start inplementing the option chosen. But a number of institutional
issues need to be resolved. These relate to who will be responsible for
the development. If the option chosen in the expansion of an existing

town, the existing municipal council of the town should take some of
the responsibility for development but must be supported by the regional
corporation. In this option, the mining enterprise may contribute very
little as the benefits are not accrued to them. If a new town is developed a new organisation like a development corporation may be created.
Within this option it is not clear how the regional corporation or the
mining firms will contribute. They may depend on the alternative location chosen. In any case, the mining firms, while in theory depending
on the regional corporation, in practice tend to act rather independently and this creates difficulties in coordinating the programmes.

This case study shows that it is possible to formulate clear questions
and to have a reasonable instrument with which to study development options. It may be that the institutional problems will be resolved in
due course, but this will depend on the political ability of the regional development corporation.

11. THE GIBRALTAR STUDY

11.1 The objectives of the study

The basic question posed in this study was how much traffic would be
attracted to a fixed crossing (either a tunnel or a bridge) of the
Straits of Gibraltar, were such a crossing to be built. As the horizon
period was very long, an exact answer was impossible, as too many impon-
derable factors needed to be taken into account. But it was necessary
to make a best estimate of at least the orders of magnitude in order to
make a rational evaluation of the desirability of such a fixed crossing.

The client for the study was SECEG, an autonomous Spanish government
organisation set up to study the options and to liaise with the Moroccan
counterpart organisation.

11.2 Details of the study

The study was concerned with forecasting the passenger and freight traffic which would be potentially diverted to the fixed crossing. The area
considered (see figure 11) included eleven European countries and twenty-
two African countries. The existing modes of transport between the two
continents included air, long distance shipping and ferries. This last
could be accessed by road or rail. Information was collected on a systematic basis for air traffic (passengers and freight) from ICAO (International Civil Aviation Organisation) and for shipping from the Lloyd's
register. Both of these sources contained computerised data for every
movement between the continents. In addition information from ferry
operators, customs and immigration controls was collected to give more
details for road and rail transport to the ferry ports.

Aggregated data in terms of population, employment, trade, incomes,
etc., were collected from published sources of international organisations such as UN, World Bank, OECD, etc.

11.3 The model

The model utilised needed to assess the behaviour of potential users
(passengers or agents) of a new mode (the fixed crossing) for which no
past experience existed. The only way to assess this was to describe
the existing crossings (air, long distance shipping, etc.) based on its
attributes such as cost of travel, time, terminal costs, reliability,

Figure 11. The Study Area

153

etc. and then estimate the sensitivity to each of these attributes by each potential user so that any variation of the attributes could be assessed in terms of changes in the utilisation of the crossings (elasticities). The new fixed crossing could then be represented by a new combination of these attributes and therefore predictions of the likely attraction could be made.

The model used was similar to that used for the TAV study (high speed train) for the corridor of Rio de Janeiro – Sao Paulo – Campinas in Brazil. The model produced the future traffic in the fixed crossing (see figure 12) as a function of :

(i) The existing traffic: this traffic reflects cultural and economic ties between European and African countries (post-colonial relationships).

(ii) The growth or decline of the traffic: this growth or decline between each pair of countries will depend on the growth of population and income in the countries concerned as well as the policies pursued in terms of trade. This last point introduced a large element of uncertainty into the forecasts.

(iii) The traffic generated or suppressed: the new fixed crossing may induce new movements generating a higher overall traffic. This would depend on whether the new fixed crossing produced a substantial change in those important attributes (as perceived by the users) of the crossing.

(iv) The proportion of the overall traffic attracted to the fixed crossing due to its attributes and in competition with the other crossings.

The model was calibrated using the data sources described above and the elasticities estimated for each group of potential users. The proportion or probability of using the fixed crossing was estimated using a hierarchical multinomial logit model (Daly and Zachary 1976) which is derived from Random Utility Theory (Domencich and McFadden 1975). In figure 12 the hierarchical structure is represented.

The traffic generated or suppressed was estimated by a consistent aggregation of the utilities in each level of the hierarchy. Using Williams' (1977) work, the increase or decrease in utilities was used to estimate the generation or suppression of traffic.

The overall framework used to estimate the final traffic was a direct demand model (Quandt and Baumol 1969) which took into account the change of traffic due to change of population, incomes and utilities. However, the basic forecast of the exogenous variables for long time horizons are very uncertain. Forecasts of population and incomes in African countries are particularly so, but the most difficulties arose from the uncertain policies of trade between Europe and Africa. On the one hand, the possible development of import controls could affect dramatically the north–south relationship. On the other hand, liberalisation of trade could affect both production and incomes in developing countries as well as trade increases.

The only way forward was to assume different scenarios to represent these options. Thus a forecast was done for each one. The European scenarios were based on the work of OECD (Interfutures) modified to take into account recent information about the economic situation of European countries. The African scenarios were assumed to be based on the outcome of the European scenarios only, as there was no equivalent forecast (like the OECD ones) for the African countries.

11.4 The policies

A number of policies are being tested at present. The alternatives are

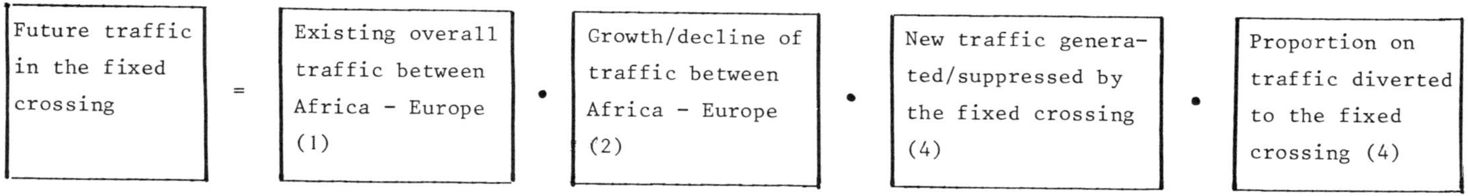

| Future traffic in the fixed crossing | = | Existing overall traffic between Africa – Europe (1) | · | Growth/decline of traffic between Africa – Europe (2) | · | New traffic genera- ted/suppressed by the fixed crossing (4) | · | Proportion on traffic diverted to the fixed crossing (4) |

(1) Existing data for each group (passenger and freight)

(2) Forecast of socio-economic and political factors (if >1 → growth, <1 → decline)

(3) Forecast of changes in utilities (if >1 → new generation, <1 → suppression)

(4) Probability of using the fixed crossing, considering all other alternative crossings (<)

Figure 12. The structural model.

155

related to the following aspects:
(i) Alternative scenarios of north-south relationship: four alternatives
    are tested here (increased trade liberalisation with renewed economic
    growth in developed countries; moderate growth in developed coun-
    tries with free trade; independent development for Africa with no
    convergence of productivity; mounting protectionism by developed
    countries).
(ii)Alternative technological and pricing policies of competing modes.
    These issues affected the speed and cost of air, shipping, rail and
    road transport which, combined with the trade scenarios, increased
    the number of alternatives.
(iii)Alternative crossings. These aspects included the forecast of the
    base situation if no fixed crossing was built, if a rail tunnel was
    built and if a road and/or rail bridge was built.
For each combination of policies, forecasts are being produced for each
of the years 1990, 2000 and 2020.

11.5 Conclusions

The study is not completed yet and presumably a number of alternative
policies will be tested more locally, which may affect the integration
between the south of Spain and the north of Marocco. Equally, there are
other policies being discussed concerning the access to the Straits by
land (road and rail), especially from the African continent which may be
determined more on the actual traffic than the crossing itself.
    In any case, the forecasts for the foreseeable future are rather low
which, taking into consideration the enormous uncertainties associated
with the forecasts, may result in a decision being taken on international
political grounds rather than on exact quantitative measurements.
    This case study shows that even if clear institutional arrangements are
set up for the planning issues and clear questions are asked, there may
still be difficulties in achieving reliable analytical techniques to
answer these questions. Of course, this problem does not ask for the
overthrow of proper analysis but for renewed effort in developing new
methods or at least limiting the uncertainties within a given range, on
which decision makers can take calculated risks.

12. CONCLUSIONS

This paper has presented eight case studies involving mathematical models
in planning. The case studies have been selected to illustrate particular combinations of issues in the use of models. These issues are concerned with the specification of the problem, the theoretical strength
and the institutional setting. In some of the case studies the specification of the problem was clear at the outset, which facilitated the
evaluation of the solutions. But in many cases, the problem is vaguely
specified, and this requires more comprehensive models. This is not a
bad thing in itself and in some cases - e.g. Bilbao - the model developed
has been in continuous use ever since, precisely because it was not developed for answering a single question.
    Models have shortcomings and some of them can be of critical importance
for the predictions. In some of the cases presented, the model used had
a reasonable theoretical basis for answering the questions posed. In
other cases, the theory used had limitations, but in the absence of any
better theory the models were used with strong alternative assumptions.
This is the case, for example, of the scenario utilised in the Gibraltar

study.

Finally, the critical aspects of the use of models is the institutional setting. Some of the failures attributed to the use of models are, in reality, failures of the planning process. Planning institutions in developing countries usually had no clear demarcation of responsibilities and even if they had them on paper, in reality they are powerless as they do not implement the decisions because they may not have control over budget expenditure.

However, some planning agencies, with only an advisory role, can still have a successful track record just because of the continuity of the staff in the agency. This has been the case in the Bilbao study.

Some of the results of using quantitative models highlight the inconsistencies of investment plans or programmes by operating agencies (this was the case with the Tehran study and the SPT study). This in turn may weaken the case for the expansion plans. In the absence of clear political leadership, the planning institutions will be attacked by the larger and more politically powerful operating agencies. The example of the SPT study shows that politicians sometimes do not want to know the answers when these are 'politically' unpopular.

ACKNOWLEDGEMENTS

All of the case studies presented in this paper have been projects in my consulting office. Acknowledgement is given to the contributions of my partners R.S. Baxter, A.D.J. Flowerdew, R.J. Stibbs and I.N. Williams. Some of the associates of the firm have also contributed substantially to some of the case studies, in particular R.G. Bullock, T. de la Barra and P.A. Geraldes. Some of the case studies presented had large contributions by individuals, in particular M.L. de Mendonca in the SISTRAN and SPT studies in Brazil, J.L. Burgos in the Bilbao study and J. Cueno in the Gibraltar study.

REFERENCES

Daly, A.J. and Zachary, S., 'Improved multiple choice models' in
  Proceedings of the PTRC Summer Annual Meeting, PTRC, London, 1976.
Domencich, T.A. and McFadden, D., Urban Travel Demand: A Behavioural
  Analysis, North Holland Publ. Co., Amsterdam, 1975.
Hesse, M., Models and Analogues in Science, Shield and Ward, London,
  1963.
OECD, Interfutures, Paris, 1979.
Quandt, R.E. and Baumol, W.H., 'The demand for abstract transport
  models: some hopes', in Journal of Regional Science, Vol. 9, No.1,
  1969.
Stone, R., Mathematics in the Social Sciences and Other Essays,
  Chapman and Hall, London, 1966.
Williams, H.C.W.L., 'On the formation of travel demand models and
  economic evaluation measures of user benefit', in Environment and
  Planning A, Vol. 9, 1977.

10 Information Systems for Urban and Regional Planning in Developing Countries

P. NIJKAMP

I. INTRODUCTION

Planning and policy analysis aims at reducing uncertainties regarding insights into or choices about future developments. Monitoring, fore-casting and scenario analysis are some of the popular tools that serve to deal explicitly with uncertain but foreseeable events in the near or distant future. Consequently, information systems have drawn a great deal of attention in planning and policy analysis (see also Nijkamp 1982a, 1982b).

Usually a distinction is made between data and information. Data is numerical representations or other symbolic surrogates aiming at char-acterising attributes of phenomena, while information may be regarded as structured data (for instance, by means of modelling, organising or con-verting data), so as to improve the insight into a certain phenomena (see also Burch et al. 1979).

The complexity of modern societies and the enormous social costs in-volved in taking wrong decisions have led to a general need for appro-priate information, not only at the level of individual decision making but also at the level of social and economic organisations (cf. Sowell 1980). The data storage capacity of modern computers also favours a much more structured use of information than in previous periods. Not only in the developed world but also in developing countries, proper and systematic information is regarded as a prerequisite for successful planning (cf. also Casley and Lury 1981).

Clearly, there are many tradeoffs involved in collecting data and developing information systems. The accuracy, adaptability and timely availability have to be traded off against the economic consequences in terms of costs and benefits. A necessary condition for a manageable information system is a permanent user-surveyor dialogue so as to guaran-tee a meaningful coordination of the various tasks in a planning process.

Braybrook and Lindblom (1979) have investigated the relationship between the necessary information level (or level of insight) and the impact (or depth) of a certain decision or choice. This relationship may be represented by means of Figure 1.

Hence, a fundamental issue in dealing with information systems is a tradeoff between the costs of producing relevant information from appropriate data and the benefits of employing this information in actual planning procedures or policy choices.

Data can be collected at various levels and from various viewpoints. From an ideal point of view, the nature of data is determined by the aims of the analysis (impact analysis, plan evaluation e.g.), but in reality one very often has to use an existing and given database in the most efficient way so as to extract the most relevant information from this data for a prespecified use in a planning context. For instance, it appeared from the international survey of multiregional economic models (carried out by the Integrated Regional and Urban Development Group of the International Institute for Applied Systems Analysis; see Issaev et al. 1982), that the majority of multiregional economic models did not produce their own specific database, but mainly employed the existing data provided by the various statistical offices.

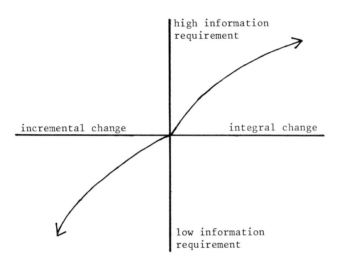

Figure 1. Necessary information and impact of a decision.

The collection of data is a problem in itself. Normally data is collected from a multi-purpose point of view, so that it is usually very difficult to obtain data with a precise and distinct focus on the problem at hand. Very often, data has to be manipulated, (dis)aggregated or adjusted in order to fit them into a precisely demarcated research or planning problem (cf. also Langefors 1966).

Data can be collected at various levels of aggregation, for instance, at individual levels (e.g. individual household income), or at aggregate levels (e.g. average regional income). Such data may be the result of interviews, questionnaires, censuses, samples, surveys or non-survey techniques. The choice for a particular data collection technique and for the level of aggregation of this data will be determined by the aim of the information systems and will also depend on the abovementioned tradeoff between costs and expected usefulness (cf. Park et al. 1981). The loss of information due to an aggregate representation of disaggregate variables can be represented by the entropy measure: entropy measures the ignorance of micro-variables when one knows only a macroscopic variable (see Gokhale and Kullback 1978).

A basic problem is of course, that one is usually not only interested in measures describing the state of a system, but also its evolution. Up-to-date data for complex systems (e.g. based on monitoring systems) however, is normally hard to obtain because of the high costs of a permanent filing system for relevant data. Sometimes interpolation or extrapolation techniques are used to cope with the lack of data for a time series. Other common techniques for updating data sets are RAS-techniques (for input-output tables) or entropy techniques (for spatial interaction data). Needless to say, none of these techniques will be able to reflect sudden jumps or shifts in a system (see also Chapter 16 of this book).

2. THE PRODUCTION OF INFORMATION

The treatment of data (e.g. restructuring, interpreting) may be based on various viewpoints and approaches (cf. Burch et al. 1979). Examples of related operations are:

-   capturing   a systematic recording of data
-   verifying   validating the correct nature of data
-   classifying   categorising data into specific classes
-   arranging   placing data in a predetermined sequence
-   summarising   aggregating data into new sets
-   calculating   manipulating data in an arithmetic way
-   forecasting   extrapolating data towards the future
-   simulating   assessing and manipulating lacking data
-   storing   placing data onto storage media
-   retrieving   selecting specific data from media
-   communicating   transferring data to other users.

All these operations are determined by the aims of the information system at hand. The choice for certain operations very much depends on the related costs caused inter alia by the personnel requirements, the modularity, flexibility and versatility of the system concerned, and the processing speed and control.

The benefits of an information system depend inter alia on its accessibility, comprehensiveness, accuracy, appropriateness, timeliness, clarity, flexibility, verifiability, freedom from bias, and quantifiability.

Clearly, a system with redundant information may lead to inefficient decisions, while lack of information may also lead to less than optimal decisions. Theoretically, an optimum level of information will be reached, if the marginal value of information equals its marginal cost. In reality, these costs and benefits can hardly be expressed into one common denominator, so that this marginality rule has only a limited practical relevance. The various aspects involved in judging the value of an information system normally require a multidimensional tradeoff.

3. USE OF INFORMATION

Information as structured data systems can be used in three stages of a planning process, viz. description, impact analysis and evaluation.

3.1 Description

A description means a structured representation of the data regarding a system. For instance, the social indicator movement may be regarded as an attempt at representing relevant features of a social system in a systematic way. The same holds true for environmental quality analysis.

In general, it appears to be meaningful to represent the main characteristics of a system by means of multidimensional profiles (Nijkamp

161

1979). Each of these profiles comprises a set of relevant indicators.
For instance, a regional system may be characterised by means of the
following profiles:

- economic   production
                    investments
                    labour market
                    consumption, etc.
- housing   quantity of dwellings
                    quality of dwellings
                    residential climate
                    prices and rents, etc.
- infrastructure   accessibility (public and private transport)
                    distance
                    mobility (migration, recreation), etc.
- finances   taxes
                    subsidies
                    public expenditures
                    distributional aspects, etc.
- facilities   health care
                    cultural
                    social
                    recreational, etc.
- environmental   air pollution
                    noise
                    sewage systems
                    congestion
                    segregation
                    density, etc.
- energy   energy consumtion
                    insulation of dwellings
                    central urban heating system
                    tariff system, etc.

Depending on the aim of a specific descriptive analysis, a choice
among the foregoing profiles (including their levels of measurement) has
to be made in order to get an integrated view of the system at hand.
Thus, such a descriptive view implies a transformation of data into
structured information classes.
    Such profiles with detailed elements are not only relevant in regional
economics, but also in many other disciplines like environmental science,
geography, and demography. In all these disciplines there is a basic
need for the systematic storage and treatment of relevant data (cf.
Blitzer et al. 1975, Hordijk et al. 1980, Rees and Willekens 1981).

3.2 Impact Analysis

In the last decade several types of impact analysis for planning and
policy purposes have been developed: environmental impact analysis,
social impact analysis, urban impact analysis, input-output analysis,
technological impact analysis, energy impact analysis, and so on. The
main aim of impact analyses was to get more complete, systematic and
comprehensive information on the effects of public policy decisions or of
exogenous shifts in the parameters or data of a system. Impact analysis
will be defined here as a method for assessing the foreseeable and expected consequences of a change in one or more exogenous stimuli that
exert effects on the element of the profiles characterising a system
(see Nijkamp 1982a, and Pleeter 1980); see also Chapter 11 of this

book). In general, impact analysis implies a transformation of first-order information into new information categories.

The need for impact analysis stems from various sources:

- a systematic investigation of consequences of public policy may lead to more justified policy decisions,
- an integrated impact analysis may avoid neglect of (potentially important) indirect or unintended effects,
- the presence of spillover effects and interactions between several compartments of a system requires a comprehensive view of its complicated mechanism,
- the hierarchical structure of many planning systems evokes the need for a multi-level impact analysis which is able to trace all relevant consequences at various levels.

Due to the pluriformity and complexity of western industrialised countries, coherent and balanced public policy strategies are usually fraught with difficulties. For instance, the integration and coordination of various aspects of physical-economic planning problems (such as public facilities, communication and infrastructure networks, residential housing programs, industrialisation programs, etc.) are often hampered due to administrative frictions, mono-disciplinary approaches, lack of information and political discrepancies.

An impact analysis may be a meaningful tool for more integrated and coordinated planning strategies, as such an analysis describes systematically the effects of changes in control variables on all other components of a system. Consequently, an impact analysis should pay attention to the variety, coherence, and institutional framework of the system at hand. This implies that economic, spatial, social and environmental variables should be included as relevant components of the system. Preferably, an impact analysis should be based on a formal model (see also Glickman 1980, and Snickars 1981). A more detailed exposition of impact analysis in a regional and urban context will be given in Chapter 11 of this book.

3.3 Evaluation

Evaluation refers to the process of analysing plans, proposals or projects with a view to searching out their comparative advantages and the act of setting down the findings of such analyses in a logical framework. Thus, the essence of evaluation in a planning context is the assessment of the comparative merits of different courses of action, so as to assist the process of decision making (see Litchfield et al. 1975). Necessary steps prior to the evaluation process itself are the descriptive analysis and the impact analyses set out above. Evaluation implies essentially a confrontation of structured information categories with policy and planning views.

Evaluation may take various forms: social cost-benefit analysis, cost-effectiveness analysis, planning balance sheet analysis, multiple criteria analysis, linear programming analysis, multiobjective programming analysis and so forth. Especially during the seventies, a whole spectrum of operational evaluation methods was developed to assess the pros and cons of effects of various courses of action (see for a survey also Nijkamp 1979; see also Chapter 14 of this book).

Evaluation requires the definition of a set of operational judgement criteria (efficiency criteria, equity criteria, environmental criteria, etc.), a set of alternative actions of strategies (including information on their technical and economic feasibility), a set of (implicit or explicit) preference parameters reflecting the relative importance attached to certain outcomes of a given action or strategy. Sometimes also scenario analyses are used as a way of dealing with hypothetical reasonable policy preference patterns (see for more details on evaluation analysis, also Chapter 14).

It should also be noted that planning has essentially a process character, so that during each state the necessary and relevant information has to be provided.

In order to make full use of information in evaluation and decision making, it is necessary to also indicate precisely the nature of the variables included (target variables, instruments, exogenous data). In general, it is also useful to indicate precisely how a certain desired end-result should be reached (for instance, by means of the well-known golden section and turnpike rules). In order to prevent decision makers from taking infeasible courses of action, threshold and bottleneck analysis may provide information about the conditions under which a certain new state of the system might evolve.

4. INFORMATION SYSTEMS FOR URBAN AND REGIONAL PLANNING

The abovementioned expositions on information systems were fairly general and did not have a distinct focus on a given problem area. Therefore, it may be worthwhile delimiting the scope of the present paper by addressing problems of information systems in a multiregional development setting so as to pay more attention to the use of information systems in urban and regional planning.

It may be meaningful to specify some general judgement criteria for information systems in urban and regional planning. In an ideal situation, the following aspects might be mentioned:

- availability of information: the relevant information should be available during the successive stages of the planning process so as to guarantee an adequate picture of the system at hand (possibly including longitudinal data);
- actuality of information: the information should be based on recent data in order to provide a representative and up-to-date picture of a complex reality;
- accessibility: the information should be accessible to both model builders and users (including policy makers and planners);
- consistency: the information should represent a set of coherent and non-contradictory data on regional processes and patterns;
- completeness: the information should take into account all (intended and unintended) effects and implications of policies upon the system at hand;
- relevance: the information produced should be in agreement with the aims of regional (or urban) management planning;
- pluriformity: the variables included in an information system should reflect the variety and multidimensionality of a multiregional system;
- comparability: the various data included in an information system should allow a comparison with other data measured at different time periods or in different areas;
- flexibility: the information system should provide comprehensive information which can be adjusted to the needs of users or to new circumstances;
- measurability: the information system should take into account the available data measured on any meaningful scale (including qualitative information);

- comprehensiveness : the various components of an information system should provide an integrated picture of a multiregional system;
- effectiveness : the information produced should allow a confrontation with a priori set policy targets, so that the effectiveness of policy measures can be gauged;
- versatility : the information provided may also be used for other planning purposes;
- validity : the reliability of the information provided and of the related statistical inferences should allow a judgement from a statistical or econometric point of view.

In addition to these general methodological criteria, also some specific regional and multiregional elements of an urban and regional information system can be mentioned (see also Bowman and Kutscher 1980, Garnick 1980, Torene and Goettee 1980).

- integration : the information system should attempt to present relevant data for each relevant spatial level and each relevant spatial unit, so as to guarantee both a comparability of data from one region to another and a coordination of various planning activities in different agencies;
- interregional interaction : an urban and regional information system should reflect the interwovenness of a spatial system by demonstrating the volumes of interregional commodity flows, migration flows, capital flows, etc.;
- specific regional bottlenecks : an information system should also indicate whether or why important regional information is lacking (for instance, the frequent lack of insight into monetary flows between regions);
- multiregional decision making : various decisions affecting a regional economy are made in the headquarters of corporate decision making entities; in addition, flows of income and profits are hard to attribute to a specific region. An urban and regional information system should try to disentangle the complexity of such a spatial system;
- standardisation : in order to make data comparable across regions, data has to be standardised (for instance, by relating them to the population size of an area). An information system should provide a sound basis for such a standardisation and should also indicate the sensitivity of the results for a specific standardisation (depending inter alia on the social demographic structure).

Some good examples of urban and regional information systems can be found in among others, Benjamin 1976, Elfick 1979, Guesnier 1978, Hägerstrand and Kuklinski 1971, Kuklinski 1974 and Perrin 1974. In an interesting article, Hermansen (1971) has given an appropriate and fairly complete representation of an information system for regional development planning.

5. CONCLUDING REMARKS

A well-known problem in any kind of urban and regional information system is the spatial demarcation of the system concerned (in terms of cities, regions, etc.). From an analytical point of view, the spatial demarcation might be based on functional linkages between the spatial entities of the system at hand, although data availability very often hampers the application of this standpoint. From a planning point of view, the spatial demarcations might be based on the existing administrative framework, although here data problems may also emerge (see also Hermansen 1971). This problem deserves much attention in a mature analysis of an urban and regional information system.

Frequently, information systems for regional and urban planning have been developed in close connection with multiregional models. Multiregional models – as an extension of traditional econometric modelling – aim at providing consistent and coherent information on a complex spatial world, so as to identify the main driving forces and the mechanism of a complicated multiregional system (see also Issaev et al. 1982). The aim of coherence and consistency will, in general, lead to a rejection of economic models that do not take account of the openness of a region. Thus, without a consideration of interregional and national-regional links, there is no consistency guarantee for the spatial system as a whole. Usually, there are various kinds of direct and indirect cross-regional linkages caused by spatio-temporal feedback and contiguity effects, so that regional and urban developments may also exert significant impacts on a spatial system; this is especially important because such developments may affect the competitive power of regions in a spatial system. For instance, a general national innovation policy may favour especially the areas with bigger agglomerations. The diversity in an open spatial economic system requires coordination of planning activities on a national and regional level, leading to the necessity of using multiregional economic models in an attempt to include regional profiles in national-regional development planning. This problem is also an important issue in future investigations.

Another important problem is related to the information loss by aggregating a system from a micro level to a meso or macro level, as this information loss may occur in each of the three abovementioned stages: data input, models and final profiles. Similar problems may emerge in attempts to disaggregate existing data into data of a lower spatial level. Such questions of consistent bottom-up aggregation or top-down disaggregation should also be addressed in further research in information systems.

Finally, also the related problem of multilevel (or hierarchical) approaches may be addressed in information systems, not only from an institutional point of view, but also from an analytical point of view (see also Issaev et al 1982).

As mentioned before, the key question of building up an information system is the search for a compromise between various conflicting criteria. At present, the existing systems of information (statistics and specialised operative systems) are incomplete, inconsistent and insufficiently oriented towards the needs of the analysis of geographical aspects of socio-economic development planning. This situation leads to a lack of data for models, gaps in adequate use of information for the decision making process, difficulties faced by users in making consistent decisions and implementing models. Hence, the obvious problem is: how to filful the needs of information for planning integrated regional-national developments?

The development of computerised information systems supporting regional and national planning and management, has in recent years been marked by much progress and has led to a variety of meaningful experiences, the accumulation of which could contribute greatly to the solution of the above problems. Therefore, a major aim in designing operational decision aid systems is to develop a systematic framework for an urban and regional information system in specific geographical, socio-economic and institutional settings. Such a framework is also important for the current practice of urban and regional planning, for the design of appropriate models, for the treatment of imprecise data and for the development of suitable evaluation methods.

REFERENCES

Benjamin, B., 'Statistics and Research in Urban Administration and Development', International Association for Regional and Urban Statistics, The Hague, 1976.

Blitzer, C.R., Clark, P.B. and Taylor, L. (eds), Economy-Wide Models and Development Planning, Oxford University Press, New York, 1975.

Bowman, C.T. and Kutscher, R.E., 'The Labor Market Data Base for Multiregional Models', in Adams, F.G. and Glickman, N.J. (eds), Modeling the Multiregional Economic System, D.C. Heath, Lexington, Massachusetts, 1980, pp. 57-64.

Braybrooke, D. and Lindblom, C.E., A Strategy of Decision, Free Press, New York, 1979.

Burch, J.G., Strater, F.R. and Grudnitski, G., Information Systems: Theory and Practice, John Wiley, New York, 1979.

Casley, D.J. and Lury, D.A., Data Collection in Developing Countries, Clarendon Press, Oxford, 1981.

Elfick, M (ed), 'URPIS Seven', The Australian Urban and Regional Information Systems Association, Melbourne, 1979.

Garnick, D.H., 'The Regional Statistics System', in Adams, F.G. and Glickman, N.J.(eds), Modeling the Multiregional Economic System, D.C. Heath, Lexington, Massachusetts, 1980, pp. 25-48.

Glickman, N.J., 'Impact Analysis with Regional Econometric Models', in Pleeter, S. (ed), Economic Impact Analysis, Martinus Nijhoff, Boston, 1980.

Gokhale, D.V. and Kullback, S., The Information in Contingency Tables, Dekker, New York, 1978.

Guesnier, B., 'Le Système d'Information Régional', Institute of Regional Economics, University of Poitiers, 1978 (mimeographed).

Hägerstrand, T. and Kuklinski, A.R. (eds), Information Systems for Regional Development, University of Lund, Lund, Sweden, 1981, pp. 1-37.

Hermansen, R., 'Information Systems for Regional Development Planning', in Hägerstrand, T. and Kuklinski, A.R. (eds), Information Systems for Regional Development, University of Lund, Lund, Sweden, 1971, pp. 1-37.

Hordijk, L., Jansen, H.M.A., Olsthoorn, A.A. and Vos, J.B., 'Reken- en Informatiesysteem Milieuhygiëne', Institute for Environmental Studies, Free University, Amsterdam, 1980.

Issaev, B., Nijiamp, P., Rietveld, P. and Snickars, F., Multiregional Economic Modelling: Practice and Prospect, North-Holland, Amsterdam, 1982.

Kuklinski, A.R. (ed), Regional Information and Regional Planning, Mouton, The Hague, 1974.

Litchfield, N., Kettle, P. and Whitbread, M., Evaluation in the Planning Process, Pergamon Press, Oxford, 1975.

Nijkamp, P., Multidimensional Spatial Data and Decision Analysis, John Wiley, Chichester/New York, 1979.

Nijkamp, P., 'Regional Planning and Urban Impact Analysis', in Funck, R. (ed)., Essays in Honor of Martin J. Beckmann, Series Karlsruhe Studies in Regional Science, 1982a (forthcoming).

Nijkamp, P., 'Information Systems for Multiregional Planning', Collaborative Paper CP-82-27, Free University, Amsterdam, 1982b.

Park, S.H., Mohtadi, M. and Kubursi, A., 'Errors in Regional Nonsurvey Input-output Models', Journal of Regional Science 21,no.3, 1981, pp. 321-329.

Perrin, J.C., Le Développement Régional, Presses Universitaires de France, Paris, 1975.

Pleeter, S., Economic Impact Analysis, Martinus Nijhoff, Boston, 1980.

Rees, P. and Willekens, F., 'Data Bases and Accounting Framework for IIASA's Comparative Migration and Settlement Study', CP-81-39, International Institute for Applied Systems Analysis, Laxenburg, 1981.

Sowell, T., Knowledge and Decision, Basic Books, New York, 1980.

Snickars, F., 'A Model System for Policy Impact Analysis in the Tuscany Region: A Progress Report', International Institute for Applied Systems, Laxenburg, 1982.

Torene, R. and Goettee, D., 'Towards a General Purpose Economic Data Base', in Adams, F.G. and Glickman, N.J. (eds), Modeling the Multi-regional Economic System, D.C. Heath, Lexington, Massachusetts, 1980, pp. 65-72.

11 Urban and Regional Impact Analysis in Development Planning

P. NIJKAMP AND M. VAN PELT

1. INTRODUCTION TO SPATIAL IMPACT ANALYSIS

Urban and regional planning has no self-regulating mechanism that guarantees an integrated approach to social, economic, environmental and physical development programming. The coordination of different policies at a local, regional or national level is a major challenge to and responsibility of governments in all parts of the world. In addition to institutional problems however, also analytical problems of integrating different policy fields do exist. This latter category has to be coped with in a scientifically justified manner by planners and scholarly experts.

It is clear that a unifying conceptual and operational framework for integrated policy analysis in less developed areas, taking into account the varying direct and indirect roles of governments requires a rigorous endeavour to structure development programming in a systematic and coherent manner. Housing policies, infrastructure policy, environmental management, manpower policy, migration policy, and urban renewal policies will never be effective, if a more comprehensive view of a complex spatial reality (and of policy thereon) is lacking (Bourne and Simmons 1978, Lapatra 1973).

The rapid spatial changes during the last decade (desurbanisation, locational changes due to new technologies, drastic shifts in geographical mobility patterns, etc.) have evoked the need for a more systematic analysis of spatial development patterns so as to provide more insight into the effects of various public policies (see also Nijkamp and Rietveld 1981, Van Lierop and Nijkamp 1981, Chatterjee and Nijkamp 1981). Many analyses have demonstrated that the geographical patterns of cities and regions were influenced, sometimes in a decisive way, by various public programs and policies. This awareness has led to an increased interest in urban and regional impact analyses in order to assess the consequences of various types of policies in a systematic and coherent way (see also Glickman 1979, Nijkamp 1981). Consequently, in the 1970's several countries like France, Great Britain, Sweden, Canada, the United States, and The Netherlands have tried to design impact analyses in order to judge the geographical implications (in cities and regions) of policies at various institutional levels so as to improve the efficiency and equity of policy making.

Spatial (urban and regional) impact analysis may be defined as a systematic and coherent organisation and application of established analytical techniques to assess the expected or foreseeable impacts (both intended and unintended) of various policies and programs at various institutional levels on cities and regions. Examples of such impact analyses are: the effectiveness of local and regional energy programs,

the geographical implications of new town developments, the socio-
economic effects of infrastructure policies, etc.

This way of systematically and coherently evaluating the geographical
dimensions of public policies has been induced by the increasing influence of the public sector in a complex society, the need to critically
judge the effectiveness of large amounts of public expenditures for
individual programs and policies, the general desire to use existing
information in a more efficient way (see Chapter 10), and the necessity
of understanding complex inter-governmental interactions in multi-level
institutional systems.

Various methodologies have been designed for spatial impact analysis,
ranging from traditional input-output models to large-scale urban and/or
(multi)regional models (see also Issaev et al. 1982, Pleeter 1980).
Many modelling efforts however, have not been very successful due to
lack of data, unjustified expectations, wrong levels of aggregation,
neglect of indirect effects, etc. On the other hand, there is a continuing trend in the developed countries to use modelling activities in
assessing the spatial dimensions of government policies, as the outcomes
of such models may shed more light on the coherence of policies and/or
programs and may provide an integrative frame of reference for such
policies and programs. This raises the question whether urban and
regional impact analysis may be a meaningful tool for policy analysis in
developing countries. This question will be answered in the next section by alluding to some key issues in analysing spatial development
patterns in economic less-advanced countries.

2. SPATIAL DEVELOPMENTS IN LESS DEVELOPED COUNTRIES

Information systems in the developed world are not always developed:
they may suffer from inconsistencies, gaps, unreliable data or wrong
levels of measurements. Even more severe shortcomings can be observed
regarding information systems in developing countries. Consequently, it
is often very hard to describe the factual developments, let alone the
impacts of various development policies. Yet it is important to obtain
more insight into the geographical aspects of public policies in developing countries, as otherwise no satisfactory tool exists to measure
the effectiveness of such policies.

In regard to regional developments, there is a general tendency in
many developing countries that interregional welfare discrepancies are
increasing, that rural areas are becoming less able to reach their first
take-off stage, that infrastructure facilities are often insufficient to
stimulate regional growth, that using energy costs affect the welfare
prospects of peripheral areas and that perpetuating interregional gaps
in welfare reinforce the trend toward more regional autonomy (Rondinelli
and Ruddle 1978).

Urban developments display also drastic changes: there is a strong
trend for cities in less developed countries to continue to grow, while
the number of jobs and dwellings is hardly increasing (Abu-Lughod and
Hay 1977, Bairoch 1973, Dholakia 1977, King 1976). In addition, a
dual (or segmented) labour market is emerging , while also the informal
sector is growing. Finally, the decay in urban quality-of-life caused
by pollution, congestion, and social alienation has led to severe
problems in large agglomerations in third world countries.

The spatial dynamics in developing countries has led to the need for
appropriate policy programs, such as demographic and migration policies,
rural development strategies, urban revitalisation programs, etc. In

addition, various policies have been developed without an explicit
geographical connotation, which have turned out to have strong spatial
repercussions (like labour market policies, national energy savings
programs, industrial development programs, etc.). Both rural and urban
policies in the developing world are aiming at inducing a process of
modernisation and progress by providing opportunities for economic and
social advancement (Misra and Sundaram 1978, Sinclair 1978).

The foregoing observations made clear that despite the poor information systems in developing countries, a rigorous attempt has been made
to assess all direct and indirect geographical (urban and rural) repercussions of public policies. Unfortunately, in many cases no formal
econometric models can be used, so that methods more adjusted to the
specific problems of developing countries have to be developed. This
will be the subject of the next section.

3. A METHODOLOGY FOR SPATIAL IMPACT ANALYSIS

A methodology for spatial impact analysis in developing countries should
aim at providing a systematic and coherent framework for impact assessment, while taking into account the weak database for policy analysis in
these countries.

The following general system may be helpful in developing such a
methodology:

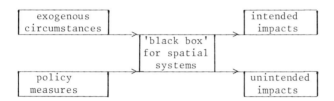

Figure 1. Illustrative system of a spatial impact analysis.

Especially the left lower block of Figure 1 is important for a spatial
impact analysis.

It is clear that Figure 1 can be extended with different policy levels,
as indicated by Figure 2. This figure illustrates that both bottom-up
and top-down policies can be dealt with in the impact system represented
in Figure 1. Furthermore, each policy level of Figure 2 may be subdivided
into policy areas (such as public facilities, infrastructure, housing,
industrial planning, energy, environmental management, etc.). Consequently, a multidimensional profile may be constructed encompassing the
various policy fields (see Figure 3). It is evident that the profile
of Figure 3 can be substituted into each policy level from Figure 2.

In conclusion, the abovementioned approach reflects, in general, the
variety, coherence, and institutional framework of the spatial system
at hand. Consequently, in this way also economic, social, energy and
environmental variables can be included as relevant elements of the system, both as policy variables in the left lower block and as targets or
impacts in the blocks on the right hand side. Policy variables may,
for instance, relate to urban housing programs, infrastructure policy,
agricultural policy, labour market policy, energy conservation programs,
etc. Impacts may, for instance, relate to changes in income levels,
distributional effects, increase in employment, decrease in pollution,

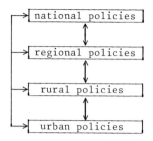

Figure 2. A multi-level policy system.

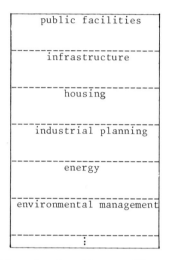

Figure 3. A multidimensional policy profile.

improvement in residential climate, improved accessibility to rural areas, etc. In this way, spatial analysis may serve several aims:

- a systematic inventory of relevant urban, regional, or rural impacts of public policies,
- an integrative approach without neglecting (potentially) important indirect (often unintended) effects,
- a consideration of spatial spillover and multitemporal effects characterising a complex spatial system,
- a consideration of multi-level policy structures.

The previous analysis has indicated that both the policy patterns and the impact pattern can be included in a multidimensional profile (see for a further introduction to multidimensional analysis, Nijkamp 1979). In this way an analytical method for taking systematic and coherent account of a wide variety of different aspects of a system is developed. If we are assuming alternative policies (denoted by $p_1, \ldots, p_N$), the respective effects on the elements of each multidimensional impact profile $c_1, \ldots, c_I$ can be included in an impact matrix (see Figure 4). Each entry of this matrix indicates the effect of a certain policy n or a certain impact on target variable i.

Having discussed now in general terms the contents of spatial (urban or regional) impacts, we now return to the systems approach which constitutes the foundation of a systematic and integrative impact analysis. In general, a system approach aims at portraying the processes and relationships in a complex system that encompasses various components which are linked together by means of functional, technical, institutional, or behavioural linkages and which can also be influenced by changing the parameters or controls from the environment outside the system itself. Currently, each compound system can be subdivided into connected subsystems. For instance, an urban-rural system can be subdivided into a transportation subsystem, a housing subsystem, an employment subsystem, an industrial subsystem, each of them linked to the other ones.

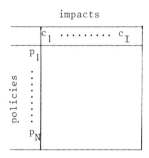

Figure 4. An impact matrix.

Thus, in an illustrative way, a compound system for spatial impact analysis may be represented in a generalised form compared to Figure 1 (see Figure 5). Thus, it is essentially a stimulus-response method, in which all policy fields translated into policy programs exert specific influences on the spatial system at hand which after some stages can be measured as final impacts. Such a systematic structure may of course be converted into a formal econometric model, but this possibility may be regarded as fairly unrealistic in the context of development programming. Yet the systematics in Figure 5 may provide an operational framework for spatial impact analysis, as will be demonstrated in the next section. Before doing so, the last column of Figure 5 will be discussed in more detail.

According to Figure 1, the impacts resulting from policy measures may be subdivided into intended and unintended effects. Other classifications of effects are: direct and indirect effects, qualitative effects, short-term and long-term effects, etc. Given the information availability in developing countries, various effects are to be measured in a qualitative (ordinal, binary, nominal, or verbal) sense. Hard modelling efforts are likely to be less successful and often even not necessary for the policy problems at hand (see also Chapter 13 of this book). Thus, the final aim of this chapter is to design, on the basis of a systemstheoretic approach, an operational methodology that is characterised by integrated coherence and easy applicability. This will be further discussed in the next section.

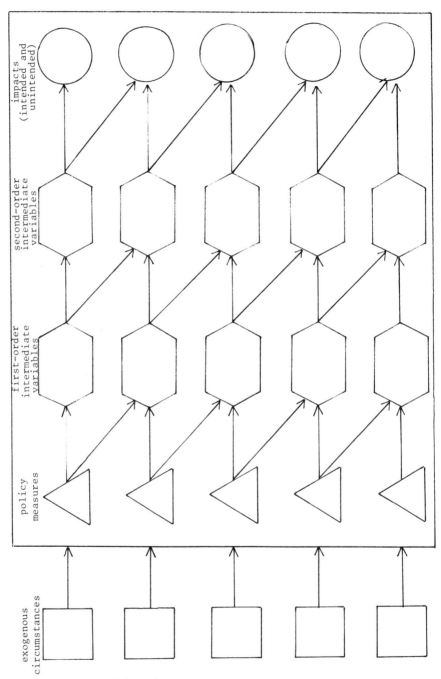

Figure 5. A multidimensional impact system.

176

4. TOWARD AN OPERATIONAL IMPACT ANALYSIS

The following conditions may be mentioned which have to be fulfilled by
a spatial impact analysis in a practical policy context (see also Nijkamp 1981):

- a focus on policy issues and instruments,
- a complete picture of all relevant impacts,
- a consistent treatment of all relevant data,
- a multidimensional representation of the system,
- a cross-regional or intertemporal comparison of effects,
- a flexible adjustment to new circumstances,
- an orientation toward the available data,
- a comprehensive picture of spatial interactions,
- a possibility for an effectiveness analysis of policy measures,
- an orientation to prevailing institutional or political structures.

With these conditions in mind, an operational spatial impact analysis
has to be designed. As mentioned already, usual econometric models are
not applicable, so that more simplified assessment systems have to be
used. In this respect, a representation of linkages in a system by means
of arrows or graphs (see Figure 5) may be very useful, as this provides
us essentially with a construction of a comprehensive spatial econometric model. Instead of 'hard' (quantitative) statements such a systematic approach may lead to 'soft' (qualitative) inferences. It goes
without saying that especially in countries with a poor information
system, the latter approach may be promising.

In general, a systems representation of a region or city may include
the following components or subsystems:

- an economic subsystem,
- a facilities subsystem,
- a demographic subsystem,
- a social subsystem.

These subsystems can be distinguished for both urban and rural areas
so as to encapsule also the urban-rural duality. An example of such a
comprehensive system for urban agglomerations is given in Figure 6.

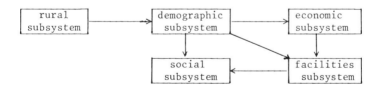

Figure 6. A spatial impact system with various subsystems.

The various subsystems can be further subdivided into interactions
between the constituent elements. For instance, the demographic subsystem can be represented as in Figure 7.

In a similar way, all other subsystems can be depicted (van Pelt 1982).
The degree of complexity of these subsystems will depend on the policy
objectives at hand and on the data availability. Each of these subsystems can be encompassed by Figure 6, so that ultimately a comprehensive,
but comprehensible picture of the spatial system concerned emerges.

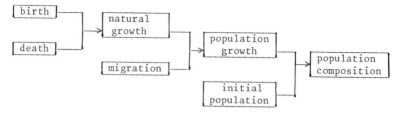

Figure 7. A simple representation of the demographic subsystem.

It should be emphasised that the successive subsystems are not closed. There are strong mutual interactions between all subsystems. Examples are:

- a rise in population affects the situation on the labour market,
- more urban in-migration requires more facilities and dwellings,
- more medical facilities influence the birth and death rates,
- high income differences cause more geographical mobility.

Thus these linkages have to be included as well. This may lead alto-gether to a fairly complex systems model, but this representation is a necessary condition for understanding the complex impacts of public policies.

The next step is now to indicate where (i.e. at which component of the abovementioned system) public policies will have a major impact. For instance, educational policy will have a first and major influence on the facilities subsystem.

Then the following logical step to be undertaken is to assess as accurately as possible the direct (first-order) effects of the policy or program at hand. During the first stage, many impacts can be gauged in quantitative terms. After the assessment of the direct effects, the second-order effects have to be estimated by just following the various arrows in the systems framework. Here again no formal models are necessary, but it may of course be problematic to assess all second-order impacts in quantitative terms. If this is not possible, also qualitative inferences may be drawn (like ordinal rankings, verbal statements such as 'good, better, best', nominal or binary information, probabilistic state-ments, etc.). This procedure can be repeated for the third- and higher-order impacts, so that the final impact matrix (see Figure 4) may con-tain both quantitative and qualitative information.

In conclusion, the arrow scheme of a system model may provide a co-herent and integrated picture of a complex spatial system and is suitable for a qualitative impact assessment in the case of weak information sys-tems. This approach may also be helpful in a coordinated national, regional, rural, and urban policy framework. An extensive empirical application can be found in Nijkamp and Van Pelt (1983).

Finally, it should be noted that such systems approaches can also be extended with scenario analysis and multicriteria evaluation analysis, so that spatial impact analysis may provide a useful contribution to an operational policy analysis in developing countries.

REFERENCES

Abu-Lughod, J. and Hay, R., Third World Urbanization, Maaroefa Press, Chicago, Illinois, 1977.

Bairoch, P., Urban Unemployment in Developing Countries, ILO, Geneva, 1973.

Bourne, L.S. and Simmons, J.W., Systems of Cities, Oxford University Press, New York, 1978.

Chatterjee, L. and Nijkamp, P. (eds), Urban Problems and Economic Development, Sijthoff and Noordhoff, Alphen a/d Rijn, Netherlands, 1981.

Dholakia, J., Unemployment and Employment Policy in India, Sterling, New Delhi, 1977.

Glickman, N.J. (ed), The Urban Impacts of Federal Policies, Johns Hopkins Press, Baltimore, Maryland, 1979.

Issaev, B., Nijkamp, P., Rietveld P. and Snickars, F., Multiregional Economic Modeling: Practice and Prospect, North-Holland, Amsterdam, 1982.

King, A.D., Colonial Urban Development, Routledge and Kegan Paul, London, 1976.

Lapatra, J.W., Applying the Systems Approach to Urban Development, Hutchinson and Ross, Dowden, U.K., 1973.

Van Lierop, W.F.J. and Nijkamp, P. (eds), Locational Developments and Urban Planning, Sijthoff and Noordhoff, Alphen a/d Rijn, Netherlands, 1981.

Misra, R.P. and Sundaram, K.V., Regional Policies in Nigeria, India and Brazil, Mouton, The Hague, 1978.

Nijkamp, P., 'Urban impact analysis in a spatial context', Research Memorandum 1981-5, Dept. of Economics, Free University, Amsterdam, 1981.

Nijkamp, P. and Van Pelt, M., 'Spatial Impact Analysis for Developing Countries; a Framework and a Case Study', Research Memorandum 1983-1, Dept. of Economics, Free University, Amsterdam, 1983.

Nijkamp, P. and Rietveld, P. (eds), Cities in Transition, Sijthoff and Noordhoff, Alphen a/d Rijn, Netherlands, 1981.

Van Pelt, M., 'Stedelijke Effect Analyse in de Derde Wereld', Master's Thesis, Dept. of Economics, Erasmus University, Rotterdam, 1982.

Pleeter, S. (ed), Economic Impact Analysis, Martinus Nijhoff, Boston, 1980.

Rondinelli, D.A. and Ruddle, K., Urbanization and Rural Development, Praeger, New York, 1978.

Sinclair, S.W., Urbanization and Labour Markets in Developing Countries, Croom Helm, 1978.

12 Regional and Interregional Accounting Systems for Development Planning Under Conditions of Limited Information

G. J. D. HEWINGS

1. INTRODUCTION

Some years ago Walter Isard coined the expression 'Anglo-Saxon bias' to describe the lack of interest and attention devoted to space by economists in the development of economic theory. It has been adequately demonstrated that Isard's early proselytising has achieved the desired results in that spatial economic theory (broadly conceived) has become an accepted part of the research agendas of the disciplines which participate in the field of regional science. However, some lingering 'bias' still exists and remains to be purged from the system: in this case, the bias lies within regional science as much as it does in those disciplines whose orientation is towards the analysis of the developing world. In the vast literature of regional science, one would be hard pressed to find more than a handful of articles dealing with the applications of regional science techniques of analysis to problems of spatial planning in developing countries. Concomitantly, one has to search equally diligently through the development economics literature to find issues of spatial planning addressed explicitly in models and policy analyses.

Hence, there exists a major gap in our understanding of issues related to the spatial development of a substantial segment of the world's population: the work reported here extends some discussion initiation in Hewings (1982) by providing more specific examples of model building and their application under conditions of limited information. The concerns of spatial planning in the developing country context are reviewed briefly in the next section together with a sample of some of the analyses and methodology used to date. Thereafter, some analysis, centering on the Sri Lankan model and a two-region simulated disaggregation of that economy will be presented. These methods will be elaborated and extended to the multiregion case, although without empirical implementation. Finally, some comments will be offered.

2. REGIONAL ANALYSIS IN DEVELOPING ECONOMIES

Regional analysis has long been characterised by the way it has successfully borrowed theory and techniques developed at the national and international levels and transformed them for application at smaller spatial scales. At the national level, a great deal of lateral transference of models and theory from the developed to the developing world has been accepted. On the other hand, at the regional level, there appears to have been little movement in this direction. Part of the reason for this may be a misperception that there are no major regional problems in the developing world (or that these issues, if they exist, are dwarfed in magnitude by national issues). Another explanation may be a certain degree of skepticism about the utility of regional science techniques in contexts of stages of development far below those in the developed world. Since the sample from which one may draw to arrive at such a conclusion is extremely limited, one might suggest that the question cannot be answered at this stage. There is no doubt that the large multi-sector multiregion models that such skeptics envision being constructed in developing countries are out of the question: the point that should be made is that our ability to undertake such models in the developed world is of only recent vintage (see Isard and Anselin 1982).[1]

While there are many scholars exhibiting extreme caution about modelling in developing countries (see Gilbert 1976), there are others such as Higgins (1973) and Brookfield (1975) who have come to view spatial issues as a necessary and integral part of overall national development planning. Perhaps, the greatest source of interest occurs in the manifestation of concerns with income distribution and marked concentrations of high or low average per capita incomes in regions within a country. The almost synergistic relationship between the structure of production and the distribution of income needs, it is suggested, a third dimension, the mapping of these characteristics and their interactions into a space-time framework. Capturing these interactions is not an impossible task but it does pose some particularly difficult problems of appropriate modelling systems. One is caught between the twin dangers of the demands for model simplicity and the need to handle the possibility of rather unstable relationships, not to mention the need for conceptualisation within a dynamic framework.

Some of these issues will be addressed in later sections of this paper. The issue to be discussed here is the need for regional analysis in the developing countries and the characteristics of models appropriate to meet these needs. In the discussion which follows, some examples will be provided, where appropriate, from work already undertaken.

One might wish to venture the notion that the rationale for attention to regional problems should be no different no matter what the stage of national development. While the argument has some merit, one would point to Williamsons' (1965) work which hypothesised an inverted 'U' relationship between the level of development and some index of regional disparities. Ceteris paribus, one would expect regional disparities to appear most prominently in countries at an intermediate level of development. The exact nature of the relationship between regional disparities and national development and the associated policy implications have provided a rich source of speculation. In particular, it should be noted that, inter alia, regions in developing economies are likely to be far more open than their counterparts in the developed world: hence, external dependence (in terms of both interregional and international) is probably much higher. The implications here are two-fold: first, external shocks are likely to have a much greater impact on regions and, secondly, interregional flows are probably a much more visible component of a single region's trading relationships. This will be true not only in terms of flows of goods and services but also in terms of flows of funds - wages and salaries, dividends, and taxes and transfers. While there has been increasing recognition that single region models have limited utility, this would appear to be a statement even more directly applicable in developing economies. Hence, the thrust of this line of argument is the proposition that any modelling system should, as far as possible, be constructed within the context of a multi-region system.

Of all the desired characteristics associated with appropriate models discussed in Hewings (1982), the interaction between the production sectors and the household sectors stands out as one of the most important elements. The link here is to the issue of income distribution, an issue which has not been a prominent feature of the vast majority of regional analytical models in the regional science literature. (Exceptions would be the work of Ledent and Gordon 1980, Schinnar 1976, 1977, Madden and Batey 1980, Batey and Madden, 1981 and Beyers 1980). As a result, the standard models of regional analysis need to be expanded, in some cases rather dramatically, to capture the important interrelationships which have often been 'lost' through aggregation over sector or space.

Figure 1 provides a view of some of the major approaches to modelling space-time interdependence: these classes of models are well known and will not be reviewed here. Since none of them alone, contains many of the desired features, it is felt that integrated models may be more appropriate. The type of integration which will form the basis for the discussion in this paper is the social accounting system (SAM). Originally proposed by Stone and associates many years ago, it has experienced a considerable degree of rejuvenation under the aegis of Pyatt and others at the World Bank (see Pyatt and Roe 1977). Figure 2 shows a simple one region social accounting system.

In this system, all the major aggregates of the macro accounting system are present but with two discernible differences. First, a great deal more detail is provided - for example, different types of consumers (classified according to income level or location, i.e., urban or rural) and, secondly, the interactions between the accounts are featured prominently. With such a system, it is possible to track the complex direct and indirect repercussions of policy decisions on all segments of the regional economy. Extended to a multi-region system, it would, of course, be possible to track the importance of different types of interregional linkages and flows and their associated feedback effects on the growth and development of individual regions.

The importance of these interregional linkages may be illustrated by reference to Figure 3. In the Muda region of Malaysia, Bell and Hazell (1980) developed a regional SAM in which the semi-input-output method pioneered by Tinbergen (1966) was incorporated. The complete system was used to measure the ex post facto impact of a large irrigation project on the region's economy. The summary which follows abstracts from Bell and Hazell's conclusions. Essentially, the project achieved its major goal of increasing regional income since it enabled the farm community to double and in some cases to triple crops in locations where only one crop per year had been grown previously. However, had one of the objectives of the project been the reduction of the disparities in levels of income between the Muda region and the rest of the country, the project would have yielded potentially conflicting results, depending on the time at which the evaluation was undertaken. In the short run, the disparities decreased through a combination of substantial contributions to regional income from the construction of the project and the increases in crop yields. However, in the long run, higher incomes became associated with higher marginal propensity to consume non-regionally produced goods with the result that non-regional (especially urban) incomes rose in association with the expenditure by the farm communities on goods and services produced in urban areas. Hence, disparities, once again, may have begun to widen. Obviously, it is impossible to generalise from this one case study but it is clear that there may be many unintended effects of projects in small very open regions. De Vries (1979) has commented

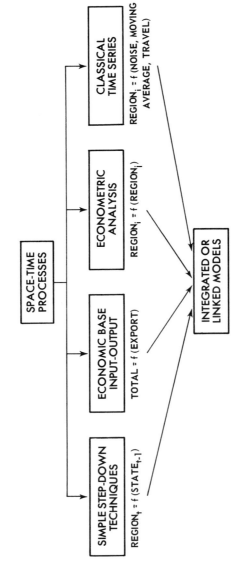

Figure 1. Approaches to Measuring and Analysing Space-Time Interdependence

	FACTORS OF PRODUCTION	INSTITUTION CURRENT ACCOUNT	PRODUCTION ACTIVITY	INTERREGIONAL & FOREIGN ACCOUNTS
FACTORS OF PRODUCTION — Labour · Capital · Firms			(Value added in production)	(Net factor incomes from other regions and rest of the world)
INSTITUTIONS — Households · Government	(Gross Profits) (Wages, Salaries)	(Transfers and taxes)		(Transfers from outside regions)
PRODUCTION ACTIVITY — Agriculture · Manufacturing · Services		(Consumer expenditures on regional goods)	(Interindustry transactions)	(Exports of goods outside the region)
INTERREGIONAL & FOREIGN ACCOUNTS		(Consumer expenditures on imports)	(Imports of intermediate goods)	

Figure 2.   Single Region Social Accounting Scheme

Note   :   Entries in the matrix provide examples of some of the transactions between accounts

Source :   After Pyatt and Roe 1977

185

STAGE	ACTIVITY	INCOME EFFECT	CONVERGENCE?
1	Project Construction	Increase Local Income	yes
2	Project Completion	Increase Local Income	yes
.	.	.	
.	.	.	
.	.	.	
3	Increased farm yields from irrigation	Increased Local Income	yes
.	.	.	
.	.	.	
.	.	.	
4	Increased spending by farmers on urban goods	Increased Non-local Income	no

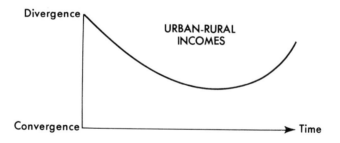

Figure 3. Spatial Impact of an Agricultural Project in a Less Developed Regional Economy.
(Based on a study of the Muda, region of Malaysia by Bell and Hazell)

similarly in the context of the role of small and medium sized manufacturing firms in the industrialisation process:

> Distribution of income and regional development have important
> consequences for small and medium sized enterprise (SME) devel-
> opment. As is well known, an increase in the income of the
> poorer segments of the population may disproportionately in-
> crease demand for labour intensive products in the SME sector.
> Similarly, regional developments may strengthen smaller local
> markets and benefit SME's. But little empirical evidence has
> been accumulated in this area. On the other hand, in the ab-
> sence of income redistribution, assistance to small scale enter-
> prises may lower the price of inputs into capital intensive
> industry to the benefit of higher income consumers; hence, in
> the absence of accompanying policies to assist the poorer seg-
> ments of the population, 'interaction' between large and small
> scale industry may primarily benefit the former.

A further point should be made about SAM system: like the input-output
structures around which they are built, they do rely on some very strong
assumptions about coefficient stability and linearity in relationships.
With large-scale projects impacting small, very open regions, one might
wish to question the reliability of such assumptions. It is in this
context that the role of identifying important parameters provides a
feasible alternative for dealing with such difficulties: these issues
will be addressed below.

The role of migration assumes no less importance in developing economies than elsewhere: the physical removal of individuals from one region
to another may set up a complex structure of interregional flows and/or
goods and services initiated by the remittance of all or part of a pay-
check to a family who may not have migrated. Hence, levels of income in
some regions may be very dependent on non-local sources and these interactions would be difficult to trace without a system of accounts. In
most models which have been developed to date, variants on the Harris-
Todaro framework for handling migration appear to have been used (see
for example, Krueger et al. 1981, Dervis et al. 1982). While this
might possibly be the best model for handling essentially rural to urban
migration flows, it does not take into account the complexity of the
region to region migration flows. In this context, one might wish to
appeal to some of the notions developed in the standard literature for
assistance: for example, the notion of channelisation of flows, condi-
tioned information emanating from friends and family who have previously
migrated to another region, might prove to be a useful construct. The
Harris-Todaro model does have the advantage of some wider applicability
and empirical testing in developing countries. Incorporation of this
framework into the model would require a certain amount of quasi-dynamics
since the model postulates, in its simplest form, that migration will
continue until there is equality between the rural wage and the expected
urban wage. (See the incorporation in the model for Korea by Adelman and
Robinson, 1978).

There are many other issues which would quickly move the model from a
static form to one attempting to handle dynamic changes - the issues of
the stability of consumption expenditures by sector and region as per
capita income rises, the problems of interregional and international
flows of capital into and out of the regional economies and the complex
interrelationships between income and savings allocations over time
would all require attention. Some models, developed to date, have
attempted to handle only a small subset of these issues since the data

problems often preclude a great deal of elaboration beyond a static accounting system. In particular, the model of Goreux and Manne (1973) for Mexico, Prastacos (1981) for Greece, Bigsten (1980) for Kenya have incorporated some spatial dimensions to the structuring of the intranational economic system. Waardenburg (1975) has tried to incorporate a Tinbergen system into a multi-level framework and their ideas are suggestive of some of the ways in which the model's sophistication in terms of data requirements could be reduced without seriously compromising the utility of the analytical framework for policy decision making.

In addition, a number of other studies have attempted to approach the problem of spatial disparities from a number of different aspects. For example, Faukert, Skolka and Maton (1981) explored the relationship between income distribution, the structure of the economy and employment distribution through case studies of the Philippines, Iran, Republic of Korea and Malaysia. Using the last named country, Mazumdar (1981) has focussed on the urban labour market and its relationship to income distribution while Meerman (1979) tried to ascertain just who benefits from public expenditure in Malaysia. On a more conceptual level, Hermansen (1975), Mohan (1979), and Van Staveren and Van Dusseldorp (1980) have explored the utility of a number of models and frameworks for regional planning.

In the next section, some experimental work will be reviewed which approaches the problem of data parsimony from a slightly different perspective. Thereafter, some extensions to the multi-regional case will be presented drawing on an entropy formulation.

3. MODELLING UNDER CONDITIONS OF LIMITED DATA

In the development of many regional models, there has been some considerable debate about the advantages of survey versus nonsurvey techniques. This literature is extensive and well-trodden and will not be reviewed here: the particular approach adopted here provides a compromise between the excessive demands of an all-survey based model and the questionable accuracy of a nonsurvey model. The analysis draws its inspiration from some early work by Sherman and Morrison (1950) which was utilised by Bullard and Sebald (1977) and, subsequently, Hewings (1981) and Hewings and Romanos (1981). The procedure begins by assuming that in any matrix representation of an economic system, it is highly unlikely that all of the elements in that system will be important - important in the sense that changes in their values will lead to 'disruptions' throughout the rest of the system. In essence, the procedure suggests that some elements in the system, by virtue of their size and/or their position contribute significant links to the functioning of the total economic system. If one is able to analyse these elements, then an alternative to the survey/nonsurvey debate will be possible - namely, a survey approach in which data is collected only for the important elements in the system.

Input-output literature, early work along these lines was undertaken by Evans (1954) and, more recently, by Byron (1978) within a SAM system. The particular algorithm used for the current analysis is contained in the Appendix. Using the SAM developed for Sri Lanka by Pyatt and Roe (1977), the analysis was performed for various parts of the system and for a hypothetical two-region model developed from the national model.

Pyatt and Roe (1977) provide two solution methods for a SAM system: in the first case, the complete matrix, such as the one shown in Figure 2,

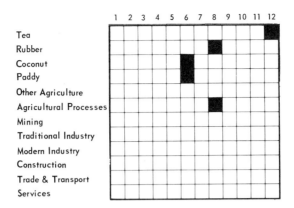

Figure 4. Inverse Important Parameters for the Interindustry Sectors of the Sri Lankan Economy

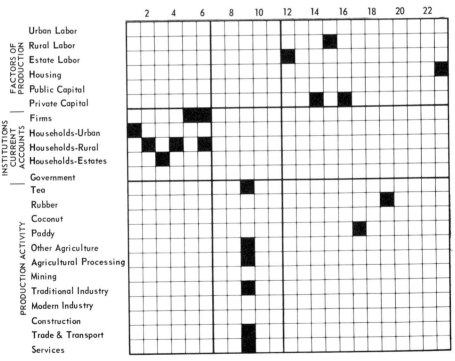

Figure 5. Inverse Important Parameters for the Complete Social Accounting System, Sri Lanka

189

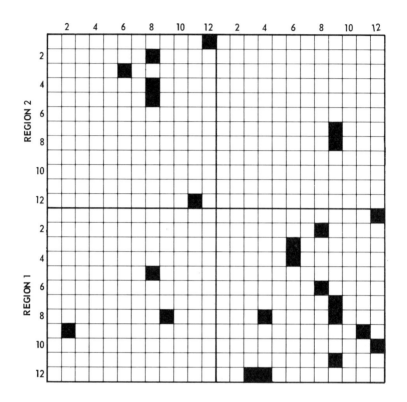

Figure 6. Inverse Important Parameters for the Interindustry Interregional Model

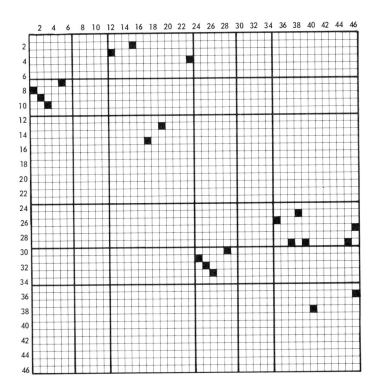

Figure 7. Inverse Important Parameters for the Two-Region SAM

is used to obtain the solution:

$$X = (I - A)^{-1} Y \qquad\qquad (1)$$

where A may be defined as T_{ij}/X_j .
Alternatively, matrix partitioning procedures may be used to obtain the
closed form solution:

$$X = M_3 M_2 M_1 Y \qquad\qquad (2)$$

where M_i represents a matrix multiplier which may, for example, contain all the interactions between the industries. The former procedure,
using the generalised inverse, was used in this analysis.

Figure 4 shows the inverse important parameters for the interindustry
section: note that they are small in number, reflecting the rather open
and unconnected nature of the Sri Lankan economy. When we expand the
analysis to include the complete SAM, the location of important parameters changes rather dramatically (see Figure 5). The greatest concentrations are in the value added submatrix (T_{13}) and the consumption
expenditure submatrix (T_{32}). The concentrations in the institution/
factor submatrices reflect the fact that most of these are pure accounting transfers with associated very large coefficients. The results of
this analysis confirm the findings of Hewings and Romanos (1981) in a
regional study of Greece and, to a great extent, the work of Bell and
Hazell (1980) alluded to in an earlier section.

The national data was divided into two somewhat arbitrary 'regions':
the data is shown in the Appendix. Figure 6 shows the important parameters for the interindustry portion of the system: the higher density
in region 2 reflects a higher concentration of industries with stronger
ties to the rest of the industrial system. The interregional linkages
do not prove to be very important – but bear in mind that this data may
not be representative of interregional connectivities in developing economies. Finally, in Figure 7, the important parameters are shown for
the full two-region SAM – again using a generalised inverse solution.
In this case, the interregional flows on any account fail to assume any
importance while there appears to be a diminshed role for consumer expenditures but not for value added. The result from this analysis is
very inconclusive and suggests that some 'real-world' data is necessary
before any definitive statement could be made.

However, there are some important issues which need to be resolved:
first how can the important parameters be identified at the regional
level without prior collection of data for all elements in the system?
On this issue, we have made little progress: using the national table
as a guide, did not yield very promising results in one study (Hewings
and Romanos 1981). Secondly, the analysis operates by changing one
parameter at a time: an alternative might be to adopt the procedure
suggested by Page, Gilmore and Hewings (1981) in which column sensitivity
in a system was evaluated. In developing economies under conditions of
rising per capita income (as a result of a project), significant changes
in one of two elements in the system could trigger significant changes
in another element which, alone, might not have been considered inverse
important.

These issues are currently being investigated and while their lack of
resolution does limit the wide applicability of the technique to de novo
developments of regional models, it does provide a useful guide to the
focus of attention on the collection of data for updating the model for

purposes of project monitoring or <u>ex post</u> evaluation.

4. THE MULTIREGIONAL APPROACH

Thus far, the analysis has been conducted in a single region and a two-region context. When one moves to a multiregional model, the incorporation of limited survey data has to be handled in a somewhat different manner. In essence, the approach would involve the allocation of major aggregates from the national level to the regional level, supplemented by the survey data. In the discussion which follows, the top down (national → regional) disaggregation procedure will be presented: the suggestions which follow draw heavily on the thinking of Boyce and Hewings (1980), Kim et al. (1982), Hewings and Syversen (1982), and Hewings and Lee (1982).

Table 1 shows the necessary notation: in the discussion of the procedure, only sectoral detail will be shown for the interindustry matrix. All other submatrices will be collapsed into vectors.

It is assumed that a social accounting system is available for the nation as a whole: the procedure then, is to allocate the major accounts, shown in Table 1, across the set of regions. Define the following formulation:

$$\text{MIN } Z = \sum_{irs} \sum Y_i^{rs} \ln Y_i^{rs} + \sum_{ijrs} \sum X_{ij}^{rs} \ln X_{ij}^{rs} \qquad (3)$$

subject to:

$$\sum_{js} X_{ij}^{rs} + \sum_s Y_i^{rs} = X_i^{r1} + M_i^{r1} - E_i^r \qquad \forall i,r \qquad (4)$$

$$\sum_{ir} X_{ij}^{rs} = X_j^{s\cdot} - V_j^s \qquad \forall j,s \qquad (5)$$

$$\sum_{rs} X_{ij}^{rs} = X_{ij} \qquad \forall i,j \qquad (6)$$

$$\sum_{rs} Y_i^{rs} = Y_i \qquad \forall i \qquad (7)$$

$$\sum_{ijs} c_i^r X_{ij}^{rs} + \sum_{is} c_i^r Y_i^{rs} \leq c^r \qquad \forall r \qquad (8)$$

$$X_{ij}^{rs} \geq 0 \; ; \; Y_i^{rs} \geq 0 \qquad (9)$$

Table 1
Notation for Solution to the Multiregion Problem
Within a Social Accounting System

X_{ij}^{rs}	intermediate deliveries from sector i in region r to sector j in region s
Y_i^{rs}	final demand deliveries from sector i in region r to region s
$X_i^{r\cdot}$	gross production of sector i in region r
$X_j^{s\cdot}$	gross production of sector j in region s
X_{ij}	intermediate deliveries from sector i to j
Y_i	final demand, excluding exports, for sector i
V_i^r	value added in sector i in region r
M_i^r	imports from abroad to sector i in region r
E_i^r	exports outside the country from sector i in region r

The objective function, equation (3) is a standard entropy formulation defined over both interregional intermediate and final flows. The constraint set (equation (4) through (9)) provides the necessary accounting balances. Equation (4) is the macro accounting balances: equation (5) defines the column sum constraint on intermediate flows for each sector in each region. Total intermediate flows from sectors i to j over all regions and to final demand are constrained by equations (6) and (7). Equation (8) provides a cost constraint on flows between sectors and regions while the usual nonnegativity constraints are shown in equation (9). The Lagrangian function, L, is defined as:

$$L = \sum_{irs}\sum Y_i^{rs}\,\ln Y_i^{rs} + \sum_{ijrs}\sum X_{ij}^{rs}\ln X_{ij}^{rs} + \alpha_i^{r\cdot}[\sum_{js}\sum X_{ij}^{rs} + \sum_s Y_i^{rs} - (X_i^{r\cdot}+M_i^{r\cdot}-E_i^r)]$$

$$+ \beta_1^{s\cdot}[\sum_{ir}\sum X_{ij}^{rs} - (X_j^{s\cdot} - V_j^s)] + \alpha_{ij}[\sum_{rs}\sum X_{ij}^{rs} - X_{ij}] + \delta_i[\sum_{rs}\sum Y_i^{rs} - Y_i]$$

$$+ \varepsilon_r[\sum_{ijs}\sum c_i^r X_{ij}^{rs} + \sum_{is}c_i^r Y_i^{rs} - c^r] \tag{10}$$

Given the usual necessary and sufficient conditions for stationary points, we have the following solutions:

$$X_{ij}^{rs} = \exp[-(X_i^{r\cdot} + \beta_j^{s\cdot} + \alpha_{ij} + \varepsilon_r c_i^r)]$$

$$= A_i^r B_j^s C_{ij} \exp(-\varepsilon_r c_i^r) \tag{11}$$

where A_i^r, B_j^s and C_{ij} are defined in terms of their associated Lagrangians.

194

Similarly:

$$Y_i^{rs} = \exp[-(\alpha_i^{r\cdot} - \delta_i - \varepsilon_r c_i^{\cdot r})]$$

$$= A_i^r D_i \exp(-\varepsilon_r c_i^r) \tag{12}$$

Through substitution, we find that

$$-\alpha_i^{r\cdot} = \ln \frac{X_i^{r\cdot} + M_i^{r\cdot} - E_i^r}{X_i + M_i - E_i} \tag{13}$$

$$-\beta_j^{s\cdot} = \ln \frac{X_j^{s\cdot} - V_j^s}{X_j - V_j} \tag{14}$$

$$-\sigma_{ij} = \ln X_{ij} \tag{15}$$

$$\delta_i = \frac{Y_i}{M} \tag{16}$$

If additional information is available for specific intersectoral relations, these may be incorporated in the model along the lines suggested
by Matuszewski et al (1964) and more recently by Hewings and Syversen
(1982).

5. CONCLUSIONS

While a number of issues have been addressed in this chapter, the major
objective has been to show that the existence of limited data at the
subnational level should not preclude the design and implementation of
social accounting matrix systems at this spatial scale. Unfortunately,
the absence of such systems precludes definitive comment about their
applicability and utility - except in a speculative manner. However,
the problems of project selection, project monitoring and project evaluation require there to be some framework in which these discussions can
be evaluated. The complexity of interregional linkages and, perhaps,
their instability, warrant careful attention to ensure that projects
selected for funding in the hope of contributing to nationally articulated goals do not increase the ability of that same economy to achieve
contributions towards goals associated with interregional equity. While
Kuyvenhoven's (1976, 1978, 1980) attempt to link social accounting systems and project evaluation methodology of the Little-Mirrles kind has
been criticised by Bell and Devaranjan (1980), it does represent the
kind of step which ought to follow in regional analysis.
    Notwithstanding these advances, one should note that the evidence
collected thus far would seem to suggest that the greatest need in
analytical modelling at the regional level in developing countries
would be in the linkages between various types of migration processes,
disposition of wage and salary income (in terms of sectoral and regional
purchases and/or savings) and the impact on the production system.
Following Pyatt and Roe (1977), one should also recognise that changes
in the structure of the production system will, in turn, change the
various forces conditioning the migration processes. These linkages

assume considerable importance in regions in which external forces of
funds generated by former residents may contribute substantial amounts
to regional incomes. Data collection of these types of flows has not,
typically, been a feature of many countries' regional statistics. If
extensive data collection is precluded, it is suggested that far more
time and effort be devoted to migration/wage and salary disposition/
income and expenditure patterns than on developing, in great detail, the
types of models characterising regional analysis in the developed world.
In this context, the focus on the developing world, with its major concerns of income distribution inter alia, may provide an important
stimulus towards a reorientation of regional models in other parts of
the world. This should prove to be an exciting area for development in
regional science.

NOTES

[1] In some cases, there is more data available in some developing
countries for more sophisticated models than in the developed world.
In Korea, for example, an interregional commodity flow matrix for
1978 is available for 18 commodities and 100 regions. (see Kim et
al. 1982).

APPENDIX

The identification of inverse important parameters follows the procedure developed by Sherman and Morrison (1950) idea by Bullard and Sebald (1977). The procedure is as follows:

$$\tilde{b}_{mn} = b_{mn} + \left[\frac{b_{mi} \cdot b_{jn} \cdot \delta a_{ij}}{1 - b_{ji} \cdot \delta r_{ij}} \right] \qquad (1)$$

where

$$\tilde{b}_{mn} \ \varepsilon \ \tilde{B} = (I - \tilde{A})^{-1} \qquad (2)$$

$$b_{mn} \ \varepsilon \ B = (I - A)^{-1} \qquad (3)$$

$$\tilde{A} = A \ \{\text{except that one element, } a_{ij}, (\varepsilon A) = \delta a_{ij} (\varepsilon \tilde{A})\} \qquad (4)$$

The decision rule suggests that the coefficient a_{ij} is _inverse important_ if:

$$b_{mi} \cdot b_{jn} \geq \beta/100 \left[\frac{1 - b_{ji} \delta a_{ij}}{\delta a_{ij}} \right] b_{mn} \qquad (5)$$

where

$$\delta a_{ij} = \left[\frac{\alpha}{100} \right] a_{ij} \qquad (6)$$

The values of α and β are degined _a priori_ and reflect the degree to which changes in the a_{ij}'s cause changes in coefficients in the associated Leontief inverse. In this analysis, these values were set at 20 and 30 respectively.

197

REGION I

Factors | Institutions | Production

Factors · Institutions · Production

Factors   Institutions   Production

```
                                                          1.      126.    0.      1.
                                                          3.      101.    0.      1.
                                                          0.      8.      0.      23.
                        0.      0.                        0.      380.    0.      24.
                        1.      0.      0.      0.         0.      43.     0.      1.
                        3.      1.      0.      0.         2.      60.     0.      19.
                                                          5.              0.      23.
                                                          7.                      3.
                                                                                  8.

                                        0.                0.      182.    0.      1.
                        0.      8.      0.                0.      198.    0.      1.
                        8.      14.     2.      0.        0.      7.      0.      8.
                        14.     17.     0.      0.        0.      0.      0.      51.
                        17.     19.     2.      11.       11.     587.    52.     45.
                        19.     2.      5.      11.       1.              0.      7.
                        2.      26.     22.     1.        10.
                        5.      8.      21.     10.       0.
                                                          1.

                20.     256.    0.      0.                22.     0.      0.      0.
                85.     364.    1.      23.     2.        43.     0.      0.      2.
                0.      4.      2.      24.     0.         2.      0.      0.      6.
                140.    1.      4.      12.     0.         8.      0.      0.      17.
                200.    0.      6.      16.     4.         286.    30.     55.     72.
                214.    0.      2.      0.      0.                 31.             2.
                31.             5.                         0.
                0.              22.                        0.
                306.            21.                        0.
                150.            1.                         0.

                4.      144.    0.      0.      1.        76.     0.      0.      1.
                23.     55.     2.      35.     2.        60.     2.      1.      1.
                0.      60.     1.      0.      0.         1.      0.      2.      1.
                106.    1.      1.      2.      1.        61.     12.     1.      296.
                56.     50.     1.      29.     7.        397.    37.     296.    101.
                1.              0.                                8.      101.    1.
                83.             1.                                7.
                14.             1.                                18.
                0.                                                0.
                152.
                88.

                                                          1.      21.     0.      0.
                18.     2.      6.      0.      1.         2.      35.     2.      2.
                26.     1.      9.      0.      2.         0.      0.      0.      0.
                0.      0.      325.    0.      0.         1.      2.      12.     14.
                0.      28.     301.    0.      0.         7.      29.     37.     3.
                0.      25.     1.      0.      0.                 8.      57.     4.
                78.     0.      53.     0.                         7.      19.
                        5.      125.    0.                        18.     23.
                        8.      0.      0.                        0.      3.
                        17.     202.    1.                                8.
                        10.     225.    1.

                                                          0.      19.     0.      0.
                        2.      0.      0.                 0.      32.     0.      0.
                        0.      0.      3.                 0.      6.      0.      0.
                        3.      0.      0.                 0.      10.     0.      30.
                        71.     0.      2.                 0.      85.     48.     395.
                        83.     0.      21.                                       19.
                        22.     0.      11.                                       20.
                        53.     3.      2.                                        0.
                        0.                                                        14.
                        51.                                                       57.
                        132.                                                      2.

                387.                                                       81.
                202.                            0.      0.                 256.    0.      66.
                926.            0.      260.                               8.      0.      8.
                                        81.                                -8.    0.      0.
                500.    117.            2.                                 766.    0.      5.
                260.    0.              184.                                       0.      35.
                1186.   0.                                                                 0.
                10.     0.                                                                 1.
                0.                                                                         1.

                66.     0.                                         12.     0.      0.      23.
                67.     1472.                           820.       295.    0.      0.      0.
                162.    0.                                          0.     0.      0.      0.
                15.     0.                                         95.     0.      14.     14.
                0.                                                         0.      0.      0.
                                                                          0.      3.      3.
                                                                          0.      4.      4.

                0.      214.                                        1.      2.     0.      0.
                0.      0.                                          9.      39.    0.      0.
                0.      0.                                          2.      43.    0.      3.
                0.      0.                                          0.      0.     0.      0.
                                                                  41.      66.    2.      2.
                                                                                  11.     21.
                                                                                  4.      11.
                                                                                  1.      2.
```

199

REFERENCES

Adelman, I. and Robinson, S., Income Distribution Policy in Developing Countries, University Press, Stanford, 1978.

Batey, P.W.J. and Madden, M., 'Demographic-Economic Forecasting within an Activity-Commodity Framework: Some Theoretical Considerations and Empirical Results', Environment and Planning A, (13), 1981, pp. 1067-1083.

Bell, C. and Davarajan, S., 'Semi-input-output and Shadow Prices: A Critical Note', Oxford Bulletin of Economics and Statistics, (42), 1980, pp. 251-256.

Bell, C. and Hazell, P., 'Measuring the Indirect Effects of an Agricultural Investment Project on Its Surrounding Region', American Journal of Agricultural Economics, (62), 1980, pp. 75-86.

Beyers, W.B., 'Migration and the Development of Multiregional Economic Systems', Economic Geography, (56), 1980, pp. 320-324.

Bigsten, A., Regional Inequality and Development, Gower, Aldershot, 1980.

Boyce, D.E. and Hewings, G.J.D., 'Interregional Commodity Flow, Input-Output and Transportation Modelling: An Entropy Formulation', Paper presented at the First World Regional Science Congress, Cambridge, Massachusetts, 1980.

Brookfield, H., Interdependent Development, Methuen, London, 1975.

Bullard, C.W. and Sebald, A.V., 'Effect of Parametric Uncertainty and Technical Change in Input-Output Models', Review of Economics and Statistics, (59), 1977, pp. 75-81.

Byron, R.P., 'The Estimation of Large Social Account Matrices', Journal Royal Statistical Society, Series A, (141), 1978, pp. 359-367.

Dervis, K., De Melo, J. and Robinson, S., General Equilibrium Models for Development Policy, University Press, Cambridge, 1981.

De Vries, B.A., 'Industrialization and Employment: The Role of Small and Medium Sized Manufacturing Firms', in Giersch, H. (ed), International Economic Development and Resource Transfer, Workshop Proceedings, Institut für Weltwirtschaft an der Universität Kiel, 1979, pp. 47-62.

Evans, W.D., 'The Effect of Structural Matrix Errors on Interindustry Relations Estimates', Econometrica, (22), 1954, pp. 461-480.

Gilbert, A.G., Development Planning and Spatial Structure, Wiley, London, 1976.

Goreux, L.M. and Manne, A.S., Multi-Level Planning: Case Studies in Mexico, North-Holland Publ. Co., Amsterdam, 1973.

Hermansen, T., 'Interregional Allocation of Investments for Social and Economic Development: An Elementary Model Approach to Analysis', in Kuklinski, A. (ed), Regional Disaggregation of National Policies and Plans, Mouton, The Hague, 1975, pp. 159-212.

Hewings, G.J.D., 'Monitoring Changes in a Regional Economy: An Input-Output Simulation Approach', Modeling and Simulation, (12), 1981, pp. 1043-1046.

Hewings, G.J.D. and Romanos, M.C., 'Simulating Less Developed Regional Economies Under Conditions of Limited Information', Geographical Analysis, (13), 1981, pp. 373-390.

Hewings, G.J.D., 'Design of Appropriate Accounting Systems for Regional Development in Developing Countries', Papers Regional Science Association, (51), 1982 (forthcoming).

Hewings, G.J.D. and Lee, Y.L., 'National-Regional Accounting Systems for Regional Development in Developing Countries', Paper presented at the Conference on Urban Planning and Regional Development in a Rapidly Changing Society, Princeton, New Jersey, 1982.

Hewings, G.J.D. and Syversen, W.M., 'A Modified Bi-Proportional Method for Updating Regional Input-Output Matrices: Holistic Accuracy Evaluation', Modeling and Simulation, (13), 1982, pp. 1115-1120.

Higgins, B., 'Trade-off Curves and Regional Gaps', in Bhagwati, J.N. and Eckaus, R.S. (eds), Development and Planning, MIT Press, Cambridge, 1973.

Isard, W. and Anselin, L., 'Integration of Multiregional Models for Policy Analysis', Environment and Planning A, (14), 1982, pp. 359-376.

Kim, T.J., Boyce, D.E. and Hewings, G.J.D., 'Combined Input-Output and Commodity Flow Models for Interregional Development Planning: Insights from a Korean Application', Paper presented at the Conference on Urban Planning and Regional Development in a Rapidly Changing Society, Princeton, New Jersey, 1982.

Krueger, O.A. et al. (eds), Trade and Employment in Developing Countries, 1: Individual Studies, University Press, Chicago, 1981.

Kuklinski, A. (ed), Regional Disaggregation of National Policies and Plans, Mouton, The Hague, 1975.

Kuyvenhoven, A., Planning with a Semi-input-output Method with Empirical Application to Nigeria, Nijhoff, Boston, 1978.

Kuyvenhoven, A., 'Semi-input-output and Shadow Prices: A Reply', Oxford Bulletin of Economics and Statistics, (42), 1980, pp. 257-259.

Ledent, J. and Gordon, P., 'A Demometric Model of Interregional Growth Rate Differences', Geographical Analysis, (12), 1980, pp. 55-67.

Madden, M. and Batey, P.W.J., 'Achieving Consistency in Demographic-Economic Forecasting', Papers Regional Science Association, (44), 1980, pp. 91-106.

Matuszewski, T.I., Pitts, P.R. and Sawyer, J.A., 'Linear Programming Estimates of Changes in Input Coefficient', Canadian Journal of Economics and Political Science, (30), 1964, pp. 203-210.

Mazumdar, D., The Urban Labor Market and Income Distribution: A Study of Malaysia, University Press, Oxford, 1981.

Meerman, J., Public Expenditures in Malaysia: Who Benefits and Why, University Press, Oxford, 1979.

Mohan, R., Urban Economics and Planning Models, Johns Hopkins Press, Baltimore, 1979.

Page, W.P., Gilmore, D. and Hewings, G.J.D., An Energy and Fuel Demand Model for the Ohio River Basin Energy Study Region, University of Illinois, Urbana, 1980.

Paukert, F., Skolka, J. and Maton, J., Income Distribution, Structure of Economy and Employment, Croom Helm, London, 1981.

Prastacos, P., Allocation of Transportation Investments and Regional Economic Growth: A Multilevel Optimization Framework, unpublished PhD, University of Illinois, Urbana, 1981.

Pyatt, G. and Roe, A., Social Accounting for Development Planning, University Press, Cambridge, 1977.

Sherman, J. and Morrison, W., 'Adjustment of an Inverse Matrix Corresponding to a Change in One Element of a Given Matrix', Annals of Mathematical Statistics, (21), 1950, pp. 124-127.

Schinnar, A.P., 'A Multidimensional Accounting Model for Demographic and Economic Planning Interactions', Environment and Planning A, (8), 1976, pp. 455-475.

Schinnar, A.P., 'An Eco-Demographic Accounting Type Multiplier Analysis of Hungary', Environment and Planning A, (9), 1977, pp. 373-384.

Tinbergen, J., 'Some Refinements of the Semi-input-output Method', Pakistan Development Review, (6), 1966, pp. 243-247.

Van Staveren, J.M. and Van Dusseldorp, D.B.W.M. (eds), <u>Framework for Regional Planning in Developing Countries</u>, IRLI, Wageningen, 1980.

Waardenburg, J.G., 'Regional Disaggregation of National Development Planning: A Framework', in Kuklinski, A. (ed), <u>Regional Disaggregation of National Policies and Plans</u>, Mouton, The Hague, 1975.

Williamson, J.G., 'Regional Inequality and the Process of National Development', <u>Economic Development and Cultural Change</u>, (13), 1965.

13 Analysis of Qualitative Data

P. RIETVELD

1. INTRODUCTION

It is well known that the quality of data for the analysis of regional
problems is in many cases unsatisfactory. For example, when measuring
important socio-economic variables such as regional production, employment, capital stock and housing stock, several conventions and approxi-
mations are used which considerably reduce the usefulness of such data
for analytical purposes.

Two dimensions can be distinguished when considering the quality of
data. First, the accuracy of data has to be mentioned. Accuracy
depends, among others, on the efforts to avoid errors during and after
the process of measurement, on the way of sampling and on sample sizes.
The other dimension concerns the validity of data. Data is valid when
the way in which it has been measured is in agreement with the purposes
for which it is used. For example, if one wants to analyse the housing
market in a certain region by using the official dwelling register, the
validity of the data is questionable when one knows that dwelling substitutes such as squatter settlements are not included in the register.

In the above examples we referred to data measured on a cardinal
scale. The interval and ratio scales are examples of this scale. A
distinguishing feature of a cardinal scale is that standard numerical
operations such as addition, subtraction and multiplication can be
applied.

In addition to a cardinal scale of measurement, one may distinguish
qualitative scales of measurement (e.g. an ordinal or a nominal scale).
In the case of an ordinal scale, only a ranking of observations is
possible; nothing can be said about the magnitude of the difference
between observations. In the case of a nominal scale, even a ranking
of observations is not possible. Examples of nominal variables are:
nationality, genus, mode of transport, etc..

There are essentially two reasons why one may decide to make use of
qualitative data. First, a variable may in principle be measurable in
a cardinal way, but one may decide to measure it in an ordinal way
because the accuracy and reliability of the data is unsatisfactory (or
can only be improved against high costs). For example, if one needs an
indicator for the quality of educational infrastructure in various
regions of a country, it may be costly to develop such an indicator
measured on a cardinal scale. An indicator measured on an ordinal scale
may be easier to arrive at, for example, by inviting a small number of
experts to indicate a rank order of regions according to the quality of
educational infrastrucutre. Obviously, an ordinal scale is less in-
formative than a cardinal one, so that for certain purposes ordinal information is not a satisfactory alternative. In Nijkamp and Rietveld

(1982) it is shown however, that for many purposes (in the field of description, analysis and explanation) ordinal information is almost as suitable as cardinal information.

A second reason for using qualitative data is that the variables concerned can only be measured in that way. Many expressions of preferences and perceptions can only be made in an ordinal way (examples are housing satisfaction or scenic beauty). Further, the impossibility of measuring nominal variables in a cardinal way is obvious.

Given these arguments, we arrive at the conclusion that there is certainly a need for methods to deal with qualitative data. Before returning to a survey of these methods, we would like to draw attention to the fact that qualitative information may not only be the point of departure, but also their anticipated result. For example, in evaluation studies, the aim may be a ranking of alternatives according to their overall attractiveness In explanatory studies, one may try to find the most important explanatory variables for a certain dependent variable. In descriptive studies, the aim may be to arrive at a clustering of more or less homogeneous sets of observations. In all these cases, the outcome is of a qualitative nature, although the inputs may be cardinal.

This paper will be devoted to a survey of methods to deal with qualitative data. In section 2, we will discuss contingency tables with nominal and ordinal data. The subject in section 3 is correlation analysis. Section 4 will be devoted to reduction and aggregation methods. In section 5, we will discuss the use of qualitative data in explanatory models.

2. CONTINGENCY TABLES WITH NOMINAL AND ORDINAL DATA

In regional analysis, qualitative data may play an important role. For example, regions may be classified in terms of degree of urbanisation (urban, rural), type of climate (oceanic, continental), availability of railroad network (yes, no), per capita income (low, medium, high). When only two classes are distinguished, one speaks of a binary or dichotomous classification. In the case of three or more classes, a classification is called polytomous.

Data of one particular nominal or ordinal variable can be used to study the regional distribution of the characteristic concerned. When data on two or more variables is available simultaneously, one may - in addition - study the interrelationships between the variables. A useful way to represent data in such a case is the contingency table (see e.g. Table 1).

Table 1.
Contingency table for two variables.

		per capita income		
		low	high	total
pattern of human settlements	rural	n_{11}	n_{12}	$n_{1.}$
	urban	n_{21}	n_{22}	$n_{2.}$
	total	$n_{.1}$	$n_{.2}$	N

204

In this table, observations on N regions are represented. The total number of rural and urban regions are $n_{1.}$ and $n_{2.}$, respectively. There are $n_{.1}$ regions with a low per capita income; n_{11} of these regions are rural, n_{21} of these regions are urban.

Contingency tables can be used to study the interrelationships between the variables concerned. In Table 2 we have distinguished two extreme cases: a) complete independence and b) complete interdependence. In the first case, the probability that a region is characterised by low income is equal for rural and urban regions (i.e. 2/3). In the second case, knowledge about the settelement pattern in a region is sufficient to come to know its income level.

Table 2.
Contingency tables with a) complete independence and
b) complete interdependence.

		per capita income			
		low	high	total	
pattern of	rural	8	4	12	a)
human settlements	urban	4	2	6	
	total	12	6	18	

		per capita income			
		low	high	total	
pattern of	rural	12	0	12	b)
human settlements	urban	0	6	6	
	total	12	6	18	

In practice, the extreme cases will seldom arise. Therefore, the following index has been proposed to measure the extent to which the observed situation departs from the situation of complete independence:

$$b = \sum_{i,j} \frac{(n_{ij} - n^*_{ij})^2}{n^*_{ij}} \qquad (1)$$

where n^*_{ij} is defined as the expected frequency in cell i,j given the assumption of complete independence and given the marginal totals in the contingency table:

$$n^*_{ij} = \frac{n_{i.} \; n_{.j}}{N} \qquad (2)$$

It can be shown that b has a chi-squared distribution of $(I-1)(J-1)$ degrees of freedom, where I and J are the numbers of classes distinguished. This result can be used to carry out tests whether the observed situation differs significantly in a statistical sense from the case of complete independence.

A related approach to study interdependence between variables in contingency tables is the log-linear model. Consider for example the two dimensional case of Table 1. The log-linear model enables one to determine the extent to which the cell elements n_{ij} are determined by the marginal totals $n_{i.}$ and $n_{.j}$ on the one hand and interaction effects between the two variables on the other hand. By applying a logarithmic transformation one may arrive at the following log-linear model:

$$\ln n_{ij} = u + u_1 (i) + u_2 (j) + u_{12} (i,j) \qquad (3)$$

where:

$$\begin{cases} u & = \tfrac{1}{4} \sum_{ij} \ln n_{ij} \\[1mm] u_1(i) & = \tfrac{1}{2} \sum_{j} \ln n_{ij} - u \\[1mm] u_2(j) & = \tfrac{1}{2} \sum_{i} \ln n_{ij} - u \\[1mm] u_{12}(i,j) & = \ln n_{ij} - \tfrac{1}{2} \sum_{j} \ln n_{ij} - \tfrac{1}{2} \sum_{i} \ln n_{ij} + u \end{cases} \qquad (4)$$

Thus u is the mean value of the $\ln n_{ij}$ in the contingency table. Further, u_1 (i) represents the effects on $\log n_{ij}$ of being in class i of the first variable. The term u_2 (j) can be interpreted in a similar way. Finally, u_{12} (i,j) represents the effect of interdependence between the two variables on the log frequencies.

Several constraints can be shown to hold for the u terms:

$$\begin{cases} u_1 (1) & = -u_1 (2) \\[1mm] u_2 (2) & = -u_2 (2) \\[1mm] u_{12}(1,1) & = -u_{12}(1,2) = -u_{12}(2,1) = u_{12}(2,2) \end{cases} \qquad (5)$$

When (3) is applied to Table 2.a, we find:

$$\begin{cases} u & = 1.38 \\[1mm] u_1 (1) & = -u_1 (2) & = .35 \\[1mm] u_2 (1) & = -u_2 (2) & = .35 \\[1mm] u_{12}(1,1) & = -u_{12}(1,2) = -u_{12} (2,1) = u_{12} (2,2) = 0 \end{cases} \qquad (6)$$

This result is specific in two respects. First, the values for u_1 (i) and u_2 (j) are equal. This is related to the fact that the marginal totals in Table 2.a are identical. Second, the interaction effect is equal to zero. This is obviously due to the independence assumption on which Table 2.a is based.

When more than two variables are distinguished, log-linear models become more complex since then several kinds of interaction effects have to be distinguished. For extensive presentations of the analysis of contingency tables and log-linear models, we refer to Birch (1963), Brouwer (1982), Cox (1970), Everitt (1977), Kullback (1968), and Payne (1977).

Note that the contingency tables discussed are based on both nominal and ordinal variables. In the case of ordinal variables, use is made of classes such as low, medium and high. Note that in the methods discussed, no use is made of the fact that there is a certain rank order in these classes. Thus, analysis of contingency tables does not give rise to different results when a re-ranking of columns or rows takes place (e.g. low-medium-high). In the next section, we will therefore present some methods of dealing with the analysis of ordinal data in a more specific way.

3. RANK-CORRELATION ANALYSIS

Correlation coefficients are a usual way of representing interdependencies between variables. These coefficients assume values between −1 and +1. A value of 0 is interpreted as a lack of interdependence.

The standard measure for expressing the correlation between two cardinal variables u and v is the Pearson product moment correlation coefficient:

$$r = \frac{\sum_i (u_i - \bar{u})(v_i - \bar{v})}{\sqrt{\sum_i (u_i - \bar{u})^2 \sum_i (v_i - \bar{v})^2}} \tag{7}$$

where $\bar{u}$ and $\bar{v}$ are the mean values of the u_i and v_i respectively.

For ordinal data, related coefficients have been developed. For example, Spearman's rank correlation coefficient is identical to Pearson's coefficient when the values of u_i and v_i are interpreted as rank numbers 1, ..., R. A theoretical disadvantage of this approach is that numerical operations such subtraction and multiplication are carried out with rank numbers. Thus, in Pearson's coefficient ordinal data is essentially treated in the same way as cardinal data.

Another correlation coefficient for ordinal data has been developed by Kendall. This coefficient is based on paired comparisons of observations (see e.g., Kendall 1970).

Consider all $\frac{1}{2} I(I-1)$ pairs of observations (i,i') of two ordinal measured variables x and y. Let S^+ be the number of pairs for which x and y are concordant, i.e. the number of pairs for which $\{x_i > x_{i'}$ and $y_i > y_{i'}\}$ or $\{x_i < x_{i'}$ and $y_i < y_{i'}\}$. Let S^- be the number of pairs for which $\{x_i > x_{i'}$ and $y_i < y_{i'}\}$ or $\{x_i < x_{i'}$ and $y_i > y_{i'}\}$. Let T_x and T_y be the number of ties in x and y, respectively. When no ties appear, Kendall's coefficient of rank correlation is defined as the number of concordant pairs minus the number of discordant pairs divided by the total number of pairs:

$$\tau = \frac{S^+ - S^-}{S^+ + S^-} \tag{8}$$

When no ties are present, the following correction is applied:

$$\tau_b = \frac{S^+ - S^-}{\sqrt{S^+ + S^- + T_x}\ \sqrt{S^+ + S^- + T_y}} \tag{9}$$

For these measures it can be proved that the extreme values are −1 and +1 respectively.

At first glance, there is not much similarity between these ordinal measures and the measure for cardinal data mentioned above: the ordinal measures being based on counting frequencies of discordant and concordant pairs, and the cardinal measure being based on measuring distances with respect to the mean. It can be shown however, that the same structure underlies the ordinal and the cardinal measures (cf. Hawkes 1971, and Ploch 1974).

The first step to prove the similarity is to rewrite (7) such that the mean values $\bar{u}$ and $\bar{v}$ disappear. It is not difficult to show that

$$
\begin{cases}
\dfrac{1}{I} \sum_i (u_i - \bar{u})^2 = \dfrac{1}{2I^2} \sum_i \sum_j (u_i - u_j)^2 \\[2ex]
\dfrac{1}{I} \sum_i (u_i - \bar{u})(v_i - \bar{v}) = \dfrac{1}{2I^2} \sum_i \sum_j (u_i - u_j)(v_i - v_j)
\end{cases}
\tag{10}
$$

Accordingly, when we set $u_{ij} = u_i - u_j$ and $v_{ij} = v_i - v_j$, (7) can be rewritten as:

$$
r = \frac{\sum u_{ij}\, v_{ij}}{\sqrt{\sum u^2_{ij}}\ \sqrt{\sum v^2_{ij}}}
\tag{7'}
$$

In (7') the sum extends over all possible pairs of observations. The second step is that we introduce the following operation for the ordinal data. For all pairs i, j:

$$
\begin{cases}
x_{ij} = 1 & \text{if } x_i > x_j \\
x_{ij} = 0 & \text{if } x_i = x_j \\
x_{ij} = -1 & \text{if } x_i < x_j
\end{cases}
\tag{11}
$$

The variable y_{ij} can be defined in the same way. Thus we arrive at two vectors consisting of $I(I-1)$ elements being equal to 1, 0 or -1. The term $(S^+ - S^-)$ can be expressed in terms of x_{ij} and y_{ij} in a straightforward way: $S^+ - S^- = \frac{1}{2} \sum x_{ij}\, y_{ij}$. Given this result, it is not difficult to see that:

$$
\tau_b = \frac{\sum x_{ij}\, y_{ij}}{\sqrt{\sum x^2_{ij}\ \sum y^2_{ij}}}
\tag{9'}
$$

When we compare (7') and (9') we conclude that although the correlation coefficients are based on different concepts, they give rise to completely identical analytical expressions. This is a very remarkable result, which indicates the usefulness of transformation (11). By means of (11), every ranking of observations can be transformed into a pairwise comparison vector with elements 1, 0 and -1. This pairwise comparison vector can then be employed for the computation of the usual product moment correlation coefficient.

This idea can obviously be generalised. It is not only possible to use pairwise comparison vectors as defined above for the computation of the coefficient r, but also for other purposes. Thus transformation (11) can also be used as a basis for the computation of regression coefficients and multiple correlation coefficients (see also, Ploch 1974, Namboodiri, Carter and Blalock 1975, and Blalock 1976). In Nijkamp and Rietveld (1982), one finds an application of this approach to ordinal principal components analysis.

4. REDUCTION AND AGGREGATION METHODS FOR QUALITATIVE DATA

One of the aims of multivariate analysis is the representation of the main features of complex datasets. If, for example, information is available on K variables for a system consisting of I regions, one may look for the main features of the regional data matrix X:

$$X = \begin{pmatrix} x_{11} \cdots \cdots x_{1I} \\ \vdots \qquad \vdots \\ \vdots \qquad \vdots \\ \vdots \qquad \vdots \\ x_{K1} \cdots \cdots x_{KI} \end{pmatrix} \qquad (12)$$

Two directions have to be indicated in which the search for basic patterns can take place. First, one may aim at gaining insight into similarities and differences between <u>regions</u>. This can be achieved among others, by the application of cluster analysis to regions. Second, one may be interested in the relationship between <u>variables</u>. In that case, principal components analysis and correlation methods (already discussed in section 3) can be mentioned as possible tools.

In this section we will subsequently pay attention to the following methods : principal components analysis, multidimensional scaling and cluster analysis.

The aim of <u>principal components analysis</u> is the representation of J variables by a smaller number of variables (called components) with a high degree of accuracy. The aim is achieved by transforming the variables to a set of independent variables (based on an orthogonal data transformation in which the original variables are substituted for independent components).

In the case of ordinal data, components can be determined in various ways. One possibility is to make use of the fact that principal components can be expressed in terms of correlation coefficients of the original variables. Therefore, transformation (11) can be used to generate the required rank correlation coefficients.

<u>Multidimensional scaling (MDS) methods</u> are related to principal components methods. Again, the aim is the representation of variables by means of a smaller number of variables. When the original data matrix X is ordinal, MDS aims at the derivation of a cardinal data matrix V with L rows (L < K) such that the values of V are as much as possible in agreement with the ordinal information contained in X.

MDS methods can be sketched as follows:
In order to avoid non-permissible mathematical manipulations with ordinal data, in MDS methods use is made of (cardinal) intermediary variables, called disparities. Disparities represent the distances between the I configuration points (for example, regions). Disparities function as an intermediary between the ordinal data matrix X and the cardinal representation to be determined. Disparities should be consistent with the information contained in X: all ordinal information (e.g. a 'larger than' expression for two observations) should be reflected by the value of the disparities. Furthermore, the ultimate cardinal configuration V should be in agreement with the disparities as much as possible.

These two requirements can be realised simultaneously via a so-called monotone regression procedure or a 'rank-image' procedure. The MDS procedure itself is an iterative procedure which yields an optimum configuration on the basis of a goodness-of-fit criterion (see Figure 1).

The result of these exercitions is a cardinal matrix V, which – in
the case of K = 2 – can be easily represented in a graphical way. For
formal descriptions and applications of MDS we refer to Carroll and
Chang (1970), Kruskal (1964), Nijkamp (1979), Roskam (1977) and Voogd
(1982).

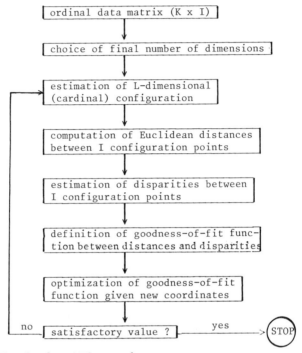

Figure 1. Sketch of an MDS procedure.

A drawback of principal components analysis and MDS is that new
artificial variables are created which are sometimes difficult to inter-
pret. It is worthwhile to mention here that another data reduction
method has been developed which does not share this drawback: interdependence analysis (see Boyce et al. 1974). Interdependence analysis
is an optimal subset selection technique by means of which a subset of
variables is derived which best represent an entire variable set. The
advantage of this approach is that no data transformations are necessary.
In Blommestein et al. (1981) and Nijkamp and Rietveld (1982) some results
are presented. It appears that also this method is not without problems.
First, it may give rise to a large number of computations to be carried
out. Second, it appears that the outcomes are not very robust when only
a small number (say 1 to 4) of variables have to be selected.
The last method to be discussed in this section is cluster analysis.
The aim of cluster analysis is a partitioning of data in separate
groups by means of a classification procedure. It is possible to
cluster both observations and variables.
A general feature of many clustering procedures is that the intersection of two clusters is empty while the union of all clusters contains the whole relevant set. Furthermore, the elements in a cluster

can be expected to display a large degree of homogeneity, while between clusters a certain degree of diversity exists.

A set of clusters can be derived on the basis of some criterion to distinguish the original elements from each other. Various (dis)similarity measures have been proposed, for example, correlation coefficients or Euclidean distances.

Another way to distinguish clustering methods is by means of the way in which the basic elements are combined, namely a hierarchical versus a non-hierarchical way. Hierarchical clustering techniques are relatively easy to carry out. The results of a hierarchical cluster-analysis can be represented by means of a dendrogram (a tree-like structure). A drawback of hierarchical cluster techniques is that there is no possibility to apply corrections in the case of a bad initial partitioning. Non-hierarchical procedures obviously do not give rise to this drawback, but give rise to a larger computational burden than hierarchical procedures.

In the case of ordinal data, the main problem is the construction of a suitable similarity criterion. When the aim is a clustering of variables one can simply employ a rank correlation coefficient (see section 3) as a similarity measure. When the aim is a clustering of observations, it is more difficult to find a suitable approach. One possibility is to carry out a clustering analysis after the ordinal data matrix has been transformed into a cardinal one by means of MDS.

For a more elaborate discussion of cluster analysis and applications we refer to Hartigan (1975) and Fisher (1982).

5. EXPLANATORY MODELS FOR QUALITATIVE DATA

Qualitative data may play an important role in explanatory models for regional and urban studies. In this section we will pay special attention to the possibility to develop explanatory models when the dependent variable is qualitative. The usual way to treat qualitative data in explanatory models is the use of dummy variables. Dummy variables can assume two values : 0 and 1. When explanatory variables are qualitative, dummy variables can be used without special problems, but as will be indicated here, this does not hold true for dependent variables.

Let y be the dependent variable and $x_1, \ldots, x_K$ the series of explanatory variables. Then a linear relationship between y and $x_1, \ldots, x_K$ can be formulated as follows:

$$y = \alpha_0 + \alpha_1 x_1 + \ldots + \alpha_K x_K + \varepsilon \tag{13}$$

where ε represents the disturbance term. In this equation the occurrence of a university in a region (y = 1: yes; y = 0: no) can be explained for example by means of regional features such as population, size and location. The problem of this specification is that the left-hand side may only assume two values as opposed to the right-hand side, apart from the disturbance term. This means that (13) only has a meaningful interpretation under very specific assumptions with respect to the disturbance term. Therefore it is better to look for an alternative specification of the relationship between y and $x_1, \ldots, x_K$.

In logit and probit analysis the relationship between y and $x_1, \ldots, x_K$ is formulated in probabilistic terms:

$$f(p) = \alpha_0 + \alpha_1 x_1 + \ldots + \alpha_K x_K \qquad (14)$$

where p is the probability that y assumes the value 1, given the values of $x_1, \ldots, x_K$. Since the right-hand side of (14) may in principle assume all values between $-\infty$ and $+\infty$, it is attractive to formulate $f(p)$ in such a way that it is a monotone increasing function of p, which may assume all values on the interval $(-\infty, +\infty)$.

There are various functions which satisfy this requirement. One possibility is the so-called logit specification:

$$\ln \left(\frac{p}{1-p}\right) = \alpha_0 + \alpha_1 x_1 + \ldots + \alpha_K x_K \qquad (15)$$

It is not difficult to see that $\lim_{p \to 0} f(p) = -\infty$, $f(\frac{1}{2})=0$ and $\lim_{p \to 1} f(p) = \infty$ in case of the logit specification. An alternative specification, which also has these properties is the so-called probit specification which is based on the inverse of the cumulative normal distribution.

There are in general two ways to estimate the parameters of (15): weighted least squares and maximum likelihood. The first method is most appropriate in the case of a limited number of categories of observations of explanatory variables. The second method is especially useful when the explanatory variables are continuous. For more elaborate discussions on logit and probit analyses, we refer to Domencich and McFadden (1975), Theil (1971), and Wrigley (1979).

We will next present an estimation method which can be used when both the dependent and all explanatory variables are ordinal: the regime method. The regime method is essentially based on a combination of logit analysis presented above and the transformation of ordinal data as given in (11).

The point of departure in regime method is an ordinal vector of dependent variables $(y_1, \ldots, y_I)$ and an ordinal matrix X with characteristic elements x_{ki} containing the information on the explanatory variables. When transformation (11) is applied to the $I(I-1)$ pairs of observations, each pair of observations on the independent variables is characterised by a K vector consisting of values 1, 0 and -1. Such a vector will be called a regime vector. In principle, there are 3^J different regimes.

Consider a particular regime vector m : e.g. $(1, -1, -1, \ldots, 1)$. Let F_m be the number of pairs of observations giving rise to this regime. For these pairs of observations (i,j) there are three possibilities: y_i may be larger than, equal to, or less than y_j. The number of these pairs will be denoted by F_{m1}, F_{m0} and F_{m-1}, respectively. Thus $f_{m1} = F_{m1}/F_m$ is the probability that, given that regime m holds for a pair of observations (i,j), the value of y_i is larger than y_j. In a similar way one can define f_{m0} and f_{m-1}.

The main idea of the regime method is that the outcomes for f_{m1} and f_{m-1} can be explained by the structure of the regime vector. Let $(z_{m1}, \ldots z_{mK})$ denote the regime vector (thus, $z_{m1} = 1$, $z_{m2} = -1$, $z_{m3} = -1, \ldots, z_{mK} = 1$). Then the relative frequencies f_{m1} and f_{m-1} can be related to the structure of regime m as follows:

$$\ln \left(\frac{f_{m1}}{f_{m-1}}\right) = \beta_0 + \beta_1 z_{m1} + \ldots + \beta_K z_{mK} \qquad (16)$$

The coefficients $\beta_0, \ldots, \beta_K$ can be estimated by means of weighted least squares, as indicated above. For more details and a numerical application, we refer to Nijkamp and Rietveld (1981, 1982).

6. CONCLUDING REMARKS

The above presentation of qualitative data methods is certainly not meant as an exhaustive survey. It is meant rather to indicate some of the possibilities for analysing qualitative data. In our opinion, the conclusion may be drawn that qualitative data methods have reached such a level of development that a large range of problems related to regional development can be analysed by means of these in an adequate way.

REFERENCES

Birch, M.W., 'Maximum Likelihood in Three-Way Contingency Tables', in
    Journal of the Royal Statistical Society, Series B, vol. 25, 1963,
    pp. 220-233.
Blalock, H.M., 'Can We Find a Genuine Ordinal Scope Analogue?', in
    Heise, D.R. (ed), Sociological Methodology, Jossey-Bass Publ., San
    Francisco, 1976, pp. 195-225.
Blommestein, H.J., Nijkamp, P., and Rietveld, P., 'A Multivariate
    Analysis of Spatial Inequalities', in Buhr, W. and Friedrich, P. (eds),
    Regional Development Under Stagnation, Nomos, Baden-Baden, 1981,
    pp. 293-316.
Boyce, D.E., Farhi, A. and Weischedel, R., Optimal Subset Selection,
    Springer, Berlin, 1974.
Brouwer, F., 'Log-Linear Analysis with Metric and Non-Metric Data: An
    Application to Spatial Data', Research Memorandum 1982-15, Dept. of
    Economics, Free University, Amsterdam, 1982.
Carroll, J.D., Chang, J.J., 'Analysis of Individual Differences in
    Multidimensional Scaling via an N-way Generalization of the
    'Eckard-Young' Decomposition', Psychometrica, vol. 25, 1970,
    pp. 283-319.
Cox, D.R., The Analysis of Binary Data, Methuen, London, 1970.
Domencich, F.A., McFadden, D., Urban Travel Demand, A Behavioural
    Analysis, North-Holland, Amsterdam, 1975.
Everitt, B.S., The Analysis of Contingency Tables, Chapman and Hall,
    London, 1977.
Fischer, M.M., 'Eine Methodologie der Regional Taxonomie, Probleme und
    Verfahren der Klassifikation und Regionalisierung in der Geographie
    und Regionalforschung', Bremer Beiträge zur Geographie und Raum-
    planung, Schwerpunkt Geographie, Universität Bremen, 1982.
Hartigan, J.A., Clustering Algorithms, Wiley, New York, 1975.
Hawkes, R.K., 'The Multivariate Analysis of Ordinal Measures', American
    Journal of Sociology, vol. 76, 1971, pp. 908-926.
Kendall, M.G., Rank Correlation Methods, Griffin, London, 1970.
Kruskal, J.B., 'Multidimensional Scaling by Optimizing Goodness of Fit
    to a Nonmetric Hypothesis', Psychometrica, vol. 29, 1964, pp. 1-27.
Kullback, S., Information Theory and Statistics, Dover Publications,
    New York, 1968.
Nambooridi, N.K., Carter, L.F., and Blalock, H.M., Applied Multivariate
    Analysis and Experimental Design, McGraw-Hill, New York, 1975.
Nijkamp, P., Multidimensional Spatial Data and Decision Analysis, Wiley,
    Chichester/New York, 1979.
Nijkamp, P., and Rietveld, P., 'Ordinal Multivariate Analysis',
    Professional Paper PP-81-2, Laxenburg, 1981.
Nijkamp, P., and Rietveld, P., 'Soft Econometrics as a Tool for Regional
    Discrepancy Analysis', Papers of the Regional Science Association,
    1982 (forthcoming).
Payne, C., 'The Log-Linear Model for Contingency Tables', in Payne, C.,
    and Muircheartaigh, C.O. (eds), The Analysis of Survey Data, vol. 2,
    Model Fitting, New York, 1977, pp. 105-144.
Ploch, D.R., 'Ordinal Measures of Association and the General Linear
    Model', in Blalock, H.M. (ed), Measurement in the Social Sciences,
    MacMillan, London, 1974, pp. 343-368.
Rietveld, P., Multiple Objective Decision Methods and Regional Planning,
    North-Holland, Amsterdam, 1980.

Roskam, E.E., 'The Nature of Data: Interpretation and Representation', in Lingoes, J.C. (ed), Geometric Representation of Relational Data, Mathesis Press, Ann Arbor, 1977.

Roy, B., 'Decision avec Critères Multiples', Metra, vol. 11, 1972, pp. 121-151.

Theil, H., Principles of Econometrics, Wiley, New York, 1971.

Voogd, H., Multicriteria Evaluation for Urban and Regional Planning, Pion, London, 1982.

Wrigley, N., 'Developments in the Statistical Analysis of Categorical Data', Progress in Human Geography, vol. 3, 1979, pp. 315-355.

14 A Survey of Multicriteria Analysis for Development Planning

P. NIJKAMP AND H. VOOGD

1. INTRODUCTION

A particularly vexing methodological difficulty in the design and evaluation of planning proposals concerns the way in which choices are made.
Clearly, the selection of the 'best' action from several alternatives,
each of which will have different outcomes or consequences, is very sub-
jective. This problem grows in importance if the actions under consideration will ultimately determine the welfare and wellbeing of a region,
as is often the case in development planning. Many planning activities
in developing countries are concerned with the construction of new infrastructure, rather than the improvement of the existing regime more typical of developed countries. Hence, methods and techniques which facilitate the treatment of choice or classification problems can be of tremendous importance in development planning.

One important subset of such tools is that composed of approaches which
use a multidimensional set of sometimes conflicting criteria or objectives to construct and solve a choice or classification problem. These
are usually called <u>multicriteria methods</u>. The purpose of this paper is
to assess various multicriteria approaches in terms of their potential
use in development planning.

The structure of the paper is as follows. In section 2 the nature of
multicriteria analysis is discussed in some detail. A distinction is
made between <u>continuous multicriteria methods</u> and <u>discrete multicriteria</u>
<u>methods</u>. The first of these classes of methods is the subject of sec-
tion 3; the second is treated in section 4. The final section summarises the conclusions of the study and points to some issues for future
research.

2. PRINCIPLES OF MULTICRITERIA ANALYSIS

A planner involved in the design or evaluation of plans or projects
begins by considering several important questions. For example, what
constitutes an exhaustive set of alternatives? Which variables are
relevant in characterising each project or plan? A fundamental question
underlying the selection of variables is whether the variables regarded
as important by the planner are in fact those perceived to be important
by the public. This raises another question, viz. who should participate in the planning process, at what stage, and in what way? Answers
to questions of this kind depend on the ability of the planning agency
to gauge public opinion. This is a very complex procedural problem,
which cannot be considered as a simple exercise in measurement or technical evaluation.

To obtain a better idea of the complexity involved, it is useful to think in more specific terms. Assume a finite and exhaustive set of alternative plans

$$P = \{p_1, p_2, \ldots, p_J\} \tag{1}$$

from which one plan must be chosen. Each plan can be evaluated by means of a finite set of variables

$$A = \{a_1, a_2, \ldots, a_N\} \tag{2}$$

which can be included in a finite set of criterion functions

$$F = \{f_1, f_2, \ldots, f_I\} \tag{3}$$

where the f's may be linear or nonlinear functions of the variables. The relationship between these factors can be illustrated as follows. Let $e_{i1}, e_{i2}, \ldots, e_{iJ}$ denote the values taken by the criterion function i for plans $1, 2, \ldots, J$. Then the set of values attained by all criterion functions for all plans can be arranged in a matrix as follows:

alternative plans

	p_1	p_2	$\cdots$	p_j	$\cdots$	p_J
f_1	e_{11}	e_{12}	$\cdots$	e_{ij}	$\cdots$	e_{1J}
f_2	e_{21}	e_{22}	$\cdots$	e_{2j}	$\cdots$	e_{2J}
f_i	e_{i1}	e_{i2}	$\cdots$	e_{ij}	$\cdots$	e_{iJ}
f_I	e_{I1}	e_{I2}	$\cdots$	e_{Ij}	$\cdots$	e_{IJ}

(criteria, left margin)

This array is also known as an evaluation matrix, project-effect matrix, or effectiveness matrix. For instance, if the aim were to plan a transportation system the criteria may be road capacity, transportation costs, maintenance costs, accessibility of service centres, visual and aesthetic appeal, levels of pollution, etc.

There are many methods that could be used to reduce the amount of information included in the above matrix, most of which use information concerning the relative importance of the various e_{ij}-scores (i.e., priorities or weights). This may result in a classification of the alternatives under consideration which may be used in the policy-making process. Such methods are called discrete multicriteria methods, where the word 'discrete' implies that a finite number of explicitly formulated alternatives is considered. Some recent surveys and discussions of discrete multicriteria methods can be found inter alia in Van Delft and Nijkamp (1977), Nijkamp (1979a, 1980), Rietveld (1980), Kmietowicz and Pearman (1981) and Voogd (1982).

Discrete multicriteria methods are especially suitable for problems in which the alternatives are precisely known. However, there are also

many cases in which only the dimensions of the alternatives are known
(i.e., a plan must include 'some' transportation infrastructure, 'some'
housing, 'some' employment, etc.), but the exact value of each dimension
is not fixed. This implies that a continuous number of alternatives
must be taken into consideration; instead of explicit alternatives,
there is additional information on the feasible area in which an optimal
solution (i.e., 'best' plan) may be situated. This may be illustrated
with the following brief example. Consider two criteria e and m
which should have values as large as possible, and the associated
feasibility spectrum (shown in Figure 1).

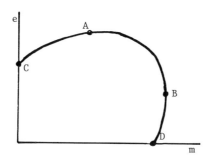

Figure 1.   A feasibility spectrum for e   and   m.

This curve is usually called the efficiency frontier (or Pareto frontier,
attainment-possibility frontier, set of nondominated points, set of non-
inferior points). It can be regarded as the locus of all points for
which e cannot be increased without a decrease in m, and vice versa.
Evidently, good solutions are represented by points on the efficient
locus AB: any other point in the feasible set is dominated by a point on
the arc AB. The choice among points on AB depends on the relative
priorities of e   and   m and may be influenced, among other things, by
institutional factors. A compromise solution (or compromise plan) of
this type can ex post be defined as that efficient point (Pareto solution) which leads implicitly to the highest weighted total utility. The
general form of such a model is:

$$\max \underline{f} \ (\underline{a}) \qquad\qquad (4)$$

$$\underline{a} \in K$$

where $\underline{f}$ is an I x 1 vector of criterion functions (also called objective function), $\underline{a}$ is a J x 1 vector of decision variables, and K is a
feasible area which defines the solution space. A multidimensional
optimisation (or programming) model of this type might, for example, be
required to maximise production and employment and energy savings and
system accessibility, subject to the constraints of limited resources
and available technology.
   Another central concept in this kind of multicriteria analysis is that
of the ideal point (or reference point or utopia point). The ideal point
$\underline{f}^0$ is defined as an I x 1 vector whose components are the maximum values
of the individual criterion functions. This means that the elements f^0_i
of $\underline{f}^0$ are defined as :

$$f_i^o = \max_i f_i \, (\underline{a})\qquad\qquad(5)$$

$$\underline{a}\in K$$

The closer a point is to the ideal point, the better the alternative it represents. Obviously, the feasibility frontier also plays a central role in this approach, since it reflects the degree of conflict or complementarity between different possible outcomes. There are in fact infinitely many options, the number of which can be reduced by using a concept such as the ideal point. Because of the continuity of the alternatives under consideration, methods of this type will be called continuous multicriteria methods. This subject is treated inter alia in Keeney and Raiffa (1976), Bromley and Sfeir-Younis (1977), Zeleny (1976b), Thiriez and Zionts (1976), Starr and Zeleny (1977), Bell et al. (1977), Nijkamp (1979a), Wierzbicki (1979a), Rietveld (1980) and Spronk (1981).

It is unfortunately the case that the information and data systems available for many regions in developing countries are rather poor; in particular, there is usually little quantitative (metric) data available for development planning. Consequently, it is also useful to classify multicriteria methods according to the accuracy of the data they require (see Table 1).

Table 1
A typology of multicriteria methods

Type of method	Type of data	
	Hard	Soft
Discrete	I	II
Continuous	III	IV

Thus, multicriteria methods may be divided into hard data methods and soft data methods. Soft data methods are based on, for example, qualitative, fuzzy or ordinal data, while hard data methods are based on cardinal or metric data. Given the previous classification into discrete and continuous methods, it is clear that at least four main categories of methods may be distinguished (Table 1). These will be discussed in more detail in the next sections, where the soft data methods (i.e., categories II and IV) will be emphasised due to their importance for development planning.

3. CONTINUOUS MULTICRITERIA METHODS

There are many different continuous multicriteria methods currently in use (see Nijkamp 1979a, Nijkamp and Spronk 1979). The class of hard continuous methods includes utility function approaches (Farquhar 1977, Fishburn 1970), penalty models (Theil 1968), goal programming (Lee 1972, Charnes and Cooper 1977, Spronk 1981), min-max approaches (Nijkamp and Rietveld 1976, Rietveld 1980), reference point approaches (Zeleny 1974, 1976a,b, Nijkamp 1979b, Wierzbicki 1979b, Lewandowski and Grauer 1982), and hierarchical models (Nijkamp 1977, Rietveld 1980).

Utility methods are based on the assumption that the whole vector of relevant criteria or objectives can be translated by means of a weighting procedure into one utility function. This implies that (4) can be respecified as:

$$\max Q = f\ (\underline{a}) \tag{6}$$

$$\underline{a} \in K$$

where Q is the master control of a scalar-valued optimisation function. This approach has only limited value, since it presupposes à priori known quantitative tradeoff rates.

Penalty models assume the existence of a set of desired achievement levels, reflected by an ideal vector f^o. Any discrepancy between an actual value $\underline{f}$ and an ideal value $\underline{f^o}$ incurs a penalty calculated by means of a penalty function which could, for instance, be quadratic:

$$\min \sum_i w_i\ (f_i - f^o)^2 \tag{7}$$

The coefficient w_i (i=1, 2, ..., I) represents the weight attached to deviating from the ideal value of criterion i. Evidently, the main difficulty in applying this kind of model is lack of information about appropriate penalty functions.

Goal programming methods are widely used to treat many different types of problems. They are essentially a subclass of penalty models, for which the penalty function is defined as:

$$\sum_i w_i\ (f_i^+ + f_i^-) \tag{8}$$

where f_i^+ and f_i^- are the respective over- and underachievement of f_i with respect to the à priori specified achievement level f_i^o for each criterion i. The plan that minimises the penalty is considered to be the most attractive option. This approach is especially appropriate when used interactively so that the users can learn about the problem and modify their aspirations (achievement levels) accordingly.

Min-max approaches are based on the use of a matrix representing the payoffs between conflicting objectives. The first step is the separate optimisation of each criterion or objective function f_i:

$$\max f_i\ (\underline{a}) \quad \text{for all} \quad i \tag{9}$$

$$\underline{a} \in K$$

The optimal value of each function (9) is then denoted by $f_i^o\ (\underline{a}^i)$, where the vector of variables associated with this individual optimum is denoted by $\underline{a}^i$. A payoff table representing the conflicts between the individual objectives is then constructed, each column corresponding to a given function and each row to the strategy $\underline{a}^i$ which represents an optimal solution with regard to the ith function. In each row i, we record the value achieved by each objective function when the strategy $\underline{a}^i$ is adopted. Thus, $f_1\ (\underline{a}^i)$ is the value of the first criterion or objective function that is obtained when strategy $\underline{a}^i$ is

221

adopted, $f_2(\underline{a}^i)$ is the value of the second criterion under strategy $\underline{a}^i$, and so forth. This payoff table can then be used in several ways. For example, an equilibrium of min-max solution may be identified - this would be the solution that is nearest to the set of ideal solutions given on the main diagonal of the payoff table (the values $f_i^o(\underline{a}^i)$, i=1, 2, ..., I).

This approach is obviously especially appropriate when it is necessary to take into account different views of a problem in some explicit way. Each view is represented by a criterion (objective) function and the information given in the payoff table may then be used to help the decision maker(s) to arrive at a compromise solution.

Reference point approaches are based on the concept of an ideal point already mentioned in the preceding section. They usually employ some kind of distance metric to assess the deviation between ideal solutions $f_i^o(\underline{a}^i)$ on the one hand and the set of efficient solutions $f_i(\underline{a}^*)$ on the other. The compromise solution is defined as the option in the set of efficient solutions for which the distance to the ideal solution is a minimum. It should be noted that there are also reference point approaches which are formulated in a goal programming framework, where the reference point represents a set of aspiration levels. This approach is also particularly appropriate when there is direct interaction between the user and the computer so that reference points can be modified during the course of the analysis.

Hierarchical models are based on the assumption that all criteria or objectives can be ranked in importance. Optimisation is then carried out in a stepwise fashion, so that higher-ranking functions are optimised before those of lower rank. A tolerance parameter (or relaxation factor) can be specified for each function (except the most important), indicating the maximum deviations from the optimum $f_i(\underline{a}_i^o)$ considered acceptable by the users.

The hard continuous multicriteria methods described above have received considerable attention in the literature. The same is not true for soft continuous approaches, however, which undoubtedly represent a much less developed area of multicriteria analysis. Three different approaches may currently be distinguished: the fuzzy set approach (Chang 1968, Bellman and Zadeh 1970, Capocelli and De Luca 1973), the stochastic approach (Donckels 1975) and the soft econometric approach (Nijkamp and Rietveld 1982).

Fuzzy set methods focus on criteria or constraints that are not sharply defined, so that the boundaries of the decision area are not marked out in an unambiguous manner. By using fuzzy set theory, it is possible to derive measures for the extent to which an element (e.g., aspect) belongs to a certain category. This information can be quantified by means of so-called membership functions, and can then be utilised in some hard optimisation method. The definition of membership functions is crucial to the use of the fuzzy set approach.

The use of stochastic approaches in continuous multicriteria analysis has been quite uncommon up to now. Nevertheless, if qualitative or ordinal decision variables can be approximated by cardinal (metric) variables with a certain probability distribution, it is possible to construct a stochastic optimisation model. The most probable compromise solution may then be identified using an appropriate hard multicriteria method. One of the main drawbacks of this approach is usually the lack of information about appropriate probability functions.

The soft econometric approach is perhaps the most promising basis for soft continuous multicriteria methods. This approach involves the transformation of qualitative or ordinal data input into metric units, which may then be analysed further by means of an appropriate hard multi-criteria method. Although no applications of this approach in the field of optimisation are known, the general principles are certainly applicable in multicriteria analysis. This is still a relatively new technique, however, and further research is necessary.

It may be concluded from the above descriptions of continuous multicriteria methods that the development of soft methods is lagging far behind that of hard methods. For this reason, the use of soft methods in development planning is currently very limited, despite promising progress in recent years. We will return to this point in the final section of this paper.

4. DISCRETE MULTICRITERIA METHODS

Discrete multicriteria methods are based on the existence of a fixed number of explicitly defined alternatives. The first step in all these methods is to construct an evaluation matrix, as explained in section 2, since the purpose of this kind of multicriteria analysis is to make some kind of evaluation of the various alternatives available. However, such an evaluation is only possible if there is a weighting scheme which expresses the relative importance of the various scores.

In the past, cost-benefit analysis has been the method most commonly used to evaluate discrete alternatives. However, many projects or plans are concerned with outcomes or consequences which cannot be discussed in terms of prices, and this makes the cost-benefit approach inappropriate for complex decision making (see Nijkamp 1977, for an extensive criticism). Related methods such as the planning-balance sheet method, cost-effectiveness analysis, and the shadow project approach are significant improvements upon traditional cost-benefit analysis for complex planning purposes, but provides no solution to the problem of judging incommensurate and intangible outcomes.

Instead of using (artificial) prices to assess the relative merits of these intangible outcomes, discrete multicriteria methods assign political priorities to certain criteria. These weights reflect the relative importance attached to the outcomes associated with each criterion. However, political weighting schemes are often difficult to infer from questionnaires or other procedures designed to reveal preferences (see Voogd 1982). When such weights cannot be assessed à priori, the analyst may proceed in one of two ways: he may either (a) use general alternative sets of weights; these scenarios may reflect alternative policy directions (views) or future policy choices (see Nijkamp and Voogd 1979) or (b) use an interactive learning procedure during which relative priorities are specified in a stepwise manner (see Van Delft and Nijkamp 1977).

There are many discrete multicriteria methods, both for hard and soft data. The following hard data methods will be considered here: the expected value method (Schimpeler and Grecco 1968, Schlager 1968, Kahne 1975), the discrepancy analysis technique (Nijkamp 1979a), the goals-achievement method (Hill 1973), and the concordance approach (see Guigou 1974, Roy 1972, Van Delft and Nijkamp 1977).

The expected value method assigns weight to the criteria and treats these weights as 'quasi-probabilities' which must add up to 1. Thus the expected value of the outcomes of each alternative plan can be calculated by multiplying the value obtained for each criterion by its appropriate weight and then summing the weighted values for all criteria. Essentially, the expected value method calculates the weighted average of all (standardised) criteria scores. This method implies a rather rigid approach since it assumes perfect linear substitution of the values of the various criteria, which is seldom true in practical applications.

Discrepancy analysis attempts to rank the plans according to their discrepancy from an optimum plan. This (hypothetical) optimum plan achieves a set of predefined goals. Statistical correlation coefficients are then used to identify the plan most similar to the reference plan. This method should be used with care, because the various discrepancies in the outcomes of a plan cannot be made sufficiently explicit.

The goals-achievement method links each criterion with a quantitative achievement level of target value. Evaluation essentially involves taking the achievement score for each criterion, and aggregating these to give a total achievement score for each alternative plan. The values are aggregated using a weighted summation procedure similar to that described above for the expected value method. The goals-achievement method is widely used in planning practice due to its simple and straightforward structure.

The concordance approach is also widely used. This method is based on a pairwise comparison of alternatives, thus using only the metric interval characteristics of the various outcome evaluations. The basic idea is to measure the degree to which the outcomes and their associated weights confirm or contradict the dominant pairwise relationships among alternatives. The differences in weights and the differences in evaluation scores are usually analysed separately. This approach uses the available information reasonably well and can be considered as a useful type of discrete multicriteria model.

In recent years, much attention has been paid to the development of qualitative or soft evaluation techniques, with considerable practical success. As a result, many operational soft discrete multicriteria methods are now available. The following approaches will be discussed here: the eigenvalue approach (Saaty 1977, Lootsma 1980), the extreme expected value method (Kmietowicz and Pearman 1981, Rietveld 1982), the permutation method (Mastenbroek and Paelinck 1976), the frequency approach (Van Delft and Nijkamp 1977, Voogd 1981a), the geometric scaling approach (Nijkamp and Voogd 1979, 1981), the regime approach (Hinloopen et al. 1983, Nijkamp 1982), the mixed data approach (Voogd 1981b, 1982).

The eigenvalue approach involves the pairwise comparison of alternatives (Saaty 1977). This comparison is carried out using a nine-point scale, where the value 1 means that the two factors being compared are of equal importance while the value 9 implies that one is of much more important than the other. A table is constructed for each criterion, in which the alternative plans are compared in a pairwise fashion with respect to that criterion. The criteria themselves are then compared in a similar way, resulting in a separate criteria evaluation table. The next step is to aggregate the information in each table using an eigenvalue procedure. This involves the calculation of quantitative evaluation scores and weights, which are then used in a weighted summation procedure to determine an aggregated appraisal score for each alternative plan. This approach therefore, has the same drawbakcs as the expected value method discussed earlier. In addition – and this is probably the most fundamental limitation of the approach – it is impossible for the user to relate the values of the criterion weights to the values obtained for the plan outcomes. In other words, the weighting is independent of the characteristics of the various plans.

The extreme expected value method can be regarded as an extension of

the expected value method discussed above. It is still assumed that
the scores achieved by each plan with respect to each criterion have
quantitative properties, but in addition it is postulated that the
probabilities (weights) are only known in a qualitative sense , i.e.,
only their ordinal properties are given. In essence, the aim of this
approach is to determine the alternative with the maximum or minimum
expected value. This is done by solving the following linear programming problem:

$$\text{max or min} \quad EV_j = \sum_i p_i \, e_{ij}$$

$$\text{subject to} \quad p_1 \geq p_2 \geq p_3 \geq \ldots, \, p_I \geq 0 \qquad (10)$$

$$\sum_i p_i = 1$$

where EV_j denotes the expected value of alternative j and p_i is
the probability associated with the evaluation e_{ij} of alternative j
with respect to criterion i. Some elementary operations lead to maximum and minimum expected values, which may be used in a final assessment
of the alternatives. However, Rietveld (1982) has shown that this
assessment should not be made solely on the basis of the extreme values,
but should also take into account certain values of EV_j generated for
intermediate values of p_i.

The permutation method is based on a compromise of all possible final
rankings of alternative plans in order to find the best 'final' ranking.
For each hypothetical final ranking a score is calculated which measures
how well this ranking corresponds to the ordinal values registered by
each plan for each criterion. Instead of the original set of alternative plans we now have a new set of alternative configurations of ranking. Then, using the ordinal weights, an appraisal score for each permutation is calculated. Given the extreme weight set used, the best
final ranking of alternatives can thus be determined. The use of this
approach is limited to problems involving only a few alternatives
because of the number of permutations, although a more heuristic extension to deal with many alternatives is possible.

The frequency approach is also based on the pairwise comparison of
alternatives. The basic idea of this approach is to transform the
available ordinal information to information on a 'lower' (i.e., binary)
scale, which is then treated as a frequency statistic. This approach
also has the disadvantage that it may become rather cumbersome if a
large number of alternatives and criteria are involved.

The geometric scaling approach is based on the principles of non-
metric multidimensional scaling. The basic idea of this approach is to
transform a large amount of ordinal data into a small amount of metric
(cardinal) data, such that the new cardinal configuration is as close
as possible (has maximum goodness-of-fit) to the ordinal data. One
limitation of this elegant approach is that it requires a fairly complicated computational algorithm. In addition, evaluation problems treated
by this method should have a sufficient number of degrees of freedom to
allow geometric scaling. This implies that unless sufficient ordinal
information is available, no metric data can be extracted.

The essence of the regime method is a pairwise comparison of all
alternatives for each criterion. By assigning binary numbers to the
results of this pairwise comparison, a long-stretched binary matrix of
regimes if obtained. The same is also done for the elements of the

225

weight factor. By combining the information from both the regimes and the ordinal weights via a successive permutation procedure, the dominance of plans (i.e., the most likely ranking of alternatives) may be inferred (see Hinloopen et al. 1983). The latter method is a recently developed, fairly simple and operational method.

Except for the extreme expected value approach, which assumes cardinal evaluation scores, all of the soft multicriteria methods mentioned above deal with qualitative weights and qualitative assessments of the alternatives with respect to individual criteria. Consequently, most of these methods have already been used in planning practice, despite the fact that they have only just been developed. However, one much-voiced and persistent criticism of these techniques is that only the ordinal characteristics of the available quantitative information are utilised. Therefore the most recent research in this area has concentrated on the development of methods capable of dealing with <u>mixed data</u>, i.e., evaluation matrices containing both quantitative scores and qualitative rankings. Nijkamp and Voogd (1981) have developed a mixed-data procedure based on the geometric scaling approach which obviously suffers from the same limitations as the simpler version mentioned above. Another set of methods has been developed by Voogd (1981b, 1982), which involves the construction of two measures: one dealing only with ordinal information and the other with cardinal information. By making various assumptions, the information from these measures can be aggregated into one appraisal score for each alternative. Thus, different mixed-data methods have been constructed using different sets of assumptions.

In conclusion, it can be said that a whole series of soft discrete multicriteria methods is now available, each method having its own particular advantage and disadvantage and making its own individual assumptions. These evaluation methods are especially useful for development planning problems because they require only a modest amount of information of modest quality.

5. EVALUATION

Multicriteria methods have become an integral part of modern planning methods and techniques. For global and macro decision problems and policy scenario analysis, hard continuous multiobjective methods have reached a stage of sufficient maturity that they can be and actually <u>are</u> applied in a wide variety of policy analyses. They may also be used to scan problems and to identify the main alternative lines of action. Hard discrete multicriteria methods have become very useful in micro decision problems and project evaluation problems. The soft variants of discrete multicriteria methods have also been successfully applied in many plan and project evaluation problems, although much work remains to be done on soft continuous models. The latter class of methods could be very useful, especially for planning and decision problems with limited or qualitative information, so that further research in this area is certainly justified.

One problem still remains to be discussed, viz., the problems of uncertainty regarding the application of various methods. Not all methods give the same results, so that a sensitivity analysis may be necessary (see especially Voogd 1982). Clearly such a sensitivity analysis should only be carried out on a set of models preselected on the basis of methodological, theoretical and empirical criteria.

The above survey has given a brief indication of the variety of multicriteria methods available for use in planning and policy problems with

conflicting objectives. Some of these techniques may play an important
role in development planning in lagging areas or countries. When reliable data is difficult to obtain, the soft variants may be especially
helpful.

REFERENCES

Bell, R.E., Keeney, R.L. and Raiffa, H., Conflicting Objectives in Decisions, Wiley, New York, 1977.

Bellman, R.E. and Zadeh, L.A., 'Decision-Making in a Fuzzy Environment', Management Science, 17, (4), 1980, B41-B164.

Bromley, D.H. and Sfeir-Younis, A., Decision-Making in Developing Countries; Multiobjective Formulation and Evaluation Methods, Praeger, New York, 1977.

Capocelli, R.M. and De Luca, A., 'Fuzzy Sets and Decision Theory', Analysis and Applications, 24, 1973, pp. 446-473.

Chang, C.L., 'Fuzzy Topological Spaces', Mathematical Analysis and Applications, 24, 1968, pp. 182-190.

Charnes, A. and Cooper, W.W., 'Goal Programming and Multiple Objective Optimization', European Journal of Operations Research 1, 1977, pp. 39-54.

Delft, A. van and Nijkamp P., Multicriteria Analysis and Regional Decision-Making, Martinus Nijhoff, The Hague/Boston, 1977.

Donckels, R., 'Regional Multiobjective Planning', Regional Science Research Paper No. 8, University of Louvain, 1975.

Farquhar, P.H., 'A Survey of Multiattribute Utility Theory and Applications', in Starr, M.K. and Zeleny, M. (eds), Multiple Criteria Decision Making, North-Holland Publ. Co., Amsterdam, 1977, pp. 59-90.

Fishburn, P., Decision and Value Theory, Wiley, New York, 1970.

Guigou, J.L., Analyse des Données et Choix à Critères Multiples, Dunod, Paris, 1974.

Hill, M., Planning for Multiple Objectives, monograph Series No. 5, Regional Science Research Institute, Philadelphia, 1973.

Hinloopen, E., Nijkamp, P. and Rietveld, P., 'Qualitative Discrete Multiple Criteria Choice Models in Regional Planning', Regional Science and Urban Economics, vol. 13, 1983 (forthcoming).

Kahne, S., 'A Contribution to Decision Making in Environmental Design', Proceedings of the IEEE 1975, 1975, pp. 518-528.

Keeney, R.L. and Raiffa, H., Decision Analysis with Multiple Conflicting Objectives, Wiley, New York, 1976.

Kmietowicz, Z.W. and Pearman, A.D., Decision Theory and Incomplete Knowledge, Gower, Aldershot, 1981.

Lee, S.M., Goal Programming for Decision Analysis, Auerback, Philadelphia, 1972.

Lewandowski, A. and Grauer, M., The Reference Point Optimization Approach; Methods of Efficient Implementation, WP-82-26, IIASA, Laxenburg, 1982.

Lootsma, T.A., 'Saaty's Priority Theory and the Nomination of a Senior Professor in Operations Research', European Journal of Operational Research 4, 1980, pp. 380-388.

Mastenbroek, P.A. and Paelinck, J.H.P., Multiple Criteria Decision Making, Netherlands Economic Institute, Rotterdam, 1976 (mimeographed).

Nijkamp, P., Theory and Application of Environmental Economics, North-Holland Publ. Co., Amsterdam, 1977.

Nijkamp, P., Multidimensional Spatial Data and Decision Analysis, Wiley, New York, 1979a.

Nijkamp, P., 'A Theory of Displaced Ideals', Environment and Planning A, 11, 1979b, pp. 1165-1178.

Nijkamp, P., Environmental Policy Analysis, Wiley, Chichester, 1980.

Nijkamp, P., 'Soft Multicriteria Analysis as a Tool in Urban Land Use Planning', Environment and Planning B, vol. 9, 1982, pp. 197-208.

Nijkamp, P. and Rietveld, P., 'Multi-Objective Programming Models, New Ways in Regional Decision-Making', Regional Science and Urban Economics 6, 1976, pp. 253-274.

Nijkamp, P. and Rietveld, P., 'Soft Econometrics as a Tool in Regional Discrepancy Analysis, Papers of the Regional Science Association 49, 1982 (forthcoming).

Nijkamp, P. and Spronk, J., 'Analysis of Production and Location Decisions by Means of Multicriteria Analysis, Engineering and Process Economics 4, 1979, pp. 285-302.

Nijkamp, P. and Voogd, J.H., 'The Use of Psychometric Techniques in Evaluation Procedures', Papers of the Regional Science Association 42, 1979, pp. 119-138.

Nijkamp, P. and Voogd, J.H., 'New Multicriteria Methods for Physical Planning by Means of Multidimensional Scaling Techniques', in Haimes, Y. and Kindler, J. (eds), Water and Related Land Resource Systems, Pergamon, Oxford, 1981, pp. 19-30.

Rietveld, P., Multiple Objective Decision Methods and Regional Planning, North-Holland Publ. Co., Amsterdam, 1980.

Rietveld, P., 'Using Ordinal Information in Decision-Making under Uncertainty', Research Memorandum 1982-12, Dept. of Economics, Free University, Amsterdam, 1982.

Roy, B., 'Decision avec Critères Multiples', Metra 11, 1972, pp. 121-151.

Saaty, T.L., 'A Scaling Method for Priorities in Hierarchical Structures', Journal of Mathematical Psychology 15, 1977, pp. 234-281.

Schimpeler, C.C. and Grecco, W.L., 'The Expected Value Method, an Approach based on Community Structures and Values', Highway Research Record 238, 1968, pp. 123-152.

Schlager, K., 'The Rank-Based Expected Value Method of Plan Evaluation', Highway Research Record 238, 1968, pp. 153-158.

Spronk, J., Interactive Multiple Goal Planning for Capital Budgeting and Financial Planning, Kluwer Nijhoff, Boston/The Hague, 1981.

Starr, M.K. and Zeleny, M. (eds), Multiple Criteria Decision Making, North-Holland Publ. Co., Amsterdam, 1977.

Theil, H., Optimal Decision Rules for Government and Industry, North-Holland Publ. Co., Amsterdam, 1968.

Thiriez, H. and Zionts, S. (eds), Multiple Criteria Decision Making, Springer, Berlin, 1976.

Voogd, J.H., 'Qualitative Multicriteria Evaluation Methods for Development Planning', The Canadian Journal of Regional Science 4, 1981a, pp. 73-87.

Voogd, J.H., 'Multicriteria Analysis with Mixed Qualitative-Quantitative Data, Dept. of Urban and Regional Planning, Planologisch Memorandum, Delft University of Technology, 1981b.

Voogd, J.H., Multicriteria Evaluation in Urban and Regional Planning, Pion, London, 1982.

Wierzbicki, A.P., A Methodological Guide to Multiobjective Optimization, Working Paper WP-79-122, IIASA, Laxenburg, 1979a.

Wierzbicki, A.P., The Use of Reference Objectives in Multiobjective Optimization; Theoretical Implications and Practical Experience, WP-79-66, IIASA, Laxenburg, 1979b.

Zeleny, M., Linear Multiobjective Programming, Springer, Berlin, 1974.

Zeleny, M. (ed), Multiple Criteria Decision Making, Springer, Berlin, 1976a.

Zeleny M., 'The Theory of Displaced Ideal', in Zeleny, M. (ed), Multiple Criteria Decision Making, Springer, Berlin, 1976b, pp. 153-206.

15 Urban and Regional Planning with Fuzzy Information

Y. LEUNG

1. INTRODUCTION

Efficient and effective policy design and management have played an important role in the shaping and monitoring of urban and regional development in the developed countries. Though they have not been equally successful in all developed countries, they have proved to be crucial mechanisms of urban and regional planning. Developing countries, on the other hand, have been plagued by urban and regional problems, such as insufficient housing, inadequate public and private facilities, high unemployment rates, inferior environmental conditions, and high disparity of regional growth, in the past decades. The feeble economic base of the countries, compounded by the relatively inadequate planning practice is possibly a major factor contributing to such urban and regional plights. To achieve a healthier state of urban and regional growth, improvement in the efficiency and effectiveness of policy design and management is thus imperative.

Successful policy design and management, to a large extent, depend on a sound database so that reliable estimation and prediction can be obtained. Unfortunately, most of the developing countries lack a sound database. Information is in general weak in nature. Weak, here, connotes limited and/or incomplete, and/or imprecise. For example, population-related planning has long suffered from a weak database (see, for instance Coale and Demeny 1966, United Nations 1967,1970, Carrier and Hobcraft 1971, Doeve 1981, and Kwon 1981). The prevailing weak information has, in turn, prevented successful applications of planning methods conventionally designed for the developed countries where data is relatively more readily available, more complete or more precise.

Thus, a sound database is mandatory for enhancing the effectiveness and efficiency of urban and regional policy design and management in developing countries. Nevertheless, existing conditions in most of these countries make the task of obtaining precise information economically, politically or socially infeasible. While a sound database is still beyond reach, methods which enable logical or formal analysis designed to account for a weak information base should be employed in the planning process.

Over the years, various methods have been developed to deal with the representation, analysis and inference with weak information. Among others, fuzzy sets theory (Zadeh 1965) is one of the methodologies which has plausible application value in the field of planning. Instead of treating precise information as obsolete, and fuzzy cognitive and decision making processes as absurd, the theory regards them as prevailing phenomena which can be formally analysed. Through the theory, human subjectivity and inexact information can be formally represented and analysed. Since information on which policy design and management in developing countries are based is imprecise, fuzzy sets theory seems to be able to serve as an appropriate framework for the analysis of the decision making processes.

The purpose of this paper is to introduce the basic idea of this theory in general, and fuzzy linear programming in particular, to researchers or practitioners in urban and regional planning, especially to those who are involved with planning in the developing countries. Through this presentation, it is hoped that more research may be stimulated and the appropriateness of the theory in planning may be further evaluated. The core of the paper deals with allocation of resources for urban and regional development in an inexact environment. To facilitate this discussion, some basic concepts of fuzzy sets theory are summarised in the following section. Concepts and techniques of fuzzy linear programming are then discussed through a framework of urban land use allocation in section 3. A simple application of the technique to a regional planning problem is then presented in section 4. To conclude the paper, section 5 provides an examination of the plausible applications of fuzzy sets theory to urban and regional planning in general, and to that of the developing countries in particular.

2. SOME BASIC CONCEPTS OF FUZZY SETS THEORY

This section summarises some basic definitions and operations of fuzzy sets theory which are relevant to the discussion in section 3. It is not intended to serve as a complete presentation of the theory. A more thorough examination of the theoretical foundation may be found in Zadeh (965), Goguen (1967) and Kaufmann (1975).

A basic idea of the theory is the concept of a fuzzy subset. In conventional set theory, we have a clear-cut boundary between membership and non-membership of an element to a set. Under fuzzy sets theory, a gradual transition from membership to non-membership is considered as more realistic.

Definition 1 (Fuzzy subset). Let U be a universe of discourse, let x be an element of U. Then a fuzzy subset A in U is a set of ordered pairs

$$\{x, \mu_A(x) \} , \text{ for all } x \in U, \tag{1}$$

where $\mu_A : U \to M$ is a membership function which takes its values in a totally ordered set M, the membership set, and $\mu_A(x)$ indicates the grade of membership of x in A. The membership set M can be the closed interval $[0, 1]$ (Zadeh 1965), or a more general structure, e.g. a lattice (Goguen 1967).

In this paper, the membership set is restricted to the closed interval $[0, 1]$, with 0 and 1 representing the lowest and highest grades of membership respectively.

Example 1. In urban planning, decision makers often encounter some types of budget constraints. Available budgets may be exactly specified. However, it may only be approximately known, sometimes. For instance, instead of 'The budget is α', the statement 'The budget is *about* α' may be the only information a planner can obtain. It is a statement which involves an inexact term ' *about* α'. The information conveyed is thus imprecise. To enable formal analysis, the term '*about* α' can be represented as a fuzzy subset defined by the following membership function

$$\mu_{about\ \alpha}(x) = e^{-k\ (x\ -\ \alpha)^2}, \quad k > 1 \quad . \tag{2}$$

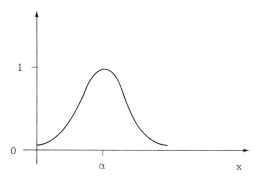

Fig. 1 Membership function of the fuzzy subset "*about* α"

Example 2. In some urban design plans, an objective may be to maximise net revenue. Nevertheless, the maximisation process may be subjected to a fuzzy condition. For example, the statement 'net revenue
should be *much greater than* β' may serve as a goal under the maximisation scheme. Its defining membership function may be specified as

$$\mu_{much\ greater\ than\ \beta}(x) = 1 - e^{-k\ (x\ -\ \beta)}, \quad k > 1 \quad . \tag{3}$$

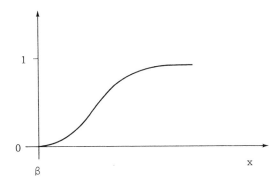

Fig. 2 Membership function of the fuzzy subset "*much greater than* β"

Example 3. Let $\{x_1, x_2, x_3, x_4\}$ be a set of objectives. With respect to the term *important*, the following subset may be derived:

$$\{0.1/x_1, 1/x_2, 0.5/x_3, 0.8/x_4\} , \qquad (4)$$

where $\mu_{important}$ (x_i) is a subjectively assigned value with 1 representing the full membership of being *important*, and 0 representing the full non-membership of being *important*. For instance, the degree of importance of x_3 is 0.5. Here, the membership function μ does not take on a specific form.

Definition 2 (Inclusion). A fuzzy subset A is included in a fuzzy subset B, denoted as $A \subset B$, if and only if $\mu_A (x) \leqq \mu_B (x)$, for all $x \in U$.

Definition 3 (Equality). Fuzzy subsets A and B are equal, denoted as $A = B$, if and only if $\mu_A (x) = \mu_B (x)$, for all $x \in U$.

Definition 4 (Complementation). Fuzzy subset B is the complement of fuzzy subset A, if and only if $\mu_B (x) = 1 - \mu_A (x)$, for all $x \in U$.

Definition 5 (Intersection). The intersection of fuzzy subsets A and B, denoted as $A \cap B$, is defined by

$$\mu_{A \cap B} (x) = \min [\mu_A(x), \mu_B(x)] , \text{ for all } x \in U , \qquad (5)$$

or employing the conjunctive symbol

$$\mu_{A \cap B} (x) = \mu_A(x) \wedge \mu_B(x) , \text{ for all } x \in U . \qquad (6)$$

Example 4. The intersection of the fuzzy subsets defined by equations (2) and (3) is depicted in Figure 3.

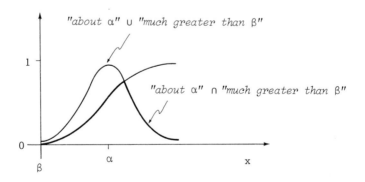

Fig. 3 Membership function of the intersection and union of fuzzy subsets "*about* α" and "*much greater than* β"

Remark Intersection corresponds to the connective 'and'. When defined by the min- operation, it is the largest fuzzy subset that is contained

234

in both A and B. Viewing example 4 in the context of urban planning, intersection of the two fuzzy subsets can be interpreted as a policy design rule 'The budget is *about* α and net revenue should be *much greater than* β'. The min-operation is usually regarded as a hard 'and' for it does not allow tradeoff between fuzzy subsets.

<u>Definition 6</u> (Union). The union of fuzzy subsets A and B, denoted as A U B, is defined by

$$\mu_{A \cup B}(x) = \max [\mu_A(x), \mu_B(x)] \text{ , for all } x \varepsilon U \text{ ,} \qquad (7)$$

or employing the disjunctive symbol

$$\mu_{A \cup B}(x) = \mu_A(x) \vee \mu_B(x) \text{ , for all } x \varepsilon U \text{ .} \qquad (8)$$

<u>Example 5.</u> The union of the fuzzy subsets defined by equations (2) and (3) is depicted in Figure 3.

<u>Remark.</u> Union corresponds to the connective 'or'. When defined by the max- operation, it becomes the smallest fuzzy subset which contains both A and B. The max- operation is usually interpreted as a hard 'or'.

<u>Definition 7</u> (Algebraic product). The algebraic product of fuzzy subsets A and B, denoted as A · B, is defined by

$$\mu_{A \cdot B}(x) = \mu_A(x) \cdot \mu_B(x) \text{ , for all } x \varepsilon U \text{ .} \qquad (9)$$

<u>Remark.</u> In the intersection of fuzzy subsets, the algebraic product is usually interpreted as the connective 'and' in a soft sense. It is employed when dependence of two fuzzy subsets is to be represented. The relationship between the two operations is $\mu_A(x) \wedge \mu_B(x) \geq \mu_A(x) \cdot \mu_B(x)$, for all $x \varepsilon U$.

<u>Defintion 8</u> (Algebraic sum). The algebraic sum of fuzzy sets A and B, denoted as A $\hat{+}$ B, is defined by

$$\mu_{A \hat{+} B}(x) = \mu_A(x) + \mu_B(x) - \mu_A(x) \cdot \mu_B(x) \text{ , for all } x \varepsilon U \text{ .} \quad (10)$$

<u>Remark.</u> In the union of fuzzy subsets, the algebraic sum is usually interpreted as the connective 'or' in the soft sense. An immediate result is $\mu_{A \hat{+} B}(x) \geq \mu_A(x) \vee \mu_B(x)$, for all $x \varepsilon U$.

Researchers should realise that the min- and the algebraic product are not the only operations defining intersections of fuzzy sets. Similarly, the max- and the algebraic sum are just two operations by which union can be defined (see for example, Giles 1976, for other definitions). The author's opinion is that in selecting or constructing a specific type of operation, we should pay attention to its mathematical justifications (for the justification of min- and max-, see Bellman and Giertz 1973) and its relevance in a specific context. Sometimes, an operation is mathematically feasible but does not possess any significant value in interpretation.

<u>Deinition 9</u> (Fuzzy relation). A n-ary fuzzy relation is a fuzzy subset in $U_1 \times U_2 \times \ldots \times U_n$ defined by

$$\mu_R (x_1, x_2, \ldots, x_n) \varepsilon [0, 1] \text{ , } x_i \varepsilon U_i \text{ , for all } i=1, 2, \ldots n \text{ .}$$
$$(11)$$

Specifically, a binary fuzzy relation is a fuzzy subset in $U_1 \times U_2$. Since a fuzzy relation is a fuzzy subset, all the operations discussed above can likewise be applied to the operations on fuzzy relations. Thus, further elaborations are not attempted here.

3. FUZZY LINEAR PROGRAMMING AND URBAN LAND USE PLANNING

Urban and regional planning in developed countries ordinarily involves the allocation of limited resources to competing activities in the most efficient way. Such a problem is especially important in developing countries where scarcity of resources is the rule rather than the exception, and selection and implementation of the most appropriate programs are crucial for development.

Mathematical programming models, especially linear programming techniques, have been applied to economic planning in developing countries (see for example, Gotsch 1968, Bowles 1969, MacEwan 1971, and Wengel 1980). In addition to a sound conceptual framework, the success of various programming models largely depends on the availability of data with exactitude. Unfortunately, the weak database in developing countries often makes the task formidable or impossible. Though probabilistic and stochastic programming have been developed to handle planning under uncertainty, they are not designed to analyse uncertainty due to vagueness in meaning of data. [1] To better handle the problem of a weak database, resource allocation in developing countries needs a flexible programming method so that inexact data can be tolerated and a higher degree of flexibility in programming can be accomplished.

In recent years, fuzzy mathematical programming (Bellman and Zadeh 1970) has become an offspring of fuzzy sets research. It deals with optimisation in a fuzzy decision making environment in which objectives, constraints, or coefficients are vague. Generally, the weak database of developing countries would likely force planners to formulate vague objectives and constraints. Thus, mathematical programming with fuzzy information seems to be appropriate for urban and regional planning in these countries.

In this section the basic concepts of fuzzy linear programming are discussed. To make the presentation more relevant to urban and regional planning, instead of introducing the method in a general context (Zimmerman 1976, Negoita and Sularia 1976), without loss of generality, I have chosen to examine it through a land use allocation problem.

Let the following be a linear programming model (modified from Schlager 1965, Reif 1973, and Leung 1976) for allocating land to activities in a land use plan design:

$$\min \sum_{i=1}^{m} \sum_{j=1}^{n} c_{ij} \, x_{ij} \tag{12}$$

$$\text{s.t.} \sum_{i=1}^{m} \sum_{j=1}^{n} P_{ij} \, x_{ij} \geq p \tag{13}$$

$$\sum_{j=1}^{n} x_{ij} \leq f_i \, , \quad \text{for} \quad i=1, \, 2, \, \ldots, \, m \tag{14}$$

$$\sum_{i=1}^{m} d_j \, x_{ij} = e_j \, , \quad \text{for} \quad j=1, \, 2, \, \ldots, \, n \tag{15}$$

$$x_{ij} \geq 0 \, , \quad \text{for} \quad i=1, \, 2, \, \ldots, \, n; \, j=1, \, 2, \, \ldots, \, n \tag{16}$$

where

m = number of zones of equal area which form an exhaustive subdivision of land area under study,

n = number of land use categories such as residential, industrial, agricultural, considered by the designer,

x_{ij} = number of acres of zone i to be allocated to land use category j,

c_{ij} = cost of developing an acre of zone i for allocation to land use category j,

p_{ij} = net revenue of developing an acre of zone i for allocation to land use j,

p = expected total net return from land use allocation,

f_i = limit on the amount of land from zone i which can be allocated to land uses,

d_j = service ratio coefficient which provides for supporting service land requirements which are necessary for development of land use category j,

e_j = total demand of land use category j .

The problem is to determine the optimal allocation of land to activities so that the total development cost is minimised and prescribed design standards are satisfied. The constraint in equation 13 requires total net revenue to be greater than a specific value p. Constraints in equation 14 set an exact limit on the total amount of land in each zone which can be allocated to varying land uses. Constraints in equation 15 ensure that the total allocation exactly equals the total demand in each land use category.

If our information becomes imprecise, the exactness of constraints in equations 13, 14 and 15 may decrease accordingly. That is, it may become impossible for planners to prescribe exact limits on the availability of land, f_i's, or it may become unrealistic to force an exact expectation on the total net revenue, p, from investment, or to set precise demands, e_j's, for each land use category. Thus, decision makers may have to specify fuzzy versions of the exact constraints.

With regard to the constraint in equation 13, a fuzzy constraint

'Net return should be *greater than* p or *not much smaller than* p'(17)

may be more realistic. This constraint implies that the total net return should preferably be greater than p. In case such a requirement cannot be satisfied, due to uncertainty, it can only be smaller than p to a *small* magnitude. Since '*greater than* p' and '*not much smaller than* p' are linguistic criteria which can be treated as fuzzy subsets, they can be approximated by the functions depicted in Figures 4a and 4b respectively. The fuzzy constraint in equation 17 is then the union of these two fuzzy subsets which imposes a fuzzy interval t on the base variable, in monetary unit (see Figure 4c).

Thus, instead of forcing the total net return to be greater than a specific value p, a permissible level of violation, t, of p is incorporated in the fuzzy constraint. The exact constraint in equation 13 is now transformed into an inexact constraint as

$$\sum_{i=1}^{m} \sum_{j=1}^{n} p_{ij} x_{ij} \gtrsim p ; p - t \qquad (18)$$

where $\gtrsim$ stands for the fuzzy version of $>$, and p and p - t are the two extreme points of the fuzzy interval.

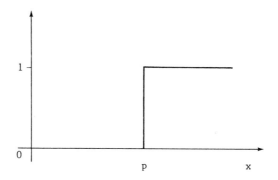

Fig. 4a Membership function of *"greater than p"*

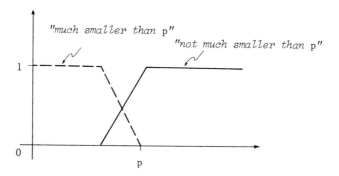

Fig. 4b Membership function of *"not much smaller than p"*

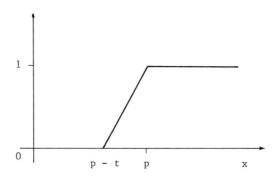

Fig. 4c Membership function of *"greater than p"* or
"not much smaller than p"

238

Accordingly, the planner's degree of satisfaction about the value $\sum\limits_{i=i}^{m} \sum\limits_{j=1}^{n} p_{ij} x_{ij}$ with respect to the statement in equation 17 may be approximated by the following membership functions:

$$\mu(\sum_{i=1}^{m} \sum_{j=1}^{n} p_{ij} x_{ij}) = \begin{cases} 0 & \text{if } \sum\limits_{i=1}^{m} \sum\limits_{j=1}^{n} p_{ij} x_{ij} < p - t \\[2em] 1 - \dfrac{p - \sum\limits_{i=1}^{m} \sum\limits_{j=1}^{n} p_{ij} x_{ij}}{t} & \text{if } p - t \leq \sum\limits_{i=1}^{m} \sum\limits_{j=1}^{n} p_{ij} x_{ij} < p \\[2em] 1 & \text{if } \sum\limits_{i=1}^{m} \sum\limits_{j=1}^{n} p_{ij} x_{ij} \geq p \end{cases}$$

(19)

That is, when the total net revenue is greater than p, the planner is completely satisfied with the grade of membership equal to 1. His degree of satisfaction then decreases monotonically to zero towards the value $p - t$.

By the same token, the imprecise information about the total amount of land available for development in each zone may force planners to replace each exact constraint in equation 14 by a fuzzy constraint

'Total area for development in zone i should be

smaller than f_i or *not much greater than* f_i .'   (20)

Symbolically, it may be stated as:

$$\sum_{j=1}^{n} x_{ij} \lesssim f_i \; ; \; f_i + d_i \; , \text{ for all } i = 1, 2, \ldots, m \qquad (21)$$

Here, we are setting tolerance levels d_i's on the availabilities of land f_i's.

$$\mu_i(\sum_{j=1}^{n} x_{ij}) = \begin{cases} 1 & \text{if } \sum\limits_{j=1}^{n} x_{ij} \leq f_i \\[2em] 1 - \dfrac{\sum\limits_{j=1}^{n} x_{ij} - f_i}{d_i} & \text{if } f_i < \sum\limits_{j=1}^{n} x_{ij} \leq f_i + d_i \\[2em] 0 & \text{if } \sum\limits_{j=1}^{n} x_{ij} > f_i + d_i \end{cases} \qquad (22)$$

(see Figure 5).

Along the same line of reasoning, uncertainty of the future demands makes the formulation of exact constraints in equation 15 unrealistic. Planners may have to replace each of them by the following fuzzy constraint

'Total allocation to land use category j

should be *equal to* e_j or *not much greater than*   (23)

e_j and *not much smaller than* e_j.'

239

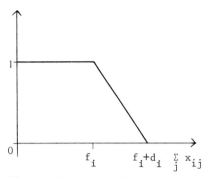

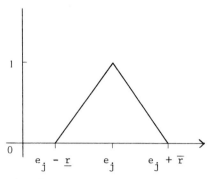

Fig. 5 Membership function of the degree of satisfaction about the value $\sum_j x_{ij}$

Fig. 6 Membership function of the degree of satisfaction about the value $\sum_i d_j x_{ij}$

Symbolically, the constraint is expressed as

$$\sum_{i=1}^{m} d_j x_{ij} \cong e_j \; ; \; e_j - \underline{r}, \; e_j + \bar{r}, \quad \text{for } j=1, 2, \ldots, n \; . \tag{24}$$

In this formulation, permissible levels of violation on the left, $\underline{r}$, and on the right, $\bar{r}$, of e_j are specified.

The planner's degree of satisfaction about the value $\sum_{i=1}^{m} d_j x_{ij}$ may then be approximated by the membership function

$$\mu_j (\sum_{i=1}^{m} d_j x_{ij}) = \begin{cases} 0 & \text{if } \sum_{i=1}^{m} d_j x_{ij} < e_j - \underline{r} \\[2ex] 1 - \dfrac{e_j - \sum_{i=1}^{m} d_j x_{ij}}{\underline{r}} & \text{if } e_j - \underline{r} \leq \sum_{i=1}^{m} d_j x_{ij} < e_j \\[2ex] 1 & \text{if } \sum_{i=1}^{m} d_j x_{ij} = e_j \\[2ex] 1 - \dfrac{\sum_{i=1}^{m} d_j x_{ij} - e_j}{\bar{r}} & \text{if } e_j < \sum_{i=1}^{m} d_j x_{ij} \leq e_j + \bar{r} \\[2ex] 0 & \text{if } \sum_{i=1}^{m} d_j x_{ij} > e_j + \bar{r} \end{cases} \tag{25}$$

(see Figure 6).

Now, let us suppose that instead of minimising the total development cost in equation 12, planners would prefer to employ a target value, c, in the minimisation process. The objective of the problem then becomes vague and may be stated as:

'Total development cost should be *smaller than*

c or *not much greater than* c.' $\tag{26}$

The fuzzy objective may then be expressed as

$$\sum_{i=1}^{m} \sum_{j=1}^{n} c_{ij} \, x_{ij} \lesseqgtr c \, , \, c + \ell \qquad (27)$$

The planner's degree of satisfaction about the value $\sum_{i=1}^{m} \sum_{j=1}^{n} c_{ij} \, x_{ij}$ may be approximated by

$$\mu \left(\sum_{i=1}^{m} \sum_{j=1}^{n} c_{ij} \, x_{ij} \right) = \begin{cases} 1 & \text{if } \sum_{i=1}^{m} \sum_{j=1}^{n} c_{ij} \, x_{ij} \leq c \\[2ex] 1 - \dfrac{\sum_{i=1}^{m} \sum_{j=1}^{n} c_{ij} \, c_{ij} - c}{\ell} & \text{if } c < \sum_{i=1}^{m} \sum_{j=1}^{n} c_{ij} x_{ij} \leq c+\ell \\[2ex] 0 & \text{if } \sum_{i=1}^{m} \sum_{j=1}^{n} c_{ij} \, x_{ij} > c + \ell \end{cases}$$

$$(28)$$

Since both the fuzzy objective and constraints are defined as fuzzy subsets, they are symmetric in the optimisation process. The feasible solutions are those which satisfy both the fuzzy objective and constraints. Thus, the decision space may then be constructed as the intersection of the fuzzy subsets defining the fuzzy objective and constraints (Bellman and Zadeh 1970). In our formulation, the decision space, D, is the intersection of the fuzzy subsets in equations 19, 22, 25 and 28. Its membership function is

$$\mu_D \, (x_{ij}) = \min \left\{ \mu \left(\sum_{i=1}^{m} \sum_{j=1}^{n} p_{ij} \, x_{ij} \right) ; \, \mu_i \left(\sum_{j=1}^{n} x_{ij} \right) , \, \text{all } i; \right.$$

$$\left. \mu_j \left(\sum_{i=1}^{m} d_j \, x_{ij} \right), \, \text{all } j; \, \mu \left(\sum_{i=1}^{m} \sum_{j=1}^{n} c_{ij} \, x_{ij} \right) \right\} \, . \qquad (29)$$

The optimisation problem is then

$$\max_{x_{ij} \geq 0} \mu_D \, (x_{ij}) \, . \qquad (30)$$

By making a simple arithmetic substitution and by dropping the 1's (Zimmerman 1976) in equations 19, 22, 25 and 28, the optimisation problem in equation 29 can be simplified to

$$\max_{x_{ij} \geq 0} \min \left\{ \frac{1}{t} \sum_{i=1}^{m} \sum_{j=1}^{n} p_{ij} \, x_{ij} - \frac{p}{t} ; \, \frac{f_i}{d_i} - \frac{1}{d_i} \sum_{j=1}^{n} x_{ij}, \, \text{all } i; \right.$$

$$\frac{e_j}{r} - \frac{1}{r} \sum_{i=1}^{m} d_j \, x_{ij} \, , \, \frac{1}{r} \sum_{i=1}^{m} d_i \, x_{ij} - \frac{e_j}{r} \, , \, \text{all } j; \qquad (31)$$

$$\left. \frac{c}{\ell} - \frac{1}{\ell} \sum_{i=1}^{m} \sum_{j=1}^{m} c_{ij} \, x_{ij} \right\}$$

Equivalently, it can be reqritten as a conventional linear program

$$\max \, \lambda \qquad (32)$$

$$\text{s.t.} \quad \frac{1}{t} \sum_{i=1}^{m} \sum_{j=1}^{n} p_{ij}\, x_{ij} - \frac{p}{t} \geq \lambda \tag{33}$$

$$\frac{f_i}{d_i} - \frac{1}{d_i} \sum_{j=1}^{n} x_{ij} \geq \lambda \quad \text{for} \quad j=1, 2, \ldots, m \tag{34}$$

$$\frac{e_j}{r} - \frac{1}{r} \sum_{i=1}^{m} d_j\, x_{ij} \geq \lambda \;, \quad \text{for} \quad j=1, 2, \ldots, n \tag{35}$$

$$\frac{1}{r} \sum_{i=1}^{m} d_j\, x_{ij} - \frac{e_j}{r} \geq \lambda \;, \quad \text{for} \quad j=1, 2, \ldots, n \tag{36}$$

$$\frac{c}{\ell} - \frac{1}{\ell} \sum_{i=1}^{m} \sum_{j=1}^{n} c_{ij}\, x_{ij} \geq \lambda \tag{37}$$

$$x_{ij} \geq 0 \;, \quad \text{for} \quad i=1, 2, \ldots, m \;;\; j=1, 2, \ldots, n \tag{38}$$

Therefore, with the linearity assumption, planning programs with fuzzy objectives and constraints can be formulated as a conventional linear program which can be readily solved by existing algorithms.

With the availability of exact information on some planning aspects, planners may be able to specify some constraints with exactitude. For example, in addition to the fuzzy constraints previously discussed, planners may want to impose the following density constraints:

$$x_{ij} \leq g_{jk}\, x_{ik} \;, \qquad \begin{aligned} &i=1, 2, \ldots, m \\ &j=1, 2, \ldots, k, \ldots, n \end{aligned} \tag{39}$$

$$x_{ij} \leq h_{jk}\, x_{hk} \;, \qquad \begin{aligned} &i=1, 2, \ldots, h, \ldots, m \\ &j=1, 2, \ldots, k, \ldots, n \end{aligned} \tag{40}$$

where,

g_{jk} = ratio of land use category j allowed relative to land use category k, with land use categories j and k in the same zone, and

k_{jk} = ratio of land use categories j allowed relative to land use category k, with land use categories j and k in different zones.

Such exact constraints can be added to the linear program, equations 32 - 38, and solved for x_{ij}'s simultaneously.

Though the basic concept of fuzzy linear programming is introduced via the context of urban land use allocation, the fundamental principles of the technique can be applied to planning in various contexts. As an illustration, fuzzy linear programming is applied to a simple regional resource allocation problem in the following section.

4. AN APPLICATION OF FUZZY LINEAR PROGRAMMING TO A REGIONAL RESOURCE ALLOCATION PROBLEM

In this section, fuzzy linear programming is applied to a simplified regional resource allocation problem (based on the example in Hillier and Lieberman 1980, pp. 27-29) which involves the communal farming communities, the system of kibbutzim, in Israel.

It is common for groups of kubbutzim to join together as a confederation, to share common technical services and to coordinate their production. Within the confederation, the overall planning is carried out by a coordinating technical office. The function of the office is to plan agricultural production of the confederation for the coming year.

The present example concerns a confederation of three kibbutzim. The agricultural output of each kittubz is limited by the amount of available irrigable land, which can be exactly prescribed, and by the quantity of water, which can only be vaguely specified, allocated for irrigation by the Water Commissioner (a national government official).

Table 1
Resources data for the Confederation of Kibbutzim

Kibbutz	Irrigable land (acres)	water allocation (acre feet)	
		fuzzy specification	associated fuzzy interval
1	400	should be less than 600 or not much greater than 600	[600,660]
2	600	should be less than 800 or not much greater than 800	[800,840]
3	300	should be less than 375 or not much greater than 375	[375,450]

The crops under consideration are sugar beets, cotton and sorghum. These crops differ in their expected net return and their consumption of water. Fuzzy maximum quota for the total amount of land that can be devoted to each of the crops are also imposed by the Ministry of Agriculture. These exact and inexact data are tabulated in Table 2.

Table 2
Crop data for the Confederation of Kibbutzim

Crop	Net Return (dollars/acre)	(acre feet/ acre)	maximum quota (acres)	
			fuzzy specification	associated fuzzy interval
Sugar beets	400	3	should be less than 600 or not much greater than 600	[600,650]
Cotton	300	2	should be less than 500 or not much greater than 500	[500,540]
Sorghum	100	1	should be less than 325 or not much greater than 325	[325,350]

The three kibbutzim of the Confederation have agreed that every kibbutz will plant the same proportion of its available irrigable land. Nevertheless, any combination of the crops may be grown at any of the kibbutzim.

For the coming year, the coordinating technical office has to determine the amount of land to be devoted to each crop in the respective kibbutzim so that the above prescribed restrictions are satisfied. In place of taking the maximisation of total net return to the confereration as an objective, it is decided that a target value, 260,000 dollars, should be employed and the total net return is required to exceed the target value of be not much below it. Thus, the objective can be stated as

'Total net return should be greater than 260,000 dollars or not much smaller than 260,000 dollars,'

with the associated fuzzy interval [250,000 , 26,000].

Based on the above information, the resource allocation problem of the confederation can be formulated as a fuzzy linear program as follows:

Objective:

$$400(x_{11} + x_{12} + x_{12}) + 300(x_{21} + x_{22} + x_{23}) + 100(x_{31} + x_{32} + x_{33}) \geq$$

$$\geq 260,000 ; 250,000 \qquad (41)$$

Constraints:

Water (fuzzy):

$$3 x_{11} + 2 x_{21} + x_{31} \leq 600; 660 \qquad (42)$$

$$3 x_{12} + 2 x_{22} + x_{32} \leq 800; 840 \qquad (43)$$

$$3 x_{13} + 2 x_{23} + x_{33} \leq 375; 450 \qquad (44)$$

Crop (fuzzy):

$$x_{11} + x_{12} + x_{13} \leq 600; 650 \qquad (45)$$

$$x_{12} + x_{22} + x_{32} \leq 500; 540 \qquad (46)$$

$$x_{31} + x_{32} + x_{33} \leq 325; 350 \qquad (47)$$

Land (exact):

$$x_{11} + x_{21} + x_{31} \leq 400 \qquad (48)$$

$$x_{12} + x_{22} + x_{32} \leq 600 \qquad (49)$$

$$x_{13} + x_{23} + x_{33} \leq 300 \qquad (50)$$

Proportional utilisation (exact):

$$\frac{1}{400} (x_{11} + x_{21} + x_{31}) = \frac{1}{600} (x_{12} + x_{22} + x_{32}) \qquad (51)$$

$$\frac{1}{600} (x_{12} + x_{22} + x_{32}) = \frac{1}{300} (x_{13} + x_{23} + x_{33}) \qquad (52)$$

$$\frac{1}{300} (x_{13} + x_{23} + x_{33}) = \frac{1}{400} (x_{11} + x_{21} + x_{31}) \qquad (53)$$

Non-negativity:

$$x_{ij} \geq 0 \text{ , for } i = 1, 2, 3, \text{ and } j = 1, 2, 3, \qquad (54)$$

where x_{ij} = number of acres of land in kibbutz j to be allocated to plant crop i (1 = sugar beets, 2 = cotton, 3 = sorghum).

Following the arguments in section 3, the above fuzzy linear program can be formulated as a regular linear program as follows:

max λ

s.t. $-26 + .04(x_{11} + x_{12} + x_{13}) + .03(x_{21} + x_{22} + x_{23}) +$

$+ .01(x_{31} + x_{32} + x_{33}) \geq \lambda \qquad (55)$

$$10 - .05 \, x_{11} - .03 \, x_{21} - .02 \, x_{31} \geq \lambda \qquad (56)$$

$$20 - .08 \, x_{12} - .05 \, x_{22} - .03 \, x_{32} \geq \lambda \qquad (57)$$

$$5 - .04 \, x_{13} - .03 \, x_{23} - .01 \, x_{33} \geq \lambda \qquad (58)$$

$$12 - .02 \, x_{11} - .02 \, x_{12} - .02 \, x_{13} \geq \lambda \qquad (59)$$

$$12.5 - .03 \, x_{21} - .03 \, x_{22} - .03 \, x_{23} \geq \lambda \qquad (60)$$

$$13 - .04 \, x_{31} - .04 \, x_{32} - .04 \, x_{33} \geq \lambda \qquad (61)$$

$$x_{11} + x_{21} + x_{31} \leq 400 \qquad (62)$$

$$x_{12} + x_{22} + x_{32} \leq 600 \qquad (63)$$

$$x_{13} + x_{23} + x_{33} \leq 300 \qquad (64)$$

$$3(x_{11} + x_{21} + x_{31}) - 2(x_{12} + x_{22} + x_{32}) = 0 \qquad (65)$$

$$x_{12} + x_{22} + x_{32} - 2(x_{13} + x_{23} + x_{33}) = 0 \qquad (66)$$

$$4(x_{13} + x_{23} + x_{33}) - 3(x_{11} + x_{21} + x_{31}) = 0 \qquad (67)$$

$$x_{ij} \geq 0 , \text{ for } i=1, 2, 3 \text{ and } j=1, 2, 3 \qquad (68)$$

The optimal solution is

$$(x_{11}, x_{12}, x_{13}, x_{21}, x_{22}, x_{23}, x_{31}, x_{32}, x_{33})$$
$$= (140, 155, 112.5, 107,778, 316,667, 0, 0, 0, 73,333) \qquad (69)$$

5. CONCLUSION

Fuzzy sets theory has been introduced as an analytical framework by which urban and regional planning with inexact information can be handled. Specifically, fuzzy linear programming has been examined via an urban land use allocation framework and has been applied to a simplified regional resource allocation problem. While fuzzy linear programming appears to be appropriate in solving optimal allocation problems with fuzzy objectives and constraints, there are several aspects which require further attention.

1. In fuzzy linear programming, membership functions are approximated by linear functions. However, well-behaved monotonically increasing or decreasing functions can also be handled with no major difficulties.

2. In constructing the decision space, the min- operation is ordinarily employed as a rule of confluence. Nevertheless, operations such as the algebraic product (Zimmermann 1978) and addition (Sommer and Pollatschek 1980) can similarly be applied. At present, there are no definitive empirical verifications on how decision makers combine fuzzy objectives and constraints. Thus, more empirical analyses are required before the most suitable operations can be determined.

3. In this paper, constraints become fuzzy when limitations on available resources become vague. Likewise, an objective becomes fuzzy when the target value of the objective function becomes ambiguous. However, they are not the only sources of fuzziness. When the coefficients of the objective functions and that of the constraints are fuzzy numbers, the optimisation problem again becomes a fuzzy mathematical programming problem with fuzzy objectives and constraints. Such a problem can also be effectively transformed into a regular linear program (Negoita and Sularia 1976, Dubois and Prade 1980).

4. Though only fuzzy linear programming with a single objective has been discussed, the framework can easily be extended to multiple objective optimisation characterising most planning problems. The symmetry of the objectives and constraints enables the formulation of a multiple objective fuzzy linear program as a single objective fuzzy linear program (Zimmermann 1978).

5. To cope with the dynamic aspects of planning, the current framework can be extended to deal with fuzzy optimisation over time (Bellman and

Zadeh 1970). In particular fuzzy linear programming can easily be extended to solve multistage planning with time-dependent fuzzy objectives and constraints.

Though our discussion in this paper is restricted to urban and regional planning in the context of fuzzy mathematical programming, it has been demonstrated that fuzzy sets theory is also applicable in analysing more general planning problems such as those involving hierarchical objectives (Leung 1979) and multicriteria conflicts (Nijkamp 1979, Leung 1981, 1982 and 1983).

To recapitulate, new methodologies such as fuzzy sets theory appear to be appropriate for dealing with urban and regional planning in developing countries suffering from acute problems of a weak database. Though the theory is not likely to be the ultimate solution for the analysis of human subjectivity and inexact information, it is, however, more realistic than most of the conventional analytical techniques. Following the argument of the present paper, one may have the misconception that planning in developed countries is free from the problem of inexact information. On the contrary, experiences have demonstrated that human subjectivity and inexact information also prevail, albeit to a lesser extent, in the highly complex urban and regional systems and decision making processes in developed countries. Thus, development of new methodologies such as fuzzy sets theory is pertinent for realistic planning.

NOTES

[1] Note that the probability and stochastic processes deal with uncertainty related to the randomness of occurrence, while fuzzy sets deals with that related to the vagueness of meaning.

REFERENCES

fort>6Bellman, R.E, and Zadeh, L.A., 'Decision-Making in a Fuzzy Environment', Management Science, 17, 1970, B141-B164.
Bellman, R.E. and Giertz, M., 'On the Analytic Formalism of the Theory of Fuzzy Sets', Information Science, 5, 1973, pp. 149-157.
Bowles, S., Planning Educational Systems for Economic Growth, Harvard University Press, Cambridge, 1969.
Carrier N. and Hobcraft, J., Demographic Estimation for Developing Societies, Population Investigation Committee, London School of Economics, London, 1971.
Coals, A.J. and Demeny, P., Regional Model Life Tables and Stable Populations, Princeton University Press, Princeton, 1966.
Doeve, W.L.J., 'Demographic Models for Third World Countries: Towards Operational Planning Tools', in Chatterjee, L. and Nijkamp, P. (eds), Urban Problems and Economic Development, Sijthoff and Noordhoff, Alphen a/d Rijn, Netherlands, 1981.
Dubois D. and Prade H., 'Systems of Linear Fuzzy Constraints', Fuzzy Sets and Systems, 3, 1980, pp. 37-48.
Goguen, J., 'L-Fuzzy Sets', Journal of Mathematical Analysis and Applications, 18, 1967 pp. 145-174.
Gotsch, C., 'A Programming Approach to Some Agricultural Policy Problems in West Pakistan', Pakistan Development Review, 8, 1968, pp. 192-225.
Giles, R., 'Lukasiewicz Logic and Fuzzy Theory', International Journal of Man-Machine Studies, 8, 1976, pp. 313-327.
Hillier, F.S. and Lieberman, G.J., Introduction to Operations Research, Holden-Day, San Fransicso, 1980.
Kaufmann, A., Introduction to the Theory of Fuzzy Subsets, Vol. 1, Academic Press, New York, 1975.
Kwon, W.Y., 'A Simulation Model for Testing Urban Population Distribution Policies in Relation to Selecting Growth Centers in Korea', in Chatterjee, L. and Nijkamp , P. (eds), Urban Problems and Economic Development, Sijthoff and Noordhoff, Alphen a/d Rijn, Netherlands, 1981.
Leung Y., 'A Quadratic Programming Model for Investment Decision Analysis in Land Use Planning', Great Plains-Rocky Mountain Geographi-Journal, 5, 1976, pp. 57-62.
Leung, Y., 'A Fuzzy Set Procedure for Project Selection with Hierarchical Objectives', Proceedings, First International Symposium on Policy Analysis and Information Systems, pp. 364-371; also in Wang, P.P. and Chang, S.K. (eds), Fuzzy Sets – Theory and Applications to Policy Analysis and Information Systems, Plenum, New York, 1980.
Leung, Y., 'A Value-based Approach to Conflict Resolution Involving Multiple Objectives and Multiple Decision-making Units', Paper presented to the International Symposium on Conflict Management held in Tokyo, Japan, August 1981.
Leung, Y., 'A Concept of a Fuzzy Ideal for Multicriteria Conflict Resolution', in Wang, P.P. (ed), Advances in Fuzzy Sets Theory and Applications, Plenum, New York, 1982.
Leung, Y., 'Dynamic Conflict Resolution through a Theory of a Displaced Fuzzy Ideal', in Gupta, M.M. and Sanchez, E. (eds), Approximate Reasoning in Decision Analysis, North-Holland, Amsterdam, 1983.
MacEwan, A., Development Alternatives in Pakistan, Harvard University Press, Cambridge, 1971.
Negoita, C.V. and Sularia, M., 'On Fuzzy Mathematical Programming and Tolerances in Planning', Economic Computation and Economic Cybernetics Studies and Research, 1, 1976, pp. 3-14.

248

Nijkamp, P., 'Conflict Patterns and Compromise Solutions in Fuzzy Choice Theory', Journal of Peace Science, 4, 1979, pp. 67-90.

Reif, B., Models in Urban and Regional Planning, Intertext Educational Publishers, New York, 1973.

Schlager, K.J., 'A Land Use Plan Design Model', Journal of the American Institute of Planners, 1965, pp. 103-111.

Sommer, G. and Pollatschek, M.A., 'A Fuzzy Programming Approach to an Air Pollution Regulation Problem', Working Paper No. 76-01, Institute Wirtschaftswiss. R.W.T.H., Aachen, West Germany, 1976.

United Nations, Methods of Estimating Basic Demographic Measures from Incomplete Data (manual IV), United Nations, New York, 1967.

United Nations, Methods of Measuring Internal Migration (manual VI), United Nations, New York, 1970.

Wengel, J., Allocation of Industry in the Andean Common Market, Martinus Nijhoff, Boston, 1980.

Zadeh, L.A., 'Fuzzy Sets', Information and Control, 8, 1965, pp. 338-353.

Zimmermann, H.J., 'Description and Optimisation of Fuzzy Systems', International Journal of General Systems, 2, 1976, pp. 209-215.

Zimmermann, H.J., 'Fuzzy programming and linear programming with several objective functions', Fuzzy Sets and Systems, 1, 1978, pp. 45-56.

16 The Estimation and Modelling of Discontinuous Change

I. ADELMAN AND J. M. HIHN

1. INTRODUCTION

The use of models that incorporate discontinuous changes in policy analysis is still in its infancy. Several major problems have retarded the
increased use of such models. But these have been at least partially
solved by recent developments.

The purpose of this paper is to bring together the recent conceptual
and statistical advances which make the estimation of systems with discontinuous and/or nonlinear dynamics possible. The main emphasis will
be on techniques for estimating the parameters of nonlinear manifolds.
It is hoped that this exposition will improve the quality of applications of catastrophe theory in the social sciences and enable their use
in policy analysis.

We shall first review some of the difficulties with existing attempts
to apply catastrophe theory to economics generally and urban and regional analysis more specifically. Then we shall disucss how these might
be overcome.

2. PROBLEMS IN DEVELOPING AN APPLIED CATASTROPHE THEORY

Urban and regional scholars showed an early interest in catastrophe
theory because of the numerous instances of discontinuous change. For
example, sudden changes in land values, land use, and urban wage rates
are commonly observed (Dendrinos 1978, Henderson 1977, Mees 1975,
Poston and Wilson 1977, and Wilson 1976).

In analysing these discontinuities by means catastrophe theory, the
existence of gradient dynamics has been assumed. This, in turn, implies
that the dynamic paths observed are the result of an adjustment process
that moves toward an optimal state of the system. The artificial impo-
sition of the assumption that some function is being optimised when this
may be totally unjustified on behavioural grounds may be implicit in the
use of catastrophe theory. In economics, the optimisation assumption
(and, hence, gradient dynamics) is often quite natural since, at the
microlevel, we usually assume that behaviour results from optimisation
of some objective function (Varian 1982). However, the generalisation
of this assumption to macrosystems is not always appropriate. And it
is not necessary when discontinuous dynamics are modelled by means of
the more general bifurcating systems which do not assume gradient dynamics and encompass catastrophe theory as a special case.

The second problem with applied catastrophe theory has been that, in
practice, the existence of a catastrophe manifold has generally been
determined intuitively and the model then forced to fit one of the

251

simple carastrophes. From an analytical perspective, the proper approach
would be to specify a general model and then determine statistically or
analytically under what conditions a particular catastrophe manifold may
arise. Hale (1977) has proposed a procedure that, when applied to a
general dynamic systen, can be used to test for the existence and form
of the catastrophe manifold.

The third problem has been the general lack of any formal, statistical
analysis in papers employing catastrophe theory. The reasons for the
paucity of statistical estimates have been the use of topology in proving
the theorems of catastrophe theory; the existence of discontinuities;
and the existence, over some ranges of the parameters, of multiple values
of the endogenous variables for a given configuration of values of the
exogenous variables. However, due to new advances in mathematical
statistics (Cobb 1978), it is now possible to estimate the highly nonlinear manifolds that arise in bifurcating processes with only a few
relatively reasonable assumptions. Furthermore, some of the insights
of Cobb can be used to arrive at other, more standard least squares
techniques for estimating such discontinuous manifolds. These developments will be discussed in depth below along with some other estimation
techniques applicable to slightly more restrictive problems.

Before presenting the estimation techniques, we shall review the
mathematical specification of dynamic systems with discontinuities.
This review will clarify the difference between bifurcating processes
and catastrophe theory and pave the way for the stochastic specifications
which must underly attempts at estimation.

3. BIFURCATING PROCESSES

Formal attempts at inforporating discontinuous change in relevant social
processes have only employed catastrophe theory. As will be seen below,
catastrophe theory is a special case of bifurcation theory. By generali-
sing the discussion to the level of bifurcation theory and stochastic
processes, a wider range of dynamic behaviour can be modelled. This
should eventually lead to a much greater understanding of how to construct appropriate policies in the face of discontinuous change.

Consider the differential equation system:

$$\dot{y} = g(y, a) \tag{1}$$

where $y \in R^n$ is a vector of endogenous or state variables and a $\in R^m$
is a vector representing a set of environment variables. The elements
of the environment consist of the parameters of the system as well as
the control variables and uncontrollable exogenous forces. (In planning
terminology, these latter variables are referred to as instrumental and
exogenous variables.) It is assumed that there exists a one-way causal
relation from the environment to the state.

The trajectory of the state, $y(t)$, $t \geq 0$, can be determined by integrating the differential equation (1) given the trajectory of the environment, $a(t)$, $t \geq 0$, and initial conditions for y. When the environment is constant, $a(t) = 1$, it is usually the case that the state
variable converges to an equilibrium, y_e, or:

$$\lim_{t \to \infty} y(t) = y_e \tag{2}$$

where

$$g(y_e, \ a) = 0 \tag{3}$$

If only one value of y_e satisfies equations (2) and (3), then the system has a unique equilibrium. If there are several values of y_e, then the system has multiple equilibria. This latter possibility is inherent in the mathematical forms chosen for $g(y, \ a)$ in bifurcation and catastrophe theories.

The usual approach to discussing the dynamics of differential equation and control theoretic models is to graph the phase diagrams of the relevant equations. These display the equilibrium solutions and can be used to infer their stability properties. Usually, a phase diagram is drawn holding all parameters constant. For example, in the optimal growth models, the production function and savings propensities are held constant. But, as the parameters of the system change, the position of the equilibrium and possibly even the number and stability properties of the equilibria can change.

The graph of the manifold defined by $g(y_e, \ a) = 0$ used in bifurcation and catastrophe theories traces how the equilibria change with changes in the parameters of the system. If the system $\dot{y} = g(y, \ a)$ is well behaved, there are only unique equilibria. It is when $\dot{y} = g(y, \ a)$ gives rise to multiple equilibria and cyclic behaviour that bifurcation theory arises.

Bifurcating processes come in all shapes and sizes. An example of a fairly simple process is displayed in Figure 1. Figure 1 is the graph of $g(y_e, \ a) = 0$ where both y_e and a are scalar variables. In this case, when $a < b$, there is only one equilibrium: and for $a > b$, there are two equilibria. The point b is referred to as a bifurcation point because, when $a = b$, there is a fundamental change in the dynamic process.

4. GRADIENT SYSTEMS AND CATASTROPHE THEORY

A special class of differential equations is the class of gradient systems in which $g(y, \ a)$ takes the form:

$$\dot{y} = g(y, \ a) = \frac{\partial F(y, \ a)}{\partial y} \tag{4}$$

In gradient systems, the trajectories always follow the path of 'steepest ascent (descent)'. Catastrophe theory concerns gradient systems that exhibit discontinuous shifts.

The purpose of Thom's (1975) work on catastrophe theory is to show that dynamic gradient systems that exhibit dicontinuous changes can, by suitable transformations, be reparametrised into one of seven canonical polynomial forms. These canonical forms are referred to as catastrophe manifolds. A catastrophe manifold is defined by the set of equilibrium values of y for all possible values of a or by $g(y_e, \ a) = 0$.

An example of a fold catastrophe, the simplest of the catastrophe manifolds, is presented below. The fold manifold is described by equation (5).

$$g(y, \ a) = \frac{\partial F(y, \ a)}{\partial y} = y^2 - a = 0 \tag{5}$$

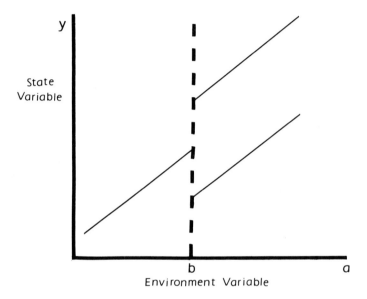

Figure 1. Illustration of a Bifurcating Process

FAMILY OF FUNCTIONS

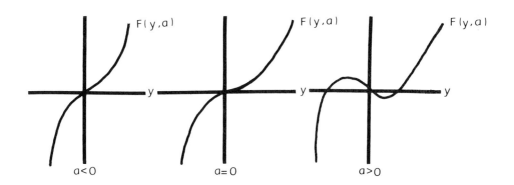

CATASTROPHE MANIFOLD

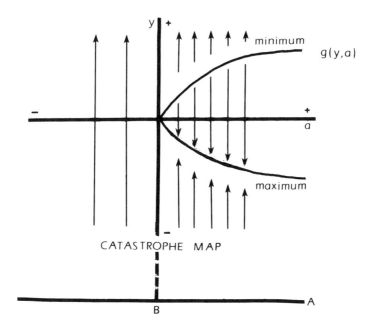

Figure 2.

The function $F(y, a)$ defines a family of functions whose solution properties change with the values of a. Since equation (5) is a gradient dynamic system, it defines the set of all values of y that correspond to the extreme points of functions defined by $F(y, a)$.

The graph of the family of functions that corresponds to the catastrophe manifold specified in equation (5) and the catastrophe map is displayed in Figure 2. The state space is represented in this case by the vertical axis and the control space by the horizontal axis.

The catastrophe manifold is a parabola in y which shows that, corresponding to different values of a, there exist two critical points - one maximum and one minimum. When the control a, is zero, the critical point is $y = 0$. This is a degenerate critical point because the second derivative is zero. If $a < 0$, then y^2 has no extreme points in the real plane. If $a > 0$, then we have $a = y^2$; and there are two symmetric values of y which satisfy the equation, namely, $y = \pm \sqrt{a}$. When $y < 0$, $F(y, a)$ reaches a maximum because the second derivative of $F(y, a)$ is negative; and when $y > 0$, $F(y, a)$ corresponds to a minimum because the second derivative is positive. The graphs in Figure 2 demonstrate how the underlying function changes as the value of the parameter changes. The bifurcation set is the set of points in the environment space that corresponds to degenerate extreme points. B is the bifurcation set. For the fold catastrophe, the bifurcation set consists of a single point. In this example, it separates the environment space into two spaces. One corresponds to the existence of two extreme points and the other corresponds to no points in the real plane (see Figure 2).

The dynamics for the fold catastrophe (equation 2) are drawn on the catastrophe manifold in Figure 2 assuming the objective is to maximise $F(y, a)$. The maxima are only locally stable; and, for large values of y, the system will converge to positive infinity.

In catastrophe theory, it is usually assumed that the endogenous variable y, moves very fast compared to changes in the control variable a. Under the assumption of 'fast dynamics', the systems will always be close to an equilibrium trajectory which greatly simplifies the analysis. Varaiya and Wiseman (1981) refer to this as the quasi-static hypothesis (QSH).

5.   TESTING FOR DISCONTINUOUS DYNAMICS

Both bifurcation theory and catastrophe theory assume the existence of discontinuously changing equilibria. In the past, the existence of discontinuities has been attributed to large exogenous shocks which change the structural parameters of the system under study. This type of approach only allows one to determine the existence of a discontinuity ex post. Bifurcation theory provides a global specification of a dynamic process in which not only do the variables determining the dynamics change, but also the parameters specifying the structure of the system. It, therefore, enables an ex ante tracing of the location of discontinuities in the parameter space. Varaiya and Wiseman (1981) argue that all proposed explanations of discontinuities in urban processes that view discontinuous change as an inherent part of the process emphasise either the existence of externalities or indivisibilities and thresholds. In political processes, discontinuities can arise because there exists multiple equilibria for specific combinations of the exogenous variables (Adelman and Hihn 1982).

Whatever the cause of a discontinuity, all processes exhibiting dis-

continuously changing equilibria have certain features in common:
(1) under certain conditions, the rate of change of the endogenous variable is disproportionate to changes in the exogenous variables and (2)
the existence of irreversibility. Hale (1977) has proposed a mathematical
procedure for determining whether such discontinuities arise and which
of the elementary catastrophe manifolds provides the appropriate description of the set of equilibrium solutions.

Assume the quasi-static hypothesis holds and that the set of equilibria
solutions is given by:

$$g(y, a) = 0 \qquad (6)$$

where $y \in R^n$, $a \in R^m$, $g_y = \partial g / \partial y$, and $g_a = \partial g / \partial a$. Taking a Taylor
expansion around the point (y, a) yields

$$g_y \Delta y + g_a \Delta a + r(y, a) = 0 \qquad (7)$$

Solving for Δy,

$$\Delta y = -g_y^{-1} g_a \Delta a - g_y^{-1} r(y, a) \qquad . \qquad (7)$$

Taking the first-order approximation of (6) linearises g(y, a) around
the point (y, a). The term g_y is an n x n matrix of partials with
respect to y; and g_a is an n x m matrix of partials with respect to
a. Hale shows that, when there is a local discontinuity, g_y will be
singular or will not be of full rank. The Lyapunov-Schmidt procedure
can then be used to partition the endogenous variables into a group of
n - k equations that are linearly independent and k equations that
are dependent. It is among the k dependent variables that discontinuous changes will occur. Once these have been identified, the system can
be reduced to a system of k equations. Varaiya and Wiseman (1981) call
the bifurcation equations to be denoted by ϕ(y, a).

Once the existence of a discontinuity has been determined, the higher
order derivatives of ϕ(y, a) must be derived in order to determine
which manifold is appropriate. For example, if the higher order derivatives of ϕ_y are nonzero and k = 1, then the relevant manifold is
either the fold or cusp. If the higher order derivatives also vanish,
then more complicated manifolds must be considered.

In practice, this procedure would be relatively difficult to implement.
An alternative approach, which is related to Hale's idea, is to take a
statistical perspective. First, note that what is of interest are the
properties of the first partial g_y(y, a) which in its most general
form is a function of both y and a. In practice, a would be of
the form a(x) where a is a vector of reduced form variables and x
is the vector of exogenous variables. For example, a might be political
participation which would be an aggregation of the existence of channels
of participation and the actual use of the channels. Therefore, g_y
can be expressed as g_y[y, a(x)]. If there is a potential discontinuity,
then this relationship is highly nonlinear with respect to y. If the
system were linear, the partial of g with respect to y would be only
a function of the exogenous variables and parameters a or $dy = g_y[a(x)] dx$.
If this is true, then one would not expect dy and y to be highly
correlated while dy and dx would be. Therefore, if a principal components matrix for dy, dx, and y were constructed, the existence or

nonexistence of linearity would imply a certain structure to the interaction among regression coefficients of variables upon the principal
components (or variable loadings). Furthermore, an examination of the
principal components matrix should help one isolate what types of bifurcation is most likely to exist. If the underlying bifurcation is a
fold, then dy should be most closely related to $1/y$; if a cusp, then
dy is most closely correlated to $1/y^2$; if a swallowtail, then dy is
most correlated to $1/(y^3 - y)$; or if a butterfly, then dy is most
correlated to $1/(y^4-y^2 - y)$.

   To determine the specific parameters of the bifurcating process, formal estimation procedures will need to be employed. These are discussed
in the following section.

6. ESTIMATION OF DISCONTINUOUS DYNAMIC PROCESSES

Having determined the existence and general shape of the catastrophe
manifold, we are now ready to turn to estimation. The very lack of continuity which causes $g(y, 1)$ to be singular is also likely to lead to
the breakdown of regression analysis when one attempts to estimate discontinuous functions. However, one can develop various procedures for
dealing with this problem.

Estimation of Bifurcating Processes

Intuitively, all the techniques employed for estimating the parameters
of a manifold with discontinuities and multiple equilibria are based on
smoothing out the actual function that is estimated and then mathematically rederiving the parameters for the original function. For example,
assume:

$$g(y, a) = y^3 - \beta y - \alpha x_1 = 0 \qquad (9)$$

where y is the endogenous variable and x_1 is an exogenous variable.
Equation (9) gives rise to the cusp catastrophe and can be rewritten as:

$$y^3 = \beta y + \alpha x_1 + u \qquad (10)$$

   For the specified equation and for purposes of estimation, y^3 can be
considered as just another endogenous variable, y_2, leaving

$$y_2 = \beta y + \alpha x_1 + u \quad . \qquad (11)$$

For estimation purposes, y_2 is being regressed on y and x_1 with y,
however, correlated to u. This problem is now linear in both the parameters and endogenous variables. The well-known solution to the difficulty posed by the correlation between y and u is to construct an
instrument for y and use instrumental variables or two-stage least
squares to estimate (11). This technique yields consistent estimates
for equation (10). Not all of the equations of interest are that simple,
but the basic idea as to how to estimate the parameters is the same.

   The advantages of using a least-squares approach is that numerous software packages exist, and the distributions of the estimated parameters
are known. The cost of using a least-squares approach is that it is not
clear under what conditions the implicit assumptions regarding the

structure of the error term are reasonable. On the other hand, the use of maximum likelihood methods gives rise to even more serious restrictions on the distribution of the error term (see Wold 1966). Also, note that other least-squares approaches could be adopted to estimate these types of nonlinear manifolds - for example, partial least squares (Wold 1966, 1973).

As examples, consider the following two specifications of the cusp catastrohpe and the estimation problems that arise. Assume $g(y, a)$ has the form

$$(y + \varepsilon)^3 - \beta(y + \varepsilon) - \alpha x = 0 \qquad (12)$$

where ε is symmetrically distributed around zero. This can be rewritten as:

$$y^3 = \gamma y + \alpha x + u \qquad (13)$$

where

$$u = 3y^2 \varepsilon + \beta \varepsilon + \varepsilon^3 \qquad (14)$$

$$\gamma = \beta + 3\varepsilon^2 \quad . \qquad (15)$$

It can be shown that, in the limit, the only problem that arises is that $\text{plim } \gamma = \beta + 3\sigma_\varepsilon^2$ and, therefore, γ is an inconsistent estimator of β. However, since a consistent estimator of σ_ε^2 exists, it is possible to compute the appropriate value of the parameter of interest after the estimation.

Another example is similar to the functional form Cobb uses. Assume $g(y, a)$ equals

$$\left(\frac{y - L}{s}\right)^3 - \beta x_1 \left(\frac{y - L}{s}\right) - \alpha x_1 = u \quad , \qquad (16)$$

then

$$\frac{y^3}{s^3} = -\frac{L^3}{s^3} + \left(\frac{\beta_1 L}{s} - \alpha_1\right) x_1 + \frac{3L^2}{s^3} y - \frac{\beta_1}{s} x_1 y - \frac{3L}{s^3} y^2 + u \qquad (17)$$

or

$$y^3 = -L^3 + s^3\left(\frac{\beta_1 L}{s} - \alpha_1\right)x_1 + 3L_y^2 - s^2\beta_1 x_1 y_1 - 3Ly^2 + u \quad . \qquad (18)$$

Clearly, equation (18) is nonlinear in both parameters and endogenous variables. This is not an easy problem to solve and requires th use of numerical optimization techniques. However, there do exist several software packages that have programs for computing the parameters for nonlinear least-squares problems. A recent procedure in which the limiting distributions of the parameters have been derived for such a case is based on the work of Amemiya (1974). Clearly, while estimation of the parameters of a nonlinear manifold may not be easy, it is possible; and there are several different ways in which one may proceed.

Estimation of Catastrophe Manifolds

When employing catastrophe theory, an additional estimation problem
arises because catastrophe theory is derived from a marriage between
differential topology, geometry, and global analysis. The derivation
of the elementary carastrophes as descriptions of the local features of
a gradient system depend crucially on topological equivalence. It is
not possible to estimate simultaneously both the parameters of the catastrophe manifold and the relevant transformations used to determine the
topologically equivalent canonical catastrophe manifold. The reason is
that the types of transformations permitted under typological equivalence
are far more varied than those which permit the use of rigorous estimation techniques. The only solution to this problem is for the model
builder to specify theoretically the appropriate nonlinear transformations on the measurable variables that bring the mathematical form of
the model to within a linear transformation of a catastrophe manifold
(Cobb 1978),

   Cobb proposed the use of an estimation procedure specifically designed
for catastrophe manifolds (Cobb 1978, 1981, Cobb and Watson 1980, and
Crain and Cobb 1981). Under most cases, Cobb's procedure will produce
a different set of consistent estimators from the least-squares approach
discussed above. Different estimation techniques can produce different
consistent estimators because they use different measures and specify
different structures for the error term.

   Cobb argues that, from a statistical standpoint, what makes a catastrophe model different from the standard linear and nonlinear models
are that the underlying distributions are multimodal and the estimation
problem is one of determining the appropriate probability distribution
function that will produce unimodal and multimodal distributions for
different parameter values.

   Just as in the least-squares case, a random element must be introduced
into $g(y, a)$. A formulation that arises in stochastic calculus (Soong
1973) is:

$$dy = g(y, a) \, dt + \sqrt{v}(y) \cdot dw(t) \tag{19}$$

where $dw(t)$ is a random input and $v(y)$ is the limiting variance of
the trajectories of y. In stochastic processes, what is of interest
is not the paricular trajectory of the endogenous variables because there
are an infinite number of such trajectories but, rather, the distribution of the trajectory.

   Cobb (1978) has developed an estimating technique for the parameters
of the limiting distribution of the family of distributions represented
by (19). The limiting distribution of the trajectory of y for the
special case in which (1) the mean trajectory equals the deterministic
part and (2) the limiting variance is constant given by

$$\lim_{t \to \infty} f(y) = k \, \exp \int_y g(y, a) \, dy \tag{20}$$

(see Cobb 1981). For a cusp catastrophe, this limiting distribution
becomes

$$\lim_{t \to \infty} f(y) = k \, \exp \left(az + \frac{1}{2} bz^2 - \frac{1}{4} z^3 \right) \tag{21}$$

when   a   and   b   are linear combinations of the exogenous variable and z is the standardised value of y. Then:

$$a = a_0 + \Sigma a_i x_i \qquad (22)$$

$$b = b_0 + \Sigma b_i x_i \qquad (23)$$

and

$$z = \left(\frac{y - 1}{s}\right) \qquad (24)$$

where l is a location parameter and s is a scale parameter. The estimation of $g(y, x, a, b, l, s)$ is then equivalent to the estimation of the parameters a_i, b_i, l and s.

Thom's (1975) equivalence theorem, which is required for representation of differential processes with discontinuously changing equilibria by one of the seven elementary catastrophe manifolds, makes use of transformations which may well be highly nonlinear. Such nonlinear mappings would be reflected in a nonlinear relationship between the parameters (a, b) of the manifold and the exogenous variables (x). The linear relationship Cobb posits for estimation purposes could be viewed as a local approximation of the nonlinear function resulting from Thom's (1975) transformations. Alternatively, one could express the parameters (a, b) as linear functions of several latent variables (x); the latent variables would then span a nonlinear space. The canonical form of the relationship between the cusp parameters and the exogenous variables would be nonlinear in the variables but linear in the coefficients, a_i, b_i, and $\forall_i$. The nonlinearities would be expressed as nonlinear transformations upon the scales of the exogenous variables. The latent variables would then be extracted so as to make them linearly independent.

When assuming that the parameters (a, b) are linear functions of the exogenous variables (x), it can be demonstrated that the distribution function of (21) is a member of the standard expoential family of distributions (Lehman 1959). For expository purposes, assume there is only one exogenous variable. Then the limiting distribution can be rewritten as

$$\lim_{t \to \infty} f(y) + K \exp(c_1 y + c_2 xy + c_3 y^2 + c_4 xy^2$$
$$+ c_5 y^3 - c_6 y^4). \qquad (25)$$

Or, more generally, it can be expressed as

$$k \exp[\Sigma c_i f_i(y, x)] \qquad (26)$$

The maximum likelihood estimates of the parameters of such an exponential distribution exist and are unique (Crain 1976) under very general conditions. However, the computations for obtaining the maximum likelihood estimates are quite involved and time consuming. As an alternative, Cobb (1978, 1981) has suggested using the method of moments.

Parameter estimation employing the method of moments requires the ability to identify n linear equations in n parameters and n moments. Conceptually, the idea underlying the method is that, if enough of the

moments of a distribution are known, then the distribution can be specified exactly. Cobb (1981) shows that, for distributions with the form
$\exp[\Sigma c_i f_i(y, x)]$, a system of equations can be derived relating n parameters to $(2n - 2)$ of the joint moments. Both the method of moments
and maximum likelihood will yield a set of consistent estimators. The
parameters of interest (a, b, l, s) are nonlinear functions of c and
are also consistent estimators because functions of consistent estimators are consistent.

While an R-square type measure can be computed as an indication of
goodness-of-fit, the method of moments does not permit parametric statistical inference because little is known about the statistical distribution of the parameters. A nonparametric technique, such as the Stone-
Geisser method, can be used for statistical evaluation of the quality of
the model (Stone 1974, Geisser 1974, 1975). This method is based on the
predictive quality of the model. When employing the method of maximum
likelihood, likelihood ratios can be constructed with known distributions
that will test the overall ability of the model to explain the data.
However, as pointed out above, the validity of these tests depends on
rather stringent and numerous assumptions on the distribution of the
error term.

7. CONCLUSIONS

There are many social and physical processes that exhibit multiple equilibria and discontinuous change. Catastrophe theory represents a major
theoretical breakthrough that will, in the years to come, extend our
ability to model these processes. However, until widely applicable techniques for the estimation of the parameters of the relevant models are
developed, a catastrophe theory or even a bifurcation theory will have
little practical value to the social sciences.

REFERENCES

Adelman, I., and Hihn, J.M., 'The Dynamics of Political Change', Giannini Foundation Working Paper no. 192, Department of Agricultural and Resource Economics, University of California, Berkeley, 1982.

Amemiya, T., 'The Nonlinear Two-Stage Least Squares Estimator', Journal of Econometrics 2, 1974, p. 109.

Cobb, L., 'The Multimodal Exponential Families of Statistical Catastrophe Theory', in Taillie, Patil, Baldessori (eds), Statistical Distributions in Scientific Work, Reidel, Holland, 1981.

Cobb, L., 'Stochastic Catastrophe Models and Multimodal Distributions', Behavioural Science, 23, 1978, pp. 360-374.

Cobb, L. and Watson, B., 'Statistical Catastrophe Theori: An Overview', Mathematical Modelling, 1, 1980, pp. 311-317.

Crain, B., 'Exponential Models, Maximum Likelihood Estimation and the Haar Condition', Journal of the American Statistical Association, 71, 1976, pp. 737-740.

Crain, B. and Cobb, L., 'Parameter Estimation for Truncated Exponential Formities', in Taillie, Patil, and Baldessori (eds), Statistical Distributions in Scientific Work, Reidel, Holland, 1981.

Dendrinos, D.S., 'Urban Dynamics and Urban Cycles', Environment and Planning A, 10, 1978, pp. 43-49.

Geisser, S., 'A Predictive Approach to the Random Effect Model', Biometrika, 61, 1974, pp. 101-107.

Geisser, S., 'The Predictive Sample Reuse Method with Applications', Journal of the American Statistical Association, 70, 1975, pp. 320-328.

Hale, J.K., 'Generic Bifurcations with Applications', in Nonlinear Analysis and Applications: Heriot Watt Symposium, vol. 1., Pitman, London, 1977.

Henderson, J.V., Economic Theory and the Cities, Academic Press, New York, 1977.

Lehman, E.L., Testing Statistical Hypotheses, John Wiley, New York, 1959.

Mees, A., 'The Revival of Cities in Medieval Europe', Journal of Regional Science and Urban Economics, 5, 1975, pp. 402-426.

Poston, T. and Wilson, A., 'Facility Size Versus Distance Travelled - Urban Services and the Fold Catastrophes', Environment and Planning A, 9, 1977, pp. 681-686.

Soong, T., Random Differential Equations in Science and Engineering, Academic Press, New York, 1973.

Stone, M., 'Cross-Validity Choice and Assessment of Statistical Prediction', Journal of the Royal Statistical Society B, 1974, pp. 111-133.

Thom, R., Structural Stability and Morphogenesis: An Outline of a General Theory of Models, Benjamin Publishing Co., Reading, 1975.

Varaiya, R. and Wiseman, M., 'Bifurcation Models of Urban Development: Survey', Welfare and Employment Studies Project WP-81-2, Institute of Business and Economic Research, University of California, Berkeley, 1981.

Varian, H., 'Dynamical Systems with Applications to Economics', in Arrow, K. and Intriligator, M. (eds), Handbook of Mathematical Economics, Vol. 1, North-Holland Publ. Co., Amsterdam, 1981.

Wilson, A.G., 'Catastrophe Theory and Urban Modelling - An Application to Modal Choice', Environment and Planning A, 8, 1976, pp. 351-356.

Wold, H., 'Nonlinear Estimation by Iterative Least Square Procedures', in, David, F.N. (ed), Festschrift for J. Newmann: Research Papers in Statistics, Wiley, London, 1966.

Wold, H., 'Nonlinear Iterative Partial Least Squares (NIPALS) Modelling: Some Current Developments', in Krishnaiah, P.R. (ed), Multivariate Analysis - II, Academic Press, New York, 1973.

PART D: CONCLUSION

17 Prospects of Policy Analysis

L. CHATTERJEE AND P. NIJKAMP

A simple query motivated this book. How can analytical methods be made more relevant for public decision making? Put another way - what methodological improvements must be made to make analysis more useful for the regional and urban decision maker? After so much investment - monetary and human capital - has been devoted to the development of analytical techniques, the policy record shows little absorption of these techniques. Some of this we believed resulted from a lack of dialogue between analysts and implementers, and some from a mismatch between the techniques used and the structural attributes of the problems. In addressing this gap between analysis and practice, this book responds to a general mood of soul searching and introspection that is characterising the policy analysis discipline.

Our approach was not to start with methods, describing their characteristics and strengths, even though there is a tremendous creative energy being devoted to the development of quantitative methods. Rather we started with identifying several key policy issues and proceeded to a discussion of current practice in order to highlight analytical imperatives. Then some of the newer techniques and their applications were discussed. The papers in this volume show that recent methodological improvements can allow a greater responsiveness to the conceptual demands placed on urban and regional decision makers, by expanded goal directives and to the need to be sensitive to existing institutional structures. The remarkable recent advances in analytical methods and their applications potential in a wide variety of problem settings is very encouraging. However, their application in urban and regional settings is still highly experimental. This volume explored only some areas of application of these newer and richer techniques for urban and regional policy.

A central message of this volume has been that if regional and urban policy and planning has to proceed beyond its current routine activities, and translate the goals of equitable and efficient development at appropriate spatial levels, then the conceptual and methodological breakthroughs are necessary. These breakthroughs have to integrate the scientific and the political aspects of policy making. Unfortunately, it has often been too easy for decision makers to criticise formal models, since formal models focus on a few key relationships. However, complete replication of the real world is neither feasible nor desirable. Even with the new advances in techniques it is not possible to have models that are both quantitatively tractable and realistically descriptive. Rather, the emphasis should be placed on the real key relationships. To the extent analysts move away from assumptions of a linear process of development and incorporate some key political and organizational variables, hitherto commonly overlooked in standard modelling, they will be able to contribute more effectively to the planning of the development process.

Policy analysis is conducted for the purpose of providing answers to questions that are critical for the choice of appropriate policy decisions. This has almost been a definition of the subject. Yet, the public policy environment in developing countries is dominated by social, organisational and political factors. There are conflicting goals - some social and others organisational - and authority is divided (often not even clearly defined), among competing decision agents. The traditional models, that were developed to answer questions of efficiency (in situations where efficiency could be clearly defined) and in contexts where 'who pays and who benefits' was not as important as 'how much was paid for what', are not particularly applicable to the complicated task of public policy. Decision makers realised that sociological and political aspects had to be considered in the project selection stage. Thus efficiency notions were replaced by qualitative judgements that have been, for the most part, not very efficient. It has been costly to have given short shift to formal analytics.

Decisions have to be made on a continuous basis, and all decision makers have to grapple with the problem of choice among competing alternatives. Strategies and projects should be selected on the basis of what will be most effective vis à vis the socially desired goals, at any point in time. The current methods of choosing among alternatives based on adhocism, alliance of vested interests of the 'squeaky wheel' principle is producing neither efficient nor equitable solutions. Moreover, the problems of development are too immense and the resources too limited for such a process of 'muddling through' to continue in developing countries that are plagued with problems of employment, hunger and shelter.

Many value laden parameters interact in urban and regional settings, giving rise to the conceptual and methodological problems highlighted in this book. Given the complexity of the decision environment there can be no easy formulae that can yield the optimal or possibly even the appropriate solution. Rather, analytical techniques that can provide intermediate outputs, that can feed into the decision making, are likely to be more useful than those that provide complete solutions to wrong or irrelevant questions. Ultimately, the decision maker will have to intuite the appropriate solution, based on political feasibility. The analytical techniques can help the decision maker with additional information and on dimensions that impinge on a particular problem that exists in that spatial level of implementation. In the final analysis the political process is integral to policy and planning. This volume advocates this role for quantitative analysis and suggests that this role can be more effectively performed when there is a better match between the structural attributes of the problem and the technique.

Each method described in this volume has different strengths and weaknesses. The authors in examining these various techniques have described their applicability to specific types of problems and drawn attention to their attributes, for each method comes with its own special problems of measurement and modelling. They have not been offered as solutions to the major problems confronting the decision maker. Rather they are tentative and require further exploration and experimentation. They certainly are a product of the reexaminations of the applicability of techniques with restrictive assumptions, and they attempt to approximate the complexity of real world responses.

Contributing Authors

Professor Irma Adelman
Department of Agriculture and Natural Resource Economics
College of Natural Resources
Berkeley, Ca. 96720
USA

Professor Lata Chatterjee
Department of Urban Affairs and
Department of Geography
Boston University
48 Cummington Street
Boston, Ma. 02215
USA

Dr. R.H. Chaudhury
Visiting Research Associate
Massachusetts Institute of Technology
Cambridge, Ma. 02215
USA

Professor Marcial Echenique
Department of Architecture
University of Cambridge
1 Scroope Terrace
Cambridge CB2 1PX
United Kingdom

Dr. Arun Elhance
Department of Geography
Boston University
48 Cummington Street
Boston, Ma. 02215
USA

Dr. J.M. Hihn
Department of Agriculture and Natural Resource Economics
College of Natural Resources
Berkeley, Ca. 96720
USA

Dr. Geoffrey J.D. Hewings
Regional Science Association
107-109 Observatory, 901 South Mathews
University of Illinois
Urbana, Ill. 61801
USA

Professor T.R. Lakshmanan
Department of Geography
Boston University
48 Cummington Street
Boston, Ma. 02215
USA

Dr. Lee Yeung
Chung Chi College
Chinese University
Shatin, N.T.
Hong Kong

Dr. R.P. Misra
United Nations Center for Regional Development
Marunouchi 20407, Naka-ku
Nagoya 460
Japan

Professor Peter Nijkamp
Department of Economics
Free University
P.O. Box 7161
1007 MC Amsterdam
The Netherlands

Drs. Michiel van Pelt
Department of Economics
Erasmus University
Burg. Oudlaan 50
Rotterdam
The Netherlands

Dr. Ed. B. Prantilla
United Nations Center for Regional Development
Marunouchi 20407, Naka-ku
Nagoya 460
Japan

Dr. Piet Rietveld
Department of Economics
Free University
P.O. Box 7161
1007 MC Amsterdam
The Netherlands

Dr. K.V. Sundaram
The Planning Commission
Government of India
Yajana Bhavan
New Delhi 110001
India

Dr. Henk Voogd
Department of Civil Engineering
Delft University of Technology
Delft
The Netherlands